Biography of the Noble Prophet

Seerat of the Prophet

Peace Be Upon Him

Copyright

Ibn Kathir, Ibn Ishaq, At-Tabari

Dar-Salam

Editor: Imam Ahmed

رَضِيتُ بِاللهِ رَبًّا،
وَبِالْإِسْلَامِ دِينًا،
وَبِمُحَمَّدٍ صَلَّى اللهُ عَلَيْهِ وَسَلَّمَ نَبِيًّا

Please give this book a good Review

Published for Allah
Not for Profit

Prophet Muhammad (peace and blessings be upon him) said:

*"Convey from me even an Ayah of the **Qur'an**; relate traditions from Banu Israel, and there is no restriction on that; but he who deliberately forges a lie against me let him have his abode in the Hellfire."*

Dua for Protection from All Evil

Recite 3 times - After Maghrib Salah and Fajr Salah

بِسْمِ اللَّهِ الَّذِي لَا يَضُرُّ مَعَ اسْمِهِ شَيْءٌ فِي الْأَرْضِ وَلَا فِي السَّمَاءِ وَهُوَ السَّمِيعُ الْعَلِيمُ

"In the Name of Allah, with Whose Name nothing on the earth or in the heaven can cause harm, and He is the All-Hearing, the All-Knowing"

أَعُوذُ بِكَلِمَاتِ اللَّهِ التَّامَّاتِ مِنْ شَرِّ مَا خَلَقَ

A'oodhu bi kalimaat Allaah al-taammaati min sharri maa khalaq

"I seek refuge in the perfect words of Allah from the evil of that which He has created."

Although there are many biographies about the Prophet (peace and blessings be upon him), they are not completely accurate.

"Those who disbelieve invent falsehood about Allah, and most of them do not reason." [5:103]

مَا جَعَلَ ٱللَّهُ مِنۢ بَحِيرَةٍ وَلَا سَآئِبَةٍ وَلَا وَصِيلَةٍ وَلَا حَامٍ وَلَٰكِنَّ ٱلَّذِينَ كَفَرُوا۟ يَفْتَرُونَ عَلَى ٱللَّهِ ٱلْكَذِبَ وَأَكْثَرُهُمْ لَا يَعْقِلُونَ ﴿١٠٣﴾

"And those whose scales are light - they are the ones who will lose themselves for what injustice they were doing toward Our verses." [7:9]

وَمَنْ خَفَّتْ مَوَٰزِينُهُ فَأُو۟لَٰٓئِكَ ٱلَّذِينَ خَسِرُوٓا۟ أَنفُسَهُم بِمَا كَانُوا۟ بِـَٔايَٰتِنَا يَظْلِمُونَ ﴿٩﴾

وَمِنَ ٱلنَّاسِ مَن يَقُولُ ءَامَنَّا بِٱللَّهِ وَبِٱلْيَوْمِ ٱلْءَاخِرِ وَمَا هُم بِمُؤْمِنِينَ ﴿٨﴾

The Prophet (peace be upon him) was sent as a mercy **NOT** only to **Mankind** but to **All** of **Creation**. His teachings further preserved the sanctity of animals and reinforced how people must honor and respect all of Allah's creation. Before you step on ant or harm a cat or a dog, please read the following: The Messenger of Allah (peace and blessings be upon him) said: *An ant had bitten Prophet Uzair (peace be upon him), one of the Prophets sent to the Children of Israel. So he ordered that the colony of the ants be burnt.*

Then **Allah** revealed to him:

"Because of an ant's bite you have burnt a community from amongst the communities which sings My Glory."

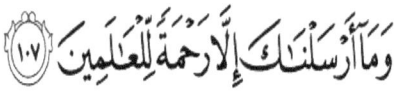

And We have not sent you, except as a mercy to the worlds.

"O Muhammad! And indeed, you are of a great moral character." [68:4]

Introduction

Without any doubts, the biography of Prophet Muhammad (Peace & Blessings be Upon Him) is authentic, truthful and complete. Prophet Muhammad (peace be upon him) was an exemplary man of intelligent mind and faultless vision. He was called "*the truthful* & the *trustworthy*" long before he became the Messenger of Allah (peace and blessings be upon him).

The Prophet (peace and blessings be upon him) preached moderation, social reform, and forgiveness. He will always be perceived and defined as an Arab. Historically, the word "**Arab**" meant desert that is waterless and treeless. And so, from the dawn of time, the Arabian Peninsula and its beautiful people have been called Arab.

Arab Tribes
Arabs were divided according to lineage into 3 groups:

#1: **Perishing Arabs**: The ancient Arabs. Their history is little known, and of whom were Thamud, Ad, Tasam, Jadis, Emlaq, and others.

#2: **Arabized Arabs**: These are the Arabs that originated from the progeny of Prophet Ishmael (peace be upon him). They are also called Adnanian Arabs.

#3: **Pure Arabs**: The people of Qahtan – originally lived in Yemen and comprised many tribes, two of which were very famous: *Himyar* and *Kahlan*.

Himyar: The most famous of whose septs were Quda'a, Sakasic, Zaid Al-Jamhur.

Kahlan: The most famous of whose septs were Anmar, Hamdan, Lakhm, Judham, Tai', Mudhhij, Kinda, Azd, Aws, Khazraj and the descendants of Jafna, the kings of old Syria. Some Kahlan emigrated from Yemen to dwell in the different parts of Arabia. Strong competition between Kahlan and Himyar led to the exodus of the first and the settlement of the second in Yemen.

The Arabized Arabs go back in ancestry to their true great grandfather **Prophet Abraham** (peace be upon him) from a town called "Ar" near the west bank of the Euphrates in Iraq. Abraham left Ar for Harran and then for Palestine, which was the headquarters for his Message.

He wandered around all over the area. In Egypt, the Pharaoh tried to do evil to his wife Sarah, but Allah Almighty saved her from the Pharaoh's evil scheme. He thus came to realize her strong love to Allah, and, in acknowledgment of her grace, the Pharaoh rendered his daughter **Hagar** at Sarah's service, but Sarah gave Hagar to Prophet Abraham as a wife.

Abraham returned to beautiful Palestine where Hagar gave birth to son Ishmael. But Sarah became jealous of Hagar that she forced Abraham to send Hagar and her baby away to a plant-less valley on a small hill in Hijaz, by the Sacred House. Abraham placed them under a lofty tree above **Zamzam** near the upper side of the Mosque in Makkah. Neither people nor water was available. Abraham then went back to **Palestine** but left his wife some dates and some water. However, not before long, they ran out of both food and water, but thanks to Allah, **Zamzam** water gushed forth to sustain them. A Yemeni tribe, Jurhum, came and lived in Makkah with Hagar's permission. It is mentioned in Sahih Al-Bukhari that this tribe came to Makkah before Ishmael was a young boy while they had passed through that valley long before this event.

Abraham went to Makkah every now and then to see his wife and son. But the exact number of these journeys is not known, but authentic historical scholars spoke of 4 trips.

Allah, the Merciful, stated in the Noble Quran that He had Abraham see, in a night dream, that he slaughtered his son Ishmael. Abraham obeyed Allah, and so he stood up to fulfill His Order.

فَلَمَّا بَلَغَ مَعَهُ ٱلسَّعْىَ قَالَ يَٰبُنَىَّ إِنِّىٓ أَرَىٰ فِى ٱلْمَنَامِ أَنِّىٓ أَذْبَحُكَ فَٱنظُرْ مَاذَا تَرَىٰ قَالَ يَٰٓأَبَتِ ٱفْعَلْ مَا تُؤْمَرُ سَتَجِدُنِىٓ إِن شَآءَ ٱللَّهُ مِنَ ٱلصَّٰبِرِينَ ﴿١٠٢﴾

And when he reached with him [the age of] exertion, he said" "O my son, indeed I have seen in a dream that I [must] sacrifice you, so see what you think." He said, "O my father, do as you are commanded. You will find me, if Allah wills, of the steadfast." [37:102-107]

فَلَمَّآ أَسْلَمَا وَتَلَّهُ لِلْجَبِينِ ﴿١٠٣﴾

"When they had both submitted and he put him down upon his forehead."

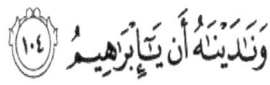

We called to him, "O Abraham."

"You have fulfilled the vision. Indeed, We thus reward the doers of good."

"Indeed, this was the clear trial."

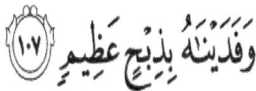

"And We ransomed him with a great sacrifice."

It is mentioned in the Bible that Ishmael was thirteen years older than his brother Ishaq. So the sequence of the story of the sacrifice of Ishmael clearly shows that it happened before Ishaq's birth, and that Allah's Promise to give Abraham another son, Ishaq, came after narration of the entire story.

When Ishmael became a young man, he learned Arabic at the hand of the tribe of Jurhum, who loved him very much with great admiration and even gave him one of their women as a wife, after his mother died. Having wanted to see his wife and son again, Abraham came to Makkah, but he did not find him at home. He asked Ishmael's wife about her husband and how they were doing.

She complained of poverty, so he asked her to tell his son Ishmael to change his doorstep. Ishmael understood quickly the message from his father, so he divorced his wife and got married to the daughter of Mudad ibn Amr, chief of the tribe of Jurhum.

When Abraham came to see his son, but again did not find him at home. He asked his new wife the same previous question, to which she thanked Allah. So Abraham asked her to tell his son Ishmael to keep his doorstep (i.e. to keep her as his wife) and Abraham went back to **Palestine**.

A third time, Abraham came to Makkah to find his son Ishmael sharpening an arrow under a lofty tree near Zamzam.

This time, father and son built **Al-Kabbah** and raised its pillars, and Abraham with Allah's order and Commandment, called unto people to make pilgrimage to it.

$$وَإِذْ يَرْفَعُ إِبْرَٰهِۦمُ ٱلْقَوَاعِدَ مِنَ ٱلْبَيْتِ وَإِسْمَٰعِيلُ رَبَّنَا تَقَبَّلْ مِنَّآ إِنَّكَ أَنتَ ٱلسَّمِيعُ ٱلْعَلِيمُ ﴿١٢٧﴾$$

And mention when Abraham was raising the foundations of the House and [with him] Ishmael, [saying], "Our Lord, accept [this] from us. You are the Hearing, the Knowing." [2:127-129]

$$رَبَّنَا وَٱجْعَلْنَا مُسْلِمَيْنِ لَكَ وَمِن ذُرِّيَّتِنَآ أُمَّةً مُّسْلِمَةً لَّكَ وَأَرِنَا مَنَاسِكَنَا وَتُبْ عَلَيْنَآ إِنَّكَ أَنتَ ٱلتَّوَّابُ ٱلرَّحِيمُ ﴿١٢٨﴾$$

Our Lord, make us Muslims and from our offspring a Muslim nation [in submission] to You. And show us our rites and accept our repentance. Indeed, You are the Accepting of repentance, the Merciful.

$$رَبَّنَا وَٱبْعَثْ فِيهِمْ رَسُولًا مِّنْهُمْ يَتْلُوا۟ عَلَيْهِمْ ءَايَٰتِكَ وَيُعَلِّمُهُمُ ٱلْكِتَٰبَ وَٱلْحِكْمَةَ وَيُزَكِّيهِمْ إِنَّكَ أَنتَ ٱلْعَزِيزُ ٱلْحَكِيمُ ﴿١٢٩﴾$$

*"Our Lord! Send amongst them a Messenger of their own (indeed Allah answered their invocation by sending **Muhammad**, peace be upon him), who shall recite unto them Your Verses and instruct them in the Book (this Quran) and Al-Hikmah (full knowledge of the Islamic laws and jurisprudence or wisdom or Prophethood, etc.), and sanctify them. Verily! You are the All-Mighty, the All-Wise."*

Ishmael had 12 sons, and who ultimately formed twelve tribes inhabiting Makkah and trading between Yemen, Syria and Egypt. Later on, these tribes spread all over the area, and outside the peninsula. All their tidings went into oblivion except for the descendants of Nabet and Qidar.

The Nabeteans, the sons of Nabet, later established a flourishing civilization in the Hijaz, they built a powerful government, and made Petra their capital. Nobody dared to challenge their authority until the Romans came and managed to destroy their kingdom.

However, the descendants of Qidar, the son of Ishmael, lived for a very long time in Makkah increasing in number, of them issued Adnan and also son Ma'ad, to whom Adnanian Arabs traced back their ancestry.

Adnan is the twenty-first grandfather in the series of the Prophetic ancestry.

It was said that whenever the Messenger of Allah (peace be upon him) spoke of his ancestry he would always stop at Adnan. The scholars said that there is exactly 40 fathers between Adnan and Abraham (peace be upon them).

Nizar, Ma'ad's only son, had 4 sons who branched out into four great tribes; Eyad, Anmar, Rabia and Mudar. These last two sub-branched into several septs. Rabia fathered Asad, Anazah, Abdul Qais, and Wa'il's two sons (Bakr & Taghlib), Hanifa and many others.

Mudar tribes branched out into 2 great divisions: Qais Ailan ibn Mudar and septs of Elias ibn Mudar. Of Qais Ailan were the Banu Saleem, Banu Hawazin, and Banu Ghatafan of whom descended Abs, Zubyan, Ashja and Ghani ibn Asur. Of

Elias ibn Mudar were Tamim ibn Murra, Hudhail ibn Mudrika, Banu Asad ibn Khuzaimah and septs of Kinana ibn Khuzaimah, of whom came Quraish, the descendants of Fahr ibn Malik ibn An-Nadr ibn Kinana.

Quraish branched out into many tribes, the most famous of whom were Jumah, Sahm, Adi, Makhzum, Tayim, Zahra and the three septs of Qusai ibn Kilab: Abdud-Dar ibn Qusai, Asad ibn Abdul Uzza ibn Qusai, and Abd Manaf ibn Qusai.

Abd Manaf branched out into four tribes: Abd Shams, Nawfal, Muttalib, and Hashim. It is, however, from the family of **Hashim** that Allah, the Almighty, chose Prophet Muhammad ibn Abdullah ibn Abdul-Muttalib ibn Hashim (peace and blessing be upon him).

Prophet Muhammad (peace be upon him) said that: "Allah selected Ishmael from the sons of Abraham, Kinana from the sons of Ishmael, Quraish from the sons of Kinana, Hashim from the sons of Quraish and He selected me from the sons of **Hashim**."

Al-Abbas ibn Abdul-Muttalib quoted the Prophet (peace be upon him): "Allah created man and chose me from the best of them, He chose the tribes and selected me from the best of them; and He chose families and selected me from the best of them. I am the best in person and family." Having increased in number, the children of Adnan, in pursuit of pastures & water, spread out all over Arabia. The tribe of Abdul Qais with some septs of Tamim & Bakr ibn Wa'il, migrated to Bahrain where they settled.

Banu Hanifa ibn Sab ibn Ali ibn Bakr went to settle in Hijr, the capital of Yamama, which is to the east of the plateau of Najd in modern-day Saudi Arabia. The tribes of Bakr ibn Wa'il settled in an area of land that included Yamama, Bahrain, Saif Kazima, and the sea shore, and the outer borders of Iraq. The tribe of Taghlib lived in the Euphrates area while some of them settled in Bakr. Banu Tamim settled in Basra semi-desert.

Banu Saleem settled near Madinah on the land stretching from Wadi Al-Qura to the eastern mountains to Harrah.

Thaqif settled in Taif and Hawazin east of Makkah. Banu Asad settled in the east of Taima and west of Kufa, while the family of Tai settled between Banu Asad and Taima. They were about 5-day-walk far from Kufa. Zubyan lived in the plot of land between Taima and Hawran. Some septs of Kinana settled in Tihama, while septs of Quraish lived in Makkah. Quraish remained divided until Qusai ibn Kilab rallied them on honorable terms attaching prominence to their status and importance.

Rulership history

By the end of the next sections, you will get to understand how the **grandfather** of the Prophet, **Abd al-Muttalib**, became in charge of the **Zamzam** well. When talking about the history of Arabia before Islam, it is necessary to explain the history of rulership and sectarianism, and the religious powers of the Arabs. The rulers of Arabia were of two groups: (a) kings, but were not independent; and (b) heads of tribes. They had the same power as kings, but independent. The kings were those of Ghassan, Heerah, and Yemen. All the other rulers of Arabia were the heads of tribes.

Yemen

Those are the folks of Sheba. They were truly one of the oldest nations of the pure Arabs and lived in Yemen. The centuries before 650 B.C., their kings were called *Makrib Sheba*. During that time, they built the *Dam of Marib*.

Sheba had so great a domain that they had settlers inside and outside Arabia.

From about 650 B.C. to 115 B.C., they gave up the name *Makrib* and assumed the designation of *Kings of Sheba*. The Holy Quran mentions Sheba as well.

$$\text{فَمَكَثَ غَيْرَ بَعِيدٍ فَقَالَ أَحَطتُ بِمَا لَمْ تُحِطْ بِهِ وَجِئْتُكَ مِن سَبَإٍ بِنَبَإٍ يَقِينٍ ﴿٢٢﴾}$$

But the hoopoe stayed not long and said: "I have encompassed [in knowledge] that which you have not encompassed, and I have come to you from Sheba with certain news. [27:22]

$$\text{إِنِّي وَجَدتُّ ٱمْرَأَةً تَمْلِكُهُمْ وَأُوتِيَتْ مِن كُلِّ شَيْءٍ وَلَهَا عَرْشٌ عَظِيمٌ ﴿٢٣﴾}$$

I found [there] a woman ruling them, and she has been given of all things, and she has a great throne. [27:23]

$$\text{وَجَدتُّهَا وَقَوْمَهَا يَسْجُدُونَ لِلشَّمْسِ مِن دُونِ ٱللَّهِ وَزَيَّنَ لَهُمُ ٱلشَّيْطَٰنُ أَعْمَٰلَهُمْ فَصَدَّهُمْ عَنِ ٱلسَّبِيلِ فَهُمْ لَا يَهْتَدُونَ ﴿٢٤﴾}$$

I found her and her people prostrating to the sun instead of Allah, and Satan has made their deeds pleasing to them and averted them from His guidance. [27:24]

$$\text{قَالَتْ يَٰٓأَيُّهَا ٱلْمَلَؤُاْ إِنِّىٓ أُلْقِىَ إِلَىَّ كِتَٰبٌ كَرِيمٌ ﴿٢٩﴾}$$

*(The Queen of **Sheba**) said (when she received the letter): O chieftains! There hath been thrown unto me a noble letter. [27:29]*

Allah mentions Sheba in other parts of the Holy Quran:

$$\text{لَقَدْ كَانَ لِسَبَإٍ فِي مَسْكَنِهِمْ ءَايَةٌ ۖ جَنَّتَانِ عَن يَمِينٍ وَشِمَالٍ ۖ كُلُوا۟ مِن رِّزْقِ رَبِّكُمْ وَٱشْكُرُوا۟ لَهُۥ ۚ بَلْدَةٌ طَيِّبَةٌ وَرَبٌّ غَفُورٌ ﴿١٥﴾}$$

*Indeed there was for Saba' (**Sheba**) a sign in their dwelling place, - two gardens on the right hand and on the left (and it was said to them) "Eat of the provision of your Lord, and be grateful to Him, a fair land and an OftForgiving Lord. [34:15]*

$$\text{فَأَعْرَضُوا۟ فَأَرْسَلْنَا عَلَيْهِمْ سَيْلَ ٱلْعَرِمِ وَبَدَّلْنَـٰهُم بِجَنَّتَيْهِمْ جَنَّتَيْنِ ذَوَاتَىْ أُكُلٍ خَمْطٍ وَأَثْلٍ وَشَىْءٍ مِّن سِدْرٍ قَلِيلٍ ﴿١٦﴾}$$

But they turned away [refusing], so We sent upon them the flood of the dam, and We replaced their two [fields of] gardens with gardens of bitter fruit, tamarisks and something of sparse lote trees. [34:16]

$$\text{ذَٰلِكَ جَزَيْنَـٰهُم بِمَا كَفَرُوا۟ ۖ وَهَلْ نُجَـٰزِىٓ إِلَّا ٱلْكَفُورَ ﴿١٧﴾}$$

By that flood We repaid them because they disbelieved. And do We [thus] repay except the ungrateful? [34:17]

From 115 B.C. until 300 A.D., the tribe of Himyar conquered the kingdom of Sheba and took Redan for their capital instead of Marib. However later, the capital of Redan was called *Zifar*. Till this day, its ruins lie on Mudawwar Mountain near the town of *Yarim*. With time, they began to decline. Their trade failed because of the Nabetean domain over the north of Hijaz, and because of the Romans control of the naval trade routes after the Romans took Egypt, Syria and the north of Hijaz. Moreover, inter-tribal warfare destroyed them further.

From 300 A.D. before Islam was brought to Yemen, they had lots of turmoil. The many civil wars destroyed them well, and so the Romans conquered Adn and even helped the Abyssinians (Ethiopians) to rule Yemen. The occupation of Yemen lasted until 378 A.D., then Yemen got its independence back.

However, later on, the Marib Dam began to crack, which led to the **Great Flood** (450 or 451 A.D.), as mentioned in the Noble Quran.

لَقَدْ كَانَ لِسَبَإٍ فِي مَسْكَنِهِمْ ءَايَةٌ ۖ جَنَّتَانِ عَن يَمِينٍ وَشِمَالٍ ۖ كُلُوا۟ مِن رِّزْقِ رَبِّكُمْ وَٱشْكُرُوا۟ لَهُۥ ۚ بَلْدَةٌ طَيِّبَةٌ وَرَبٌّ غَفُورٌ ﴿١٥﴾

There was for [the tribe of] Saba' in their dwelling place a sign: two [fields of] gardens on the right and on the left. [They were told], "Eat from the provisions of your Lord and be grateful to Him." [34:15]

فَأَعْرَضُوا۟ فَأَرْسَلْنَا عَلَيْهِمْ سَيْلَ ٱلْعَرِمِ وَبَدَّلْنَٰهُم بِجَنَّتَيْهِمْ جَنَّتَيْنِ ذَوَاتَيْ أُكُلٍ خَمْطٍ وَأَثْلٍ وَشَىْءٍ مِّن سِدْرٍ قَلِيلٍ ﴿١٦﴾

But they turned away [refusing], so We sent upon them the flood of the dam, and We replaced their two [fields of] gardens with gardens of bitter fruit, tamarisks and something of sparse lote trees. [34:16]

وَجَعَلْنَا بَيْنَهُمْ وَبَيْنَ ٱلْقُرَى ٱلَّتِي بَٰرَكْنَا فِيهَا قُرًى ظَٰهِرَةً وَقَدَّرْنَا فِيهَا ٱلسَّيْرَ ۖ سِيرُوا۟ فِيهَا لَيَالِيَ وَأَيَّامًا ءَامِنِينَ ﴿١٨﴾

And We placed between them and the cities which We had blessed many visible cities. And We determined between them the distances of journey, [saying], "Travel between them in safety." [37:18]

23

This was truly a big event that caused the fall of the entire Yemeni civilization. In 523, Dhu Nawas, a truly evil Jew, sent an army against the Christians of Najran to force them to convert to Judaism. But they refused, so they were thrown alive into a ditch where a huge fire had been set. The Quran referred to this event:

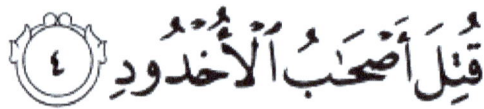

Cursed were the people of the ditch (the story of the Boy and the King). [85:4]
This short story is in the back of this book.

This aroused a great anger among the Romans and the Christians. The Roman emperors assembled a large army which helped the Abyssinian army, of 70,000 warriors, to conquest Yemen again.

525 A.D., under the control of Eriat, who was given rulership over Yemen, the job he held until he was assassinated by his own army leaders. Abraha took rulership over Yemen, but then deployed his army to demolish **Al-Kabbah**, and, hence, they came to be known as the "People of the Elephant".

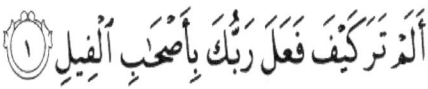

Have you not considered, how your Lord dealt with the companions of the elephant? [105:1]

Did He not make their plot go astray? [105: 2]

After the "Elephant" incident, Persians maintained rulership of Yemen until Badhan, the last of them, embraced Islam in 638 A.D., ending the Persian control over Yemen.

Heerah

Korosh the Great (557-529 B.C.) united the Persians, and they ruled Iraq and its neighborhood. They kept strong control until Alexander the Great destroyed their king Dara I subduing the Persians in 326 B.C. The Persian lands were then divided and ruled by kings known as "the Kings of Sects". This era lasted until 230 A.D.

In 226 A.D., the Persian leader Ardashir established the Sasanian state. He then subdued the Arabs living in the vicinity of his kingdom, and so that left the people of Heerah and Anbar under the Persian control.

During the time of Ardashir, Juzaima Alwaddah ruled Heerah, Rabia, Mudar, and Mesopotamia. Ardashir knew that it was impossible for him to rule the Arabs and to prevent them from attacking his borders, unless he appointed an Arab king who had support of his tribe. He also made use of them against the Byzantine kings who always used to harass him. At the same time, the Arabs of Iraq could repel the Arabs of Syria who were in the hold of Byzantine kings. But he kept the Persian battalion under the command of the king of Heerah to defend against any Arabs that might rebel against him.

In 268 A.D., after the death of Juzaima, Amr ibn Adi ibn Nasr Al-Lakhmi was appointed king by Sabour ibn Ardashir, the Persian King. Amr ruled Heerah until the Persians appointed Qabaz ibn Fairuz in whose time came Mazdak, who called for dissoluteness in social life.

So Qabaz, and many of his own people, embraced Mazdak's religion and even asked king of Heerah, Al-Munzir ibn Ma As-Sama, to follow them, but he rejected. So Qabaz discharged him and appointed Harith ibn Amr ibn Hajar Al-Kindi, and he accepted the Mazdaki doctrine.

Kisra Anu Shairwan succeed Qabaz. He killed Mazdak and his followers, and he restored Munzir to the throne of Heerah. Kisra ordered the arrest of Harith, but Harith took refuge with the Al-Kalb tribe, and he spent the rest of his life with them. Kisra appointed Eyas ibn Qubaisa At-Tai as king of Heerah after Munzir. And after Eyas, a Persian ruler was appointed over Heerah. In 632 A.D. the authority was returned to the family of Lukhm when Al-Munzir Al-Ma'rur came to power. Hardly had the latter's reign lasted for 8 months when **Khalid ibn Al-Walid** fell upon him with Muslim soldiers.

Syria

During emigration, some septs of Quda'a settled near Syria. They belonged to the family of Sulaih ibn Halwan. The sons of Dujam ibn Sulaih known as Ad-Dujaima.

The septs of Quda'a were often used by the Byzantines to defend the Byzantine borders against both Bedouin raiders and the Persians. Their most well-known king was Zyiad ibn Al-Habula. However, their power came to an end upon defeat by the Ghassanides. Their last king was Jabala ibn Al-Aihum. He embraced Islam during the reign of the Chief of the Believers, Omar ibn Al-Khattab (may Allah grant him peace).

Hijaz

Prophet Ishmael, (peace be upon him), governed Makkah as well as the Holy Sanctuary throughout his lifetime. When Prophet Ishmael died, at the age of 137, his sons, Qidar and Nabet, succeeded him. But later on, Mudad ibn Amr AlJurhumi, their maternal grandfather, took over. Thus transferring control of Makkah to the tribe of Jurhum. They held control over Makkah until their decline before the rise of Bukhtanassar.

The Adnanides gained strong power over Makkah. However, when Bukhtanassar's invaded in 587 B.C., the Adnanides left to Yemen.

When the Bukhtanassar's control and power declined, some tribes returned to Makkah, but found none of the tribe of Jurhum, but Jursham ibn Jalhamah, whose daughter, Mu'ana, was given to Ma'ad, which later she had a son by him and named Nizar.

During that time, because of the difficult life in Makkah, the tribe of Jurhum began to mistreat visitors of the Holy Sanctuary and extort funds. This stirred resentment and hatred of the Adnanides. So with the help of the tribe of Khuza'a that had come to settle in a nearby land, they invaded and frightened Jurhum out of Makkah. This gave Quda'a the control of Makkah in the middle of the second century A.D.

But prior to their tragic escape to Yemen, Jurhum filled up the Zamzam well with sand, and buried two gold deer, jewelry, swords, and the Black Stone. Jurhum lived in Makkah for about 21-centuries and had control over Makkah for at least 20-centuries. Khuza'a controlled Makkah for about 300 years. During that time, the Adnanides spread all over Arabia, Syria, and Iraq, while small septs of Quraish settled near Makkah; they were Harum, Haloul, and some families of Kinana.

But they had no privileges in Makkah at all until Qusai ibn Kilab, whose father had died when he was a child, and then his mother married Rabi'a ibn Haram, from the tribe of Bani Udhra.

Rabi'a took his wife and her child Qusai to his homeland near Syria. When Qusai became older, he went back to Makkah, which was ruled then by Halil ibn Habsha from Khuza'a. Habsha gave Qusai his daughter, Hobba, as wife. When Habsha died, Qusai's took control of Makkah and the Sacred House.

Khuza'a tried to keep the custodianship of the Sacred House away from Qusai, but with the help of Quraish and Kinana, managed to take over and to expel Khuza'a completely from Makkah.

Qusai brought his kinspeople to Makkah and allocated it to them, allowing Quraish some dwellings there. Adwan, An-Nus'a, the families of Safwan, Murra ibn Awf got the same privileges they used to enjoy. Qusai's reign over Makkah and also the Sacred House began in 440 A.D. giving Quraish absolute control over Makkah and custodianship of the Sacred House.

Due to the fact that Qusai was loved and his orders inviolable, his death gave no rise to conflicts, but it later did among his grandchildren. When Abd Munaf died, his sons left the control of providing water to pilgrims to Hashim ibn Abd Munaf, then the control was given to brother **Muttalib**. Afterwards the control was given to **Abd Al-Muttalib ibn Hashim**, the **Prophet's grandfather**, whose sons assumed this job until the rise of Islam, during which Abbas ibn Abdul-Muttalib was in control.

Religions of the Arab Tribes

Most of the Arabs had obeyed the call of Prophet Ishmael (peace be upon him), and accepted the religion of his father, Prophet Abraham (peace be upon him). Prophet Abraham (peace be upon him) worshipped Allah alone, professed His Oneness.

So the Arabs followed this religion for a long time until they forgot parts of it, but they continued to obey the fundamental beliefs such as monotheism as well as other important aspects of Abraham's religion, until the time when a chief of Khuza'a, namely Amr ibn Luhai, ruled.

Amr ibn Luhai was very well-known for righteousness, charity, respect and care for religion, and therefore he was given unreserved love and obedience by his tribesmen. When he went to visit Syria he saw people worshiping idols. Amr ibn Luhai approved of and believed it to be very righteous since Syria was the origin of Messengers and Scriptures, so he brought with him an idol (Hubal) which he placed in the middle of Al-Kabbah and summoned people to worship Hubal.

In a very short time, paganism spread all over Makkah, and so very quickly many stone and wood idols, bearing different names, were introduced into Makkah.

Before paganism and all of its vices, Christianity arrived in Arabia following the entry of the Abyssinian (Ethiopian) and Roman colonists.

The Abyssinian colonization forces in league with Christian missions attacked Yemen as a retaliatory reaction for the iniquities (injustices) of Dhu Nawas, and started vehemently to spread their faith.

Dhu Nawas (Yosef Nu'as) was a Judaic king of Ḥimyar (A kingdom in ancient Yemen) between 517 and 525 CE, who came to prominence on account of his military exploits against people of other religions that lived in his kingdom. Ibn Hisham (a well-known biographer) wrote that Yosef was an evil Jew who grew out his sidelocks (nuwas meaning, "forelock" or "sidelock"), and who became known as "lord of the sidelocks."

And so the Abyssinian attacked Yemen. They even built a church in Yemen, and called it Yemeni Al-Kabbah with the goal of directing the Arab pilgrimage caravans towards Yemen, and then tried to demolish the Sacred House in Makkah. Allah, the Almighty, however punished them and made an example of them. Such were the religions of the Arabs in the Arabian Peninsula before Islam.

Christianity similarly opened its doors wide to polytheism, and got too difficult to comprehend as a heavenly religion. As a religious practice, it developed a sort of peculiar mixture of man and God. It exercised no bearing whatsoever on the souls of the Arabs who accepted it simply because it was different.

Prophet Muhammad's family (peace be upon him) is called the Hashemite family after the Prophet's grandfather Hashim ibn Abd Manaf. The Prophet's great grandfather Hashim. He gave food and water to the pilgrims.

Hashim was wealthy and very honest. He offered the pilgrims soup, bread in broth. His first name was Amr but he was called Hashim because he crumbled bread for the pilgrims. He was the first man who started Quraish's journeys of the summer and winter. So Hashim went to Syria as a merchant often.

In Madinah, Hashim married Salma, the daughter of Amr from Bani Adi ibn An-Najjar. He spent time with Salma in Madinah, but then he left for Syria while she was pregnant. As fate would have it, he died in **Gaza**, **Palestine** in 497 A.D.

Salma gave birth to a son, the Prophet's grandfather, Abdul-Muttalib, and named him Shaiba for the white hair in his head. She brought him up in her father's house in Madinah. And so none of his family in Makkah knew of his birth.

The great grandfather of the Prophet, Hashim, had four sons; Asad, Abu Saifi, Nadla and also Abdul-Muttalib, and five daughters Ash-Shifa, Khalida, Ruqyah, Daifa, and Jannah.

After the death of Hashim, the charge of pilgrims' food and water went to his brother Al-Muttalib ibn Abd Mznaf. He was honest, generous and trustworthy. And when Abdul-Muttalib reached the age of boyhood, his uncle Al-Muttalib heard of him and went to Madinah to see him. When he saw him, tears filled his eyes and rolled down his cheeks. He embraced him and took him with him on his camel.

The boy, however refused to go with him to Makkah until he asked and took his mother's consent. So Al-Muttalib asked Salma to send the boy with him to Makkah, but she refused. However, he managed to convince her by saying: "My nephew is going to Makkah to restore his father's authority, and to live in the vicinity of the Sacred House."

In Makkah, the people, thought and considered Abdul-Muttalib the slave of Muttalib. But Al-Muttalib said: "He is my nephew, the son of my brother Hashim."

And so the boy was brought up in Al-Muttalib's house. However, later Al-Muttalib died in Bardman in Yemen.

Abdul-Muttalib took over, and managed to maintain the people's prestige and he outdid his grandfathers in his honorable behavior which gained him Makkah's deep love and high esteem.

One day, Abdul-Muttalib received an order from God, in a dream, to dig the Zamzam well at a particular place. He dug the well, and found the things that Jurhum men had buried there when they were forced to evacuate Makkah.

Abdul-Muttalib found the swords, armors and the two deer of gold. The gate of Al-Kabbah was stamped from the gold swords and the two deer of gold, and the tradition of providing Zamzam water to pilgrims was established.

When the Zamzam gushed water up, the tribe of Quraish quickly made a claim to partnership in the enterprise, but Abdul-Muttalib refused their demands on the grounds that God had singled only him out for this honorable job. To settle the dispute, they agreed to consult Bani Sa'd's diviner. But on their way, God showed them His Signs that confirmed Abdul-Muttalib's right to the sacred spring.

Abdul-Muttalib then made a solemn vow to sacrifice one of his children to Al-Kabbah if he had ten children.

When Abraha As-Sabah Al-Habashi, the Abyssinian (Ethiopian) ruler in Yemen, saw that the Arabs made their pilgrimage to Al-Kabbah, he built a large church in Sana, Yemen, to attract the Arab pilgrims to it. A man from Kinana tribe understood the reason why the church was built, so he entered the church stealthily at night and covered its front wall with excrement. When Abraha heard of that, he got very angry and so led a big army, of 60,000 warriors, to demolish Al-Kabbah.

Abraha selected the biggest elephant for himself. His army had many elephants (9 to 13). Abraha continued to move until he reached a place called Al-Magmas.

At Al-Magmas he prepared his army and his elephants to enter to destroy Makkah. However, when Abraha and his army reached the Muhassar Valley, between Muzdalifah and Mina, Allah made the elephants kneel down and to refuse to move further.

Whenever Abraha directed the elephants northwards, southwards or eastwards, the elephant stoop up and moved quickly but when he directed westwards towards Al-Kabbah, the elephants knelt down for God (Allah).

Allah, the Almighty, sent upon them birds in flights. The bird hurled against them stones of baked clay. The birds were like sparrows and swallows, each carried 3 stones. One stone in its peak and two in its claws.

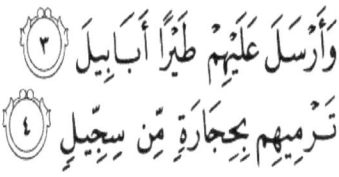

Allah sent against them birds, in flocks. Striking them with stones of Sijjil. [105:3-4]

The stones fell and sped like bullets and hit Abraha's army and destroyed them. Abraha survived the attack and fled back to Sa'na. By the time he arrived he had wounds everywhere and skin falling off. Normally when an army is defeated they make plans to avenge that defeat but the condition of Abraha meant that they were severely afraid to return to the area.

The event of the Elephant War took place in the month of Al-Muharram, only 50 or 55 days before the birth of Prophet Muhammad (peace be upon him), which corresponded to late February or early March 571 A.D. This for certain was a gift from Allah to His Messenger (peace be upon him). This was a Divine auspicious precursor of the Noor (light) to come and accompany the advent of the Prophet (peace be upon him) and his family.

News of the Elephant War had reached the most distant corners of the world. Abyssinia (Ethiopia) had strong ties with the Romans, and the Persians sped very quickly to take Yemen. Incidentally, the Persians and the Romans stood for the powerful civilized world at that time. The Elephant Raid Event riveted the world's attention to the sacredness of Allah's House in Makkah, and showed that this House had been chosen and protected by Allah.

Allah gave the grandfather of the Prophet (peace be upon him) Abdul-Muttalib ten sons. Abdullah was the father of Prophet Muhammad (peace be upon him). His mother was Fatimah, daughter of Amr Ibn A'idh ibn Murra.

Abdullah was the smartest of Abdul-Muttalib's sons and also the most loved. He was also the son whom the prophecy arrows pointed at to be slaughtered as a sacrifice to Al-Kabbah. So when Abdul-Muttalib had ten sons and they reached maturity, he told them about the promise that he made to Allah.

Their names were written on arrows and then were given to their most beloved goddess, Hubal. The arrows were shuffled and drawn. An arrow showed that it was the Prophet's father, Abdullah, to be sacrificed. Abdul-Muttalib then took the boy to Al-Kabbah with a razor to slaughter him.

Quraish, his uncles, and his brother Abu Talib, tried to stop him from completing his purpose. They suggested that they should summon a she-diviner to judge. She said that the arrows should be drawn again with respect to Abdullah as well as 10 camels. She then added that drawing the lots should be repeated with an additional 10 camels every time the arrow pointed to Abdullah.

The game was thus repeated until the number of the camels amounted to **100**. At that point the arrow pointed to the camels, consequently they were all slaughtered instead of Abdullah, his son. The slaughtered camels were given to anyone to eat, from human to animal.

This incident changed the amount of blood-money usually accepted in Arabia. It had been 10 camels, but after this event it was increased to 100. Islam, later on, approved of this. Another thing related to the above issue goes to the effect that the **Prophet** (peace be upon him) once said: I am the offspring of the slaughtered two," meaning Abdullah and Ishmael.

Abdul-Muttalib later selected Amina, the daughter of Wahab ibn Abd Manaf ibn Zahra ibn Kilab, as a wife for his son, Abdullah. Her father was the chief of Bani Zahra to whom great honor was attributed. They were married in Makkah, but soon after Abdullah was sent by his father to buy dates in Madinah, he fell ill and died. In another version of the story, Abdullah went to Syria on a business journey and died in Madinah on his way back.

Abdul-Muttalib, the father of the Prophet, was buried in the house of An-Nabigha Al-Ju'di. He was 25 years old when he died. Most scholars said that his death was two months before the birth of **Muhammad** (peace be upon him).

Before Prophethood

Muhammad (peace be upon him), was born in Bani Hashim lane in Makkah al-Mukarramahon on Monday morning, 29th of August, the ninth of Rabi Al-Awwal, the same year of the Elephant Event, and 40 years of the reign of Khosru Nushirwan (Kisra), the 20th or 22 of April, 571 A.D.

Ibn Sa'd said that Prophet Muhammad's mother said: "When the baby was born, a light came out with Muhammad that lit the palaces of Syria."

It was also reported that significant signs accompanied his birth. For example, 14 galleries of Khosru's palace broke and fell down, the Magians' sacred fires died down and many Christian churches on the Lake of Sawa were destroyed.

Muhammad's mother immediately asked someone to tell his grandfather, Abdul-Muttalib, of the beautiful event. Abdul-Muttalib took Muhammad to Al-Kabbah, and he prayed and thanked Allah. He named the baby Muhammad, and he circumcised him on the 7th day as was the custom of the Arab tribes.

The first woman that suckled him after his mother Amina was Thuyebah. She was the concubine of Abu Lahab (he was the half-uncle of Muhammad), with her son, Masrouh. She had suckled Hamzah ibn Abdul-Muttalib and she also suckled Abu Salamah ibn Abd Al-Asad Al-Makhzumi.

Childhood

It was the custom of the Arab tribes that lived in towns to send their children away to Bedouin wet nurses who would breast feed and care for their children. Living in the desert and with Bedouins had many benefits: the children grew up in a healthy surroundings whereby they developed a robust frame and acquired unpolluted pure speech and manners. The Bedouins were also free from many vices that often afflict many villeges and towns.

The Prophet (peace be upon him) was entrusted to Haleemah bint Abi Dhuaib from Bani Sa'd ibn Bakr. Haleemah's husband was from the same tribe. His name was Al-Harith ibn Abdul Uzza called Abi Kabshah.

The Prophet (peace be upon him) had several foster sisters, Aneesah bint Al-Harith, Abdullah ibn Al-Harith, Hudhafah or Judhamah bint Al-Harith (also known as Ash-Shayma). She used to nurse the Prophet (peace be upon him) and the Prophet's cousin, Abu Sufyan ibn Al-Harith ibn Abdul-Muttalib.

The Prophet's uncle Hamzah ibn Abdul-Muttalib, was also suckled by the same two wet nurses, Thuyeba and Haleemah As-Sadiyah.

Haleemah and her family were favored by many strokes of good fortune while the Muhammad (peace and be upon him) lived under their care. Ibn Ishaq said that Haleemah said that she along with her husband and the baby, set out from their village with some women of her clan in quest of babies to suckle. She said that it was a year of drought and famine and they had nothing to eat. She rode on a brown female donkey. Others rode an old she-camel. None had any milk. They could not sleep during the night because the baby kept crying from hunger. They kept praying for rain and relief.

When they arrived in Makkah, no woman amongst them accepted the Messenger of Allah (peace be upon him), because peace be upon him was an orphan. The women refused him quickly. They wanted a money and reward from the father, but an orphan had nothing. So they rejected him.

Every woman who came with Haleemah got a suckling and when they were about to leave, Haleemah said to her husband: "By Allah, I do not want to go back without a baby. The orphan is fine." Haleemah's husband said: "Maybe Allah might bless us through him."

So Haleemah took the Prophet (peace be upon him) because there was no other babies to take. When Haleemah put him on her breast, Allah gave her lots of milk. The baby (peace be upon him) drank to his heart's content, and his foster brother drank too. Both babies went to sleep very well. Haleemah's baby could not sleep many previous nights. Then Haleemah's husband went to the she-camel to milk her, and to his surprise, he was so happy. He found so much milk. He milked and drank so much, and everyone enjoyed a sound sleep that night.

The baby (peace be upon him) brought so much good fortune to Haleemah. For example, the donkey that Haleemah rode when she went to Makkah was very lean and tired, but it became stronger. By the time Haleemah reached the camp of the clan of Sa'd, Haleemah found that the barren land had sprouted forth with lush grass. Many beasts came back satisfied and full of milk. Baby Muhammad (peace be upon him) stayed with Haleemah for two years until he was weaned.

We she took the baby back to his family, she begged to have him stay with her longer. And so, the Prophet (peace be upon him) stayed with Haleemah until he was 4 or 5 years of age.

Anas related in Sahih Muslim, that when the angel, Jibril, (peace be upon him) came down, he ripped the child's chest open and took out his heart. He then removed a blood-clot out of the heart and said: "That was the part of Satan in you." Jibril then washed the Prophet's heart with the water of Zamzam in a gold basin. Then the heart was restored to its place. A boy went running to his mother, i.e. his nurse, and said:

"Muhammad (peace be upon him) has been killed." Everyone ran towards him, and found him okay, but his face was white. However, Haleemah was worried about the boy and so she returned him to his mother Amina.

Amina then went to visit her husband's grave in Yathrib (Madinah). She set out to cover a journey of 310 miles with her boy, and Abdul-Muttalib. Amina spent a month in Madinah. On the way back home, Amina became very ill and died in Abwa, on the road between Madinah and Makkah.

Abdul-Muttalib loved his grandson more than his children. Ibn Hisham said that a mattress was often placed in the shade of Al-Kabbah for Abdul-Muttalib. His own children used to sit around that mattress in honor to their father, but Muhammad (peace be upon him) would often sit on it. The children, his uncles, would take him back, but if Abdul-Muttalib was present, he said: "Leave my grandson be. I swear by Allah that my grandson will hold a high position one day."

When Muhammad, the little boy, (peace be upon him) was 8 years, two months and 10 days old, his grandfather died in Makkah. So his uncle Abu Talib, who was the brother of the Prophet's father, put him with his children and preferred him to them. For 40 years he loved his nephew and extending all possible protection and support to him.

Ibn Asakir reported, on the authority of Jalhamah ibn Arfuta, who said: "I came to Makkah when there was drought. No rain had fallen in a long time. Quraish said: 'O Abu Talib, the valley has become dry and leafless and the children are very hungry, let us all go and pray for rain.' Abu Talib took his grandson and went to Al-Kabbah. Abu Talib and the boy stood by the wall of Al-Kabbah and prayed for rain. Immediately Allah sent clouds from all directions. Rain fell heavily and it caused the flow of springs and growth of plants everywhere.

When Prophet Muhammad (peace be upon him) was 12 years old, he went with his uncle Abu Talib on a long business trip to Syria. When they reached Busra, they met a monk, a Roman. His name was Bahira (his real name was Georges).

The monk showed lots of kindness, and he entertained very lavishly. He then held the Prophet's hand and said: "You will be the master of all humans. Allah will send him with a Message that will be a mercy to all beings." Abu Talib asked: "How do you know all this?" The monk replied: "When you and your nephew appeared from the direction of Aqabah, I saw everything, trees, stones prostrated to the boy, which they never do except for a Prophet. And I recognized him also by the seal of Prophethood that is below his shoulder, like an apple. We learned this from our books."

He also asked Abu Talib to send the boy back home to Makkah because the Jews might kill him. Abu Talib obeyed and sent the Prophet (peace be upon him) back to Makkah with some of his servants.

The Prophet (peace be upon him) was about 15 years old when the sacrilegious wars began. Many people died. It broke out between Quraish and Banu Kinana on the one side and Qais Ailan tribe on the other. The war was a result of an unsettled murder. There was growing discontent with the form of justice that required sacrilegious war.

Many Quraysh leaders had travelled to Syria, where they found relative justice prevailed. Similar conditions also existed in Abyssinia. No such system, however, existed in Arabia.

Harb Ibn Omaiyah, due to his honorable lineage, was the leader of Quraish and their allies. In one of those battles, the Prophet (peace and blessings be upon him) attended the battle but did not raise arms against the enemy. His efforts were limited to collecting the arrows as they fell, and giving them over to his uncles.

Confederacy in Makkah

At the conclusion of the war, when peace returned, they tried to form confederacy in Makkah for suppressing violence and injustice, and for vindicating the rights of the weak and the poor.

Representatives from Banu Al-Muttalib, Banu Hashim, Zahrah ibn Kilab, Asad ibn Abd Al-Uzza, and Taim ibn Murra met in the habitation of an honorable man called Abdullah ibn Jadaan At-Taimy to enter into some form of confederacy that would provide for the above-mentioned needs.

The Prophet (peace be upon him) shortly after Allah had honored him with the ministry of Prophethood, observed this confederacy, and he said: "I witnessed a confederacy in the house of Abdullah ibn Jadaan. It was much more appealing to me than a herd of cattle. Even now in the period of Islam I would respond positively to going to such a meeting, if invited."

The confederacy marked a big departure from the pre-Islamic tribal-pride and war. The event that led to its convention says a man from Zubaid clan came to Makkah to sell commodities to Al-As ibn Wail As-Sahmy. However, they tried not to pay for the goods. The man sought help from the many different clans in Quraish but none helped him. He sought Allah's help. He went to a mountain top and began, at the top of his voice, to ask Allah for help, and he recited verses stating the injustices he sustained. Az-Zubair ibn Abdul-Muttalib heard of him and asked about the matter. Subsequently, the tribes to the above-stated confederacy forced Al-As ibn Wail to pay Az-Zubaidy.

The Prophet's first job

The Messenger of Allah (peace be upon him) worked as a shepherd for Bani Sa'd for many years. When he was 25 years old, he traveled to Syria as a merchant for Khadijah (may Allah be pleased with her). Ibn Ishaq reported that Khadijah was the daughter of Khwailid. She was a woman of great intellect and fortune. She often employed men for a percentage of the profits. Quraish were tradespeople. Therefore, when Khadijah learned of the Muhammad's truthfulness, honesty, and kindness, she sent for him. She asked him to go to Syria to do her business. She said that she would give him a higher rate than the other men. The Prophet (peace be upon him) agreed and traveled with her servant to Syria.

Marrying Khadijah

When the Prophet (peace be upon him) returned to Makkah, Khadijah saw a lot more profits and blessings. Her servant also told Khadijah of Muhammad's great honesty, truthfulness, sincerity, and faith. Many prominent men wanted to marry Khadijah, but she always rejected them.

Khadijah told her friend Nafisa, daughter of Maniya, about wanting to marry the Prophet (peace be upon him). Nafisa immediately went to the Prophet. He agreed and asked his uncles to go to Khadijah's family. Subsequently, they were married. The marriage agreement was witnessed by Bani Hashim and the heads of Mudar. The Prophet (peace be upon him) gave Khadijah 20 camels as dowry. She was 40 years old. She was the first woman whom the Prophet (peace be upon him) married. The Prophet did not marry any other woman until Khadijah died. He loved her very much.

Khadijah gave birth to all of the Prophet's children, but Ibrahim: Zainab, Al-Qasim, Ruqaiyah, Umm Kulthum, Fatimah, and Abdullah who was also called Tahir and Taiyib. However, for reasons only known to Allah, all the Prophet's sons died in their childhood, and all his daughters, but Fatimah only, died during the Prophet's lifetime. Fatimah died 6 months after the Prophet's death (peace be upon them). All of the Prophet's daughters witnessed Islam, accepted Islam, and emigrated to Madinah (peace and blessings be upon them all).

Rebuilding the House of Allah

When the Prophet (peace be upon him) was 35 years old, Quraish wanted to rebuild the House of Allah. The building at that time was low and of white stones, about 20.6 feet high, from the days and time of Prophet Ishmael (peace be upon him and his father, Prophet Ibrahim).

The House of Allah was also roofless. This gave the thieves a quick access to the treasures inside. It was also exposed to the sun and to rain. And since it was built centuries ago, its walls were broken and cracked. Moreover, five years before Prophethood, a great drought then flood almost demolished it.

Quraish was very compelled to rebuild it in order to safeguard its holiness and position. Quraish wanted to use only licit donations in rebuilding it. Therefore any money that was derived from prostitution, moneylending, and illegal practices were excluded. At first, they were too afraid to destroy its wall, however, Al-Waleed ibn Al-Mugheerah Al-Mukhzumi had already started the work. So seeing that no harm had happened to Al-Waleed, the others participated in demolishing its walls.

They stopped when they had reached the basis laid by Prophet Ibrahim (peace be upon him). When they began to rebuild its walls, they distributed the work among the tribes. The tribes collected stones and every tribe was responsible for rebuilding a part of the wall. The man that laid the stones was a Roman mason. His name was Baqum. The rebuilding went on in harmony till it was time to put the sacred Black Stone. Then anger broke out. Each tribe's chief wanted the honor of placing the stone in its proper position. Swords were out and bloodshed was imminent. However, the oldest chief, Abu Omaiyah ibn Mugheerah Al-Makhzumi made a suggestion that was accepted. He said: "Let the man who enters the Sanctuary next, decide." It was then Allah's Will that the Prophet (peace be upon him) should be that man to enter. On seeing him, all the people, cried out with one loud voice: "Al-Ameen (the trustworthy) has come. We will accept his decision."

The Messenger of Allah (peace be upon him) asked for a mantle, which he spread on the ground, then he placed the Black Stone in its middle. He asked the chiefs to lift the mantle together.

When the Black Stone had reached its proper position, the Messenger of Allah (peace and blessings be upon him) laid it with his own hands. The Prophet and his wisdom averted war between the tribes.

Quraish ran out of the licit donations that they had collected. So they decided to eliminate six yards from the northern part of Al-Kabbah, which is called Al-Hateem or Al-Hijr. They also raised the door two meters from the ground in order to let in only the people whom they liked. When the building was 43 feet high they added the roof, which rested on 6 columns.

The Message

When the Prophet (peace be upon him) was nearly 40 years old, he passed long hours in meditation and prayer, thinking about all the aspects of creation that was around him. He took some Sawiq (barley porridge) and water, and went to the hills. His favorite spot was the cave of Hira, in Mount An-Nour. The cave is 2 miles from Makkah. It is a small cave that is about 12 feet long and 5 feet wide. If he saw a traveler, he would invite him to share his modest provision. He spent most of his time, and Ramadan in particular, praying. His heart was tired and sad about the moral evils that were widespread among Quraish. This period of time must be understood in its Divine perspective. It was an initial stage to the period of grave responsibilities that the Prophet (peace be upon him) was about to accept.

When the Messenger of Allah (peace be upon him) was 40 years old, signs of his Prophethood from Allah began to appear. They signs began as visions, and he experienced them for six months. The visions came true all the time.

In Ramadan, in his 3rd year of solitude in the cave of Hira, Allah's message came. Allah's Will desired His mercy to flow on earth and Prophet Muhammad (peace be upon him) was honored with Prophethood on **Monday, the 21st of Ramadan, at night**. The Prophet (peace be upon him) was exactly 40 years, 6 months, and 12 days of age. When Truth (angel Jibril (Gabriel)) came down, he said: "Recite." "I cannot recite," the Prophet, replied. The Prophet described this to us: "The angel Jibril then took me and squeezed me very vehemently, then he let me go, and he repeated the order again, 'Recite!' 'I cannot recite,' I replied. Jibril (peace be upon him) once again he squeezed me hard and held me until I was exhausted. Then he said: 'Recite!' I replied: 'I cannot recite.' Jibril then held me and squeezed me very hard again, for a third time, and then he let me go, and said:

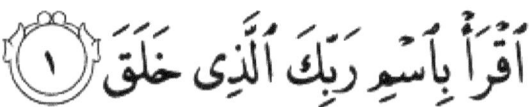

"*Recite! In the Name of your Lord, Who has created everything that exists. He created man from a clot (a piece of thick coagulated blood). Recite! And your Lord is the Most Generous.*" [96:1-3]

The night of the first revelation was at the end of the month of Ramadan, which was later named **lailatul Qadr**, or the Night of Power.

The Messenger of Allah (peace be upon him) repeated these verses. Perplexed by what had happened, the Messenger of Allah (peace be upon him) went home where he was comforted by his wife Khadijah. He said, "Cover me, cover me!" Khadijah held him and covered him till he felt better. The Prophet then described to Khadijah of the incident in the cave. She tried to reassure him and she said: "Allah will never disgrace you. For you uphold ties of kinship, you help the weak, you give charity to the poor, you entertain your guests, and you endure hardships in the path of honesty and truthfulness."

Khadijah then set out with Messenger of Allah (peace be upon him) to her Ebionite cousin Waraqah ibn Nawfal. Her cousin was familiar with Jewish and Christian scriptures. He had embraced Christianity in the pre-Islamic period, and used to write the Bible in Hebrew. At this time he was an old man and blind. Khadijah said: "Please listen to your nephew." Waraqah said: "O my nephew, what is the matter?"

The Prophet (peace be upon him) told him what had happened to him. Waraqah replied: "This is **Namus**, which meant the **angel Jibril** that Allah sent to Moses. I wish I were younger and could live up to the time when your people turn you out."

The Prophet (peace be upon him) asked: "They drive me out?" Waraqah answered in the affirmative and said: "Anyone who came with something similar to what you have brought was treated with hostility, and if I should be alive until that day, then I would support you strongly." However, a few days later Waraqah died, and the revelation also subsided.

The initial revelation was followed by a pause and a second encounter with Jibril when Prophet Muhammad heard a voice from the sky and saw the same angel sitting between the sky and the earth, and the revelations resumed with the first verses of chapter 74: *"O you who covers himself [with a garment]. Arise and warn. And your Lord glorify. And your clothing purify. And uncleanliness avoid."* (74:1-5)

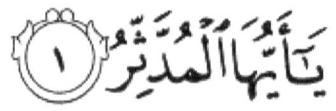

Ibn Hisham and At-Tabari related that the Prophet (peace be upon him) left the cave of Hira after the revelation, but later returned to the cave and continued his solitude.

Ibn Ishaq and At-Tabari wrote that the Prophet told Zubayr: "when I was midway on the mountain, I heard a voice from the sky saying: 'O Muhammad!' I raised my head towards the heavens to see who was speaking to me, and Jibril in the form of a man with feet astride the horizon, saying: 'O Muhammad! You are the apostle of Allah and I am the angel Jibril.' I stood looking at him. I was not moving forward nor backwards, then I began to turn my face away from him, but towards whatever region of the heavens I looked, I saw him as before."

Many scholars disagree about the period of time between Prophet Muhammad's 1st and 2nd experiences of revelation. Ibn Ishaq said that three years had elapsed from the time that Prophet Muhammad (peace be upon him) received the first revelation till he began to preach publicly. Bukhari takes chapter 74 as the second revelation however chapter 68 has strong claims to be the second revelation.

Nun. By the pen and what they inscribe. You are not, [O Muhammad], by the favor of your Lord, a madman. And indeed, for you is a reward uninterrupted. And indeed, you are of a great moral character. (68:1-4)

The Revelation stopped on the 4th verse on the letter Meem. The Revelation has exactly 68 Arabic characters in it. It has been placed in the Quran as chapter 68. The total number of verses in chapter 68 is equal to 52. This is the 25th position of the letter 'Noon' in the first Revelation transposed to arrive at 52 verses. Noon's position in the Arabic character set is 25.

The Prophet stood transfixed looking at Jibril. He tried to shift his eyes away but Jibril was in every direction the Prophet looked at. The Prophet stood without any movement until Khadijah sent someone to look for him. When the Prophet went back home, he sat close to Khadijah.

Khadijah asked the Prophet: "Father of Al-Qasim! Where have you been? I sent someone to Makkah to look for you." The Prophet told her what he had seen. She said: "It is a great sign from Allah. Please do not be afraid. Pull yourself together, for I swear by Allah that you are the Messenger for our nation." Khadijah then stood up and went to her uncle Waraqah. Waraqah said: "I swear by Allah that he is the Messenger. Tell him to be patient." She went back home and told him of Waraqah's words.

Revelation

Al-Bukhari reported that the Revelation paused for a few days, but some scholars said that it lasted for over 3.5 years. This is not correct. Still the Messenger of Allah (peace be upon him) was in a sort of depression. He tried a few times to throw himself from the tops of high mountains, but every time he went up the mountain, the angel Jibril appeared before him and said: "O Muhammad! Indeed you are Allah's Messenger in truth," whereupon his heart would calm down and he would return home.

Ibn Hajar reported that the pause of the revelation was to relieve the Prophet (peace and blessings be upon him) of the fear that he had experienced and to make him want the Revelation. When the darkness lifted, the Messenger of Allah (peace be upon him) was a different person. He began to see what he had to do. He knew for certain that he had become the Messenger of Allah. The revelation then began coming regularly and frequently.

The first revelations came to the prophets (peace & blessings be upon them) while they were sleeping until their hearts were reassured. Haykal said: "One day, while Muhammad (peace and blessings be upon him) was asleep in the cave, an angel approached him with a sheet in his hand." The angel asked Muhammad to read.

Jibril used to visit the Prophet (peace be upon him) in human form and spoke to him directly. This enabled the Prophet to fully understand what was said. Jibril was also seen in human form by the Prophet's Companions.

The Prophet (peace be upon him) said: "The Noble Spirit revealed to me that no soul will expire until it exhausts its due course, so fear Allah always. Never get so impatient to the point of disobedience. What Allah has can never be obtained but through obedience to Allah."

Jibril also used to come like the toll of a bell. This was the most exhausting form. He seized the Messenger of Allah (peace be upon him) so firmly that sweat would stream from the Prophet's forehead even on the coolest day. If the Messenger of Allah was sitting on his camel, the camel would quickly kneel down on the ground. Once the Prophet (peace and blessings be upon him) had such a revelation when he was sitting, and his thigh was touching Zaid's. Zaid felt the pressure and almost injured his thigh. The Messenger of Allah (peace be upon him) also saw Jibril's actual form. Jibril would reveal to the Prophet what he was ordered by Allah. This is mentioned in the Quran, Surat An-Najm (53): *Nor does he speak from [his own] inclination.*

It is not but a revelation revealed. Taught to him by one intense in strength. One of soundness. And he rose to his true form.

إِنْ هُوَ إِلَّا وَحْيٌ يُوحَىٰ ﴿٤﴾

عَلَّمَهُ شَدِيدُ ٱلْقُوَىٰ ﴿٥﴾

ذُو مِرَّةٍ فَٱسْتَوَىٰ ﴿٦﴾

Allah Himself talked to the Prophet when he ascended and received the order of prayer (Salat). (Chapter 17, the Journey by Night). *Exalted is He who took His Servant by night from al-Masjid al-Haram to al-Masjid al-Aqsa, whose surroundings We have blessed, to show him of Our signs. Indeed, He is the Hearing, the Seeing.* (17:1)

سُبْحَانَ ٱلَّذِي أَسْرَىٰ بِعَبْدِهِ لَيْلًا مِنَ ٱلْمَسْجِدِ ٱلْحَرَامِ إِلَى ٱلْمَسْجِدِ ٱلْأَقْصَا ٱلَّذِي بَارَكْنَا حَوْلَهُ لِنُرِيَهُ مِنْ آيَاتِنَا إِنَّهُ هُوَ ٱلسَّمِيعُ ٱلْبَصِيرُ ﴿١﴾

Some scholars stated that Allah spoke to the Prophet (peace be upon him) without a curtain in between. However, this issue remains unconfirmed.

When the Jews boasted that Moses did not require the angel Jibril to talk to Allah, Allah sent down the following verse: *And it is not for any human being that Allah should speak to him except by revelation or from behind a partition or that He sends a messenger to reveal, by His permission, what He wills. Indeed, He is Most High and Wise.* (42:51)

وَمَا كَانَ لِبَشَرٍ أَن يُكَلِّمَهُ ٱللَّهُ إِلَّا وَحْيًا أَوْ مِن وَرَآئِ حِجَابٍ أَوْ يُرْسِلَ رَسُولًا فَيُوحِيَ بِإِذْنِهِۦ مَا يَشَآءُ إِنَّهُۥ عَلِيٌّ حَكِيمٌ ۝

My Lord! Show me (Thy Self) so that I may gaze upon Thee. He said: Thou wilt not see Me, but gaze upon the mountain! If it stand still in its place, then thou wilt see Me. And when his Lord revealed (His) glory to the mountain He sent it crashing down. And Moses fell down senseless. And when he woke he said: Glory unto Thee! I turn unto Thee repentant, and I am the first of (true) believers. (7:143)

وَلَمَّا جَاءَ مُوسَىٰ لِمِيقَٰتِنَا وَكَلَّمَهُۥ رَبُّهُۥ قَالَ رَبِّ أَرِنِىٓ أَنظُرْ إِلَيْكَ قَالَ لَن تَرَىٰنِى وَلَٰكِنِ ٱنظُرْ إِلَى ٱلْجَبَلِ فَإِنِ ٱسْتَقَرَّ مَكَانَهُۥ فَسَوْفَ تَرَىٰنِى فَلَمَّا تَجَلَّىٰ رَبُّهُۥ لِلْجَبَلِ جَعَلَهُۥ دَكًّا وَخَرَّ مُوسَىٰ صَعِقًا فَلَمَّآ أَفَاقَ قَالَ سُبْحَٰنَكَ تُبْتُ إِلَيْكَ وَأَنَا۠ أَوَّلُ ٱلْمُؤْمِنِينَ ﴿١٤٣﴾

Three Years of Secret Call

Makkah was the center for the Arabs. It housed the guardians of Al-Kabbah. Also guardianship of the idols and the carved images was in the hands of the Makkans. Thus it was very difficult and dangerous to begin calling people to Islam in a place considered the den of idolatry. So the call unto Islam was conducted in clandestine locations so that the Makkans would not be angered by the unexpected surprise.

The First Converts

The Messenger of Allah (peace be upon him) naturally began his sacred mission at home, then invited friends and anyone that was closely associated with him. So he called unto Islam those people that he thought would quickly attest the truth that had come from Allah. Many immediately responded and embraced the true faith. In his immediate family circle not only his wife Khadijah, but his freed slave Zaid ibn Harithah, his cousin Ali ibn Abi Talib, who was living with him since childhood, and next came his best friend, Abu Bakr As-Siddiq (*the truth verifier*), all immediately entered the fold of Islam.

From the first day that he accepted Islam, Abu Bakr As-Siddiq was a great activist. Abu Bakr As-Siddiq was wealthy, honest, and kind. Through his hard efforts many people embraced Islam, such as Uthman ibn affan Al-Umawi, Abdur Rahman ibn Awf, Sa'd ibn Abi Waqqas, Az-Zuhri Talhah ibn Ubaidullah At-Tamimy, and Az-Zubair ibn Awwam Al-Asadi. These 6 men, plus Ali ibn Abi Talib and Zaid were the forerunners of the new faith in Arabia.

Among the early Muslims were Bilal ibn Rabah (the Abyssinian), Abu Salamah ibn Abd Al-Asad, Abu Ubaidah ibn Al-Jarrah from Bani Harith ibn Fahr (the most trustworthy), Uthman ibn Mazoun and his brothers Abdullah and Qudama, Al-Arqam ibn Abi Al-Arqam from the tribe of Makhzum, Ubaidah ibn Al-Harith ibn Al-Muttalib ibn Abd Munaf, Sa'id ibn Zaid Al-Adawi and his wife Fatimah (the sister of Omar ibn Al-Khattab), Khabbab ibn Al-Aratt, Abdullah ibn Masud Al-Hadhali and many others. These were the first companions of the Prophet (peace and blessing be upon him). These men and women were from various septs of Quraish. Ibn Hisham, a biographer, counted them to be more than 40.

Ibn Ishaq said the people then entered the folds of Islam in big groups and the new faith could no longer be kept hidden. The prophet (peace be upon him) used to teach the converts the religion in private. Revelation then accelerated. The verses revealed at this time were short ones with nice pauses and with fascinating rhythms in harmony with that delicate whispering setting. The central theme focused on purifying the soul. The early verses gave an accurate account of Paradise and the Hellfire.

The Prayer (As-Salat)

Prayer was established as a mandatory ritual at an early stage of the Islamic Call, two rakats after sunset and two before sunrise. Allah sent down the following verse: *So be patient, [O Muhammad]. Indeed, the promise of Allah is truth. And ask forgiveness for your sin and exalt [Allah] with praise of your Lord in the evening and the morning.* (40:55)

فَٱصْبِرْ إِنَّ وَعْدَ ٱللَّهِ حَقٌّ وَٱسْتَغْفِرْ لِذَنۢبِكَ وَسَبِّحْ بِحَمْدِ رَبِّكَ بِٱلْعَشِىِّ وَٱلْإِبْكَٰرِ ﴿٥٥﴾

Ibn Hijr stated that definitely the Prophet (peace and blessing be upon him) used to pray long before *The Night Journey*. It is reported through a chain of narrators that when the Messenger of Allah (peace and blessings be upon him) received the first Revelation, Jibril taught the Prophet (peace be upon him) how to do Wudu (ablution). When the Prophet (peace be upon him) was done, he took a handful of water and sprinkled it on his loins.

Ibn Hisham reported that before the time for prayer began, the Prophet (peace be upon him) and his Companions went to a mountain valley to pray. Abu Talib once saw the Prophet (peace be upon him) and Ali praying. When he understood that it was obligatory prayer, he told them to stay constant in their practice.

Quraishites Hearing the Call

The news about the call to Islam leaked out and assumed a public interest all over Makkah. In the beginning, the leaders of Makkah took no heed of the Prophet and his teachings. At first, they thought that the Prophet (peace be upon him) was a poet or a religious philosophist like Quss ibn Saidah, Omaiyah ibn Abi As-Salt, Amr ibn Nufail and their kind. However, this indifference quickly changed into real apprehension. The polytheists of Quraish then started to watch the Prophet closely and intently fearing his call.

For three underground years of activism, the Prophet (peace be upon him) had been content to teach within his narrow circle. However, the time had come to preach the faith openly.

Moreover, Jibril (peace be upon him) had brought the Prophet (peace be upon him) a further Revelation of Allah's Will to challenge his people, and to invalidate their falsehood, and to crush down their idolatrous ways.

Phase 2: Open Preaching

And warn, [O Muhammad], your closest kindred. [26:214]

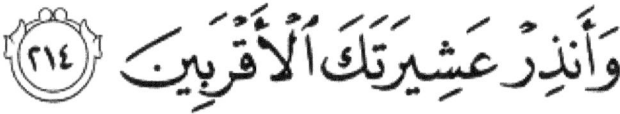

This verse was revealed to the Prophet (peace be upon him) about his tribe. It is from Surat Ash-Shu'ara (The Poets, 26). It tells the story of Prophet Musa (Moses) (peace be upon him) going through his migration with the Children of Israel, and their escape from the Pharaoh, and the drowning Pharaoh and his army.

Surat Ash-Shu'ara narrates the different stages that Musa (peace be upon him) went through in his struggle with Pharaoh and the mission of calling the people unto Allah. It includes stories that speak about the terrible punishment in store for those who denied the Messengers such as the people of Nuh, Ad, Thamud, Ibrahim, Lut and Ahlul-Aikah (The companions of the Wood). They were a group of people who worshiped a tree called Aikah.

The message that Surat Ash-Shu'ara communicates is very simple: "The Truth is undefeatable." When Message of Allah came to them, it was resisted, but truth will always prevail over falsehoods.

His Kinship

The Prophet (peace be upon him) rallied his family of Bani Hashim and Bani Al-Muttalib ibn Abd Munaf. There were 45 men in the meeting.

Abu Lahab immediately took the lead and addressed Prophet Muhammad (peace and blessings be upon him): "These are your cousins and uncles, speak on to the point, but you must understand that we are not in a position to withstand all the Arabs. Follow our traditions and it will be easier to face the other tribes. Verily, I have never heard of any man who has done more harm to his family than you."

The Prophet (peace and blessings be upon him) said nothing in that meeting. However, he invited everyone to another meeting and managed again to secure an audience.

The Messenger of Allah (peace be upon him) explained clearly what was at stake. The Messenger of Allah said: "I celebrate Allah's praise. I believe in Him. I put all my trust in Allah alone. I seek His help. I bear witness that there is no deity to be worshipped but Allah. A guide can never lie to his family. I have been sent to you, and I am the seal of the Prophets. I swear by Allah that everyone will die just as they sleep, and they will be resurrected just as they wake up. Allah will then call you to account for your deeds and actions. Then it is either the Garden (Paradise) forever, or Hellfire forever."

Abu Talib replied: "We want to help, and to accept your advice, and to believe in your words. We are you family and I am the fastest to do what you want. Please do what you have been ordered to do. I shall defend and protect you, but I cannot leave the religion of Abdul- Muttalib."

Abu Lahab quickly replied to Abu Talib: "This is a bad thing. You must ask him to stop him before the others do." Abu Talib replied: "I swear by Allah that I will protect him as long as I am alive."

From Mount As-Safa

Al-Bukhari reported part of this story on the authority of Ibn Abbas (May Allah be pleased with them). After the Messenger of Allah (peace and blessings be upon him) was certain of Abu Talib's pledge of protection, the Prophet stood on Mount As-Safa, and began to call the people: "O Bani Adi! And Bani Fahr! (Two Septs of Quraish).

Many people from Quraish gathered. Abu Lahab also went. The Prophet (peace be upon him) said: "If I were to tell you that there were some bandits in the valley that were planning to attack you, would you believe me?"

They answered: "Yes we would believe you. You have never lied to us."

The Prophet (peace be upon him) said: "Then please believe that I am a warner to you before a severe punishment."

Abu Lahab immediately said: "Perish you all! You have summoned us for such a thing?"

The following verses were immediately revealed:

Perish the two hands of Abu Lahab (an uncle of the Prophet), and perish he! His wealth and his children will not benefit him! He will be burnt in a Fire of blazing flames! And his wife, who carries wood (thorns of Sadan which she used to put on the way of the Prophet (peace be upon him), or use to slander him). In her neck is a twisted rope of Masad (palm fibre). (111:1-5)

The Polytheists Reaction

The Prophet's voice kept reverberating in every corner of Makkah until the following verse was sent down:

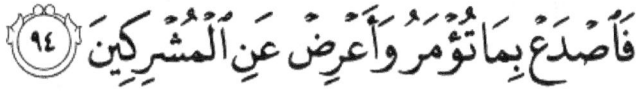

"*Then declare what you are commanded openly (Allah's Message) and turn away from the polytheists.*" [15:94]

The Prophet (peace be upon him) and his words infuriated the Makkans. They did not want to hear someone attacking their gods. They wanted to deal a pre-emptive strike before the Prophet destroyed their heritage. Their claimed religiously-based supremacy would no longer be in effect. Their pleasures would be subordinated to the pleasures of Allah and His Prophet. Allah talks about this in Surat Al-Qiyāmah (The Resurrection): *"Nay! Man denies Resurrection & Reckoning so to continue committing sins."* [75:5]

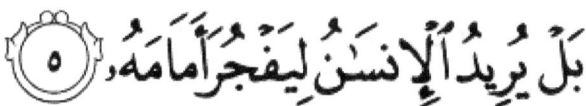

They were aware of the consequences of their behavior, but they pretended not to know.

After long, heated debates, they agreed to contact the Messenger's uncle, Abu Talib, and to ask him to stop his nephew. In order to attach a serious and heartfelt note to their demand, they chose to touch the most delicate thing in Arabian life, ancestral pride. They spoke to Abu Talib in the following fashion: "Abu Talib! Your nephew curses and mocks our idols and gods, and criticizes our way of life, either you must stop him, or you must let us kill him. For you are in the same position as we are in opposition to him, and we will free you of him." Abu Talib tried to calm their rage with the utmost kindness. The Messenger of Allah (peace be upon him) still continued preaching Allah's message and calling others to embrace it. Quraish had another concern. They were worried since the season of pilgrimage was about to begin and the pilgrims, who came from all over Arabia, could be swayed to follow the Prophet. This would be very bad for their pockets. The Kabbah was filled with their idols. Quraish made a lot of money, selling and maintaining their stone idols.

If people began to believe that there is only one God and that He listens to you from everywhere without the need to buy anything, this would be very disastrous for their business.

The pilgrims were coming within a short time. Quraish knew they had to come up with a plan to destroy the Prophet (peace and blessings be upon him) quickly.

They all agreed that it was necessary to contemplate a device that was bound to alienate the pilgrims from the new faith preached by Messenger of Allah (peace be upon him). So they decided to see Al-Waleed ibn Al-Mugheerah to deliberate on this issue. Al-Mugheerah was one of the main leaders of Quraish.

So they began plotting the attack. They considered calling the Prophet (peace be upon him) a liar, or a soothsayer, a poet, or a madman. But they decided the best thing to do, to ward off people, was to say that Muhammad was an evil magician, so if anyone listened to his message, he would separate a father from his son, and a wife from her husband.

So this is exactly what they did. When the pilgrims came, they ridiculed the Prophet (peace be upon him) in front of them. They would make fun of him and call him all sorts of names. But he, peace be upon him, was not discouraged. He continued his call to everyone and anyone.

Allah revealed sixteen verses in Surat Al-Muddaththir (The Cloaked One) about Al-Waleed and the cunning evil methods he contemplated to manipulate the pilgrims. Allah said:

"Indeed, he thought and plotted. So let him be cursed! How he plotted! Then he considered [again]; then he frowned and scowled; then he turned back and was arrogant and said: 'This is not but magic imitated [from others]. This is nothing but the word of a human being.'" [74:18-25]

The most wicked of them was the sworn enemy of the Messenger of Allah (peace and blessings be upon him), his uncle, Abu Lahab. He shadowed the Prophet's steps and shouted: "O men, do not listen to him for he is a liar. He is a madman."

However, the Prophet (peace be upon him) managed to awaken their minds and hearts. And some pilgrims accepted his Message.

The First Migration

A series of harassments began late in the fourth year of Prophethood, They began slowly at first, but sped up and worsened, and became awfully grave and no longer tolerable in the middle of the 5th year. So the Prophet (peace be upon him) wanted to find a way to deter the pains.

It was at that gloomy and desperate time that Surat Al-Kahf (The Cave, 18) was sent down. It contains definite answers to the questions with which the polytheists constantly harassed the Prophet (peace be upon him) about.

Surat Al-Kahf contains 3 beautiful stories that include highly suggestive parables for the true believers to think about. First, the story of the *Companions of the Cave*. It gives implicit guidance for the believers to abandon the land of disbelief.

وَإِذِ ٱعْتَزَلْتُمُوهُمْ وَمَا يَعْبُدُونَ إِلَّا ٱللَّهَ فَأْوُۥٓا إِلَى ٱلْكَهْفِ يَنشُرْ لَكُمْ رَبُّكُم مِّن رَّحْمَتِهِۦ وَيُهَيِّئْ لَكُم مِّنْ أَمْرِكُم مِّرْفَقًا ﴿١٦﴾

[The youths said to one another], "And when you have withdrawn from them and that which they worship other than Allah retreat to the cave. Your Lord will spread out for you of His mercy and will prepare for you from your affair facility." 18:16]

Next, there is also the story of Prophet Al-Khidr and Prophet Musa (Peace be upon them).

فَوَجَدَا عَبْدًا مِّنْ عِبَادِنَآ ءَاتَيْنَٰهُ رَحْمَةً مِّنْ عِندِنَا وَعَلَّمْنَٰهُ مِن لَّدُنَّا عِلْمًا ﴿٦٥﴾

"And they found a servant from among Our servants to whom we had given mercy from us and had taught him from Us a [certain] knowledge." [18:65]

From this aayah it is understood that the mercy mentioned here was the mercy of Prophethood. One of the indications that the mercy and knowledge with which Allah blessed His slave al-Khidr came by way of Prophethood and revelation is the aayah: *I did it not of my own accord. That is the interpretation of that about which you could not have patience.* [18:82]

So al-Khidr did them by the command of Allah, and the command of Allah is only conveyed by revelation. There is no way for the commands of Allah to be known except through revelation from Allah, especially with regard to the killing of an innocent soul, the little boy.

The al-Khidr story tells the believers to be patient, and to fight against oppression.

قَالَ سَتَجِدُنِىٓ إِن شَآءَ ٱللَّهُ صَابِرًا وَلَآ أَعْصِى لَكَ أَمْرًا ﴿٦٩﴾

"You will find me, if Allah wills, patient, and I will not disobey you in [any] order." [18:69]

There is also the story of Dhul-Qarnain (The Two Horned One).

وَيَسْـَٔلُونَكَ عَن ذِى ٱلْقَرْنَيْنِ قُلْ سَأَتْلُواْ عَلَيْكُم مِّنْهُ ذِكْرًا ﴿٨٣﴾

"And they ask you about Dhul-Qarnain. Say: "I shall recite to you something of his story." [18:83]

He was a powerful ruler of the east and west. This story tells us that Allah raises his righteous servants in order to protect the weak against the oppressors.

Surat Az-Zumar (The Troops, 39) was then sent down. It talks about migration and says that the earth is spacious. The believers must not consider themselves prisoners and constrained by the forces of tyranny and evil.

قُلْ يَـٰعِبَادِ ٱلَّذِينَ ءَامَنُوا۟ ٱتَّقُوا۟ رَبَّكُمْ ۚ لِلَّذِينَ أَحْسَنُوا۟ فِى هَـٰذِهِ ٱلدُّنْيَا حَسَنَةٌ ۗ وَأَرْضُ ٱللَّهِ وَٰسِعَةٌ ۗ إِنَّمَا يُوَفَّى ٱلصَّـٰبِرُونَ أَجْرَهُم بِغَيْرِ حِسَابٍ ﴿١٠﴾

"O My servants who have believed, fear your Lord. For those who do good in this world is good, and the earth of Allah is spacious. Indeed, the patient will be given their reward without account." [39:10].

The Messenger of Allah (peace be upon him) knew that Ashamah Negus, king of Abyssinia (Ethiopia), was a fair ruler who would not wrong any person. Therefore, he permitted some of his followers to seek asylum in Abyssinia (Ethiopia).

In Rajab of the 5th year of Prophethood, 12 men and 4 women moved to Ethiopia (Abyssinia). Amongst the emigrants were Uthman ibn Affan and his wife Ruqaiyah. She was the daughter of the Messenger of Allah (peace be upon him). About these two people, the Prophet (peace be and blessing be upon him) said:

"They are the first people to emigrate in the cause of Allah after Prophet Ibrahim and Prophet Lut (peace be upon them)."

They left Makkah and traveled under the darkness of night. They sailed on 2 boats that were sailing to Abyssinia (Ethiopia). However, Quraish heard about them. So men were dispatched to kill them, but the believers had already left the Port of Shuaibah headed towards their secure destination.

In that same year, during the month of Ramadan, the Prophet (peace be upon him) went into Quraish's Holy Sanctuary where there was a large host of Quraish polytheists, including many notables and celebrities. All of a sudden, the Prophet (peace be upon him) began reciting Surat An-Najm (The Star, Chapter 53).

The awe-inspiring Words of Allah, the Master and King of the Day of Judgment, descended unexpectedly upon them and they immediately got stunned by them. It was the first time for them to hear such truthful Revelation. In the past, each time they wished to dishonor Revelation, not only they did not listen to it but also talked loudly and disrespectfully when it was being read, so that even the true listeners could not hear a thing. They thought that they were drowning the Voice of Allah, but in fact, they were piling up sorrow for themselves, for Allah's Voice can never ever be silenced.

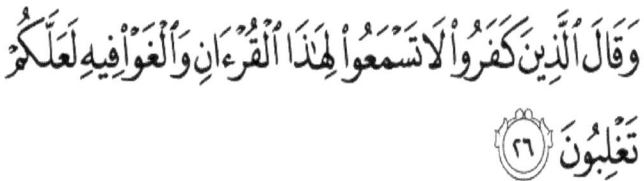

And those who disbelieve say, "Do not listen to this Qur'an and speak noisily during [the recitation of] it that perhaps you will overcome." [41:26]

When the amazing Words of Allah came down into direct contact with their ears and hearts, they were so entranced and were caught in a state of paralyzing fear, surprise, and bewilderment. They were in a state of full attentiveness to the Divine Words to such an extent that when the Messenger of Allah (peace and blessings be upon him) reached the stormy heart-beating ending:

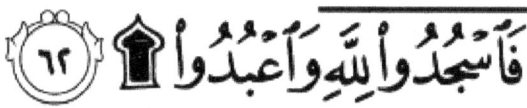

"So fall down in prostration to Allah and worship Allah (Alone)." [53:62]

إِذْ يَغْشَى ٱلسِّدْرَةَ مَا يَغْشَىٰ ﴿١٦﴾ مَا زَاغَ ٱلْبَصَرُ وَمَا طَغَىٰ ﴿١٧﴾ لَقَدْ رَأَىٰ مِنْ ءَايَٰتِ رَبِّهِ ٱلْكُبْرَىٰٓ ﴿١٨﴾ أَفَرَءَيْتُمُ ٱللَّٰتَ وَٱلْعُزَّىٰ ﴿١٩﴾ وَمَنَوٰةَ ٱلثَّالِثَةَ ٱلْأُخْرَىٰٓ ﴿٢٠﴾ أَلَكُمُ ٱلذَّكَرُ وَلَهُ ٱلْأُنثَىٰ ﴿٢١﴾ تِلْكَ إِذًا قِسْمَةٌ ضِيزَىٰٓ ﴿٢٢﴾ إِنْ هِيَ إِلَّآ أَسْمَآءٌ سَمَّيْتُمُوهَآ أَنتُمْ وَءَابَآؤُكُم مَّآ أَنزَلَ ٱللَّهُ بِهَا مِن سُلْطَٰنٍ ۚ إِن يَتَّبِعُونَ إِلَّا ٱلظَّنَّ وَمَا تَهْوَى ٱلْأَنفُسُ ۖ وَلَقَدْ جَآءَهُم مِّن رَّبِّهِمُ ٱلْهُدَىٰٓ ﴿٢٣﴾ أَمْ لِلْإِنسَٰنِ مَا تَمَنَّىٰ ﴿٢٤﴾ فَلِلَّهِ ٱلْءَاخِرَةُ وَٱلْأُولَىٰ ﴿٢٥﴾ ۞ وَكَم مِّن مَّلَكٍ فِى ٱلسَّمَٰوَٰتِ لَا تُغْنِى شَفَٰعَتُهُمْ شَيْـًٔا إِلَّا مِنۢ بَعْدِ أَن يَأْذَنَ ٱللَّهُ لِمَن يَشَآءُ وَيَرْضَىٰٓ ﴿٢٦﴾

The idolaters, unconsciously and with full compliance, prostrated in absolute Allah-fearing and devotion. They stood aghast when they sensed that Allah's Words had conquered their soul and heart and done what they had been trying hard to destroy and annihilate. The polytheists who had not been present there admonished them harshly. Afterwards they started again to fabricate more lies about the Messenger of Allah (peace be upon him). They were desperate attempts made to establish an excuse for their prostrating themselves with the Prophet on that day.

The Return to Makkah

News of the polytheists prostrating was misreported to the Muslim expatriates in Abyssinia (Ethiopia). They heard that all of Quraish had embraced Islam, so they returned back to Makkah.

They reached in Makkah in Shawwal of that same year. When they were only an hour's away from Makkah, they learned the truth. Some of them quickly returned to Abyssinia (Ethiopia), but others went secretly into Makkah. However, when the polytheists heard that the Muslims were treated kindly in Abyssinia (Ethiopia), the polytheists became more enraged. They began to dispense harsher treatment and more tortures. Therefore, the Messenger of Allah (peace be upon him) permitted the helpless to seek asylum in Abyssinia (Ethiopia) for the second time. However, migration this time was tougher, for the polytheists were on the alert. In spite of this, the Muslims escaped. The group of emigrants this time included 83 men and 19 women.

The Envoys of Quraish

Quraish could not bear the prospect of a secure refuge for the Muslims in Ethiopia (Abyssinia), so they sent 2 faithful envoys to demand the Muslim extradition. They were Abdullah ibn Abi Rabi'a and Amr ibn Al-As. This is before they both embraced Islam. They took with them valuable gifts to the king of Abyssinia and to his clergy. The pagan envoys said that the Muslims must be expelled because they had left the religion of their forefathers, and their leader was preaching a religion different from their own and of that of the king.

The king quickly summoned the Muslims to his court and asked them to explain the teachings of Muhammad (peace be upon him). Ja'far ibn Abi Talib addressed the king as such: "O king! Before Islam, we were plunged in the depth of ignorance. We worshipped idols. We ate the dead. We abandoned our family, and neglected our neighbors and friends. Our laws were unjust. The strong forced their will upon the weak. But then Allah raised amongst us a man, of whose birth, purity, honesty, and truthfulness we knew, and he called to the Oneness of Allah, and taught us not to associate anything with Him.

The Messenger of Allah (peace be upon him) forbade us from worshiping images and idols. He ordered us to speak the truth always, to be faithful, to be merciful, and to honor the rights of our friends and neighbors. And not to encroach upon the rights of the orphans, and not speak evil of women. He ordered us to stay away from vices, to offer prayers, to give alms to the poor, and to observe fast.

We have accepted the Message given to him, and the command to worship Allah alone, and not to associate anything with Him. For these reasons, our own people have persecuted us to make us abandon worshiping Allah. They have tortured and crucified us. So we came here, and hope that you will protect us from oppression."

Ashamah Negus, king of Abyssinia, was very impressed by Ja'far's speech. The king asked the Muslims to recite some of Allah's Revelation. So Ja'far recited the opening verses of Surat Maryam (Mary), which tells the story of Maryam and of the birth of both Prophet Jesus and Prophet John (peace be upon them).

بِسْمِ اللَّهِ الرَّحْمَٰنِ الرَّحِيمِ

كهيعص ﴿١﴾ ذِكْرُ رَحْمَتِ رَبِّكَ عَبْدَهُ زَكَرِيَّا ﴿٢﴾ إِذْ نَادَىٰ رَبَّهُ نِدَاءً خَفِيًّا ﴿٣﴾ قَالَ رَبِّ إِنِّي وَهَنَ الْعَظْمُ مِنِّي وَاشْتَعَلَ الرَّأْسُ شَيْبًا وَلَمْ أَكُن بِدُعَائِكَ رَبِّ شَقِيًّا ﴿٤﴾ وَإِنِّي خِفْتُ الْمَوَالِيَ مِن وَرَائِي وَكَانَتِ امْرَأَتِي عَاقِرًا فَهَبْ لِي مِن لَّدُنكَ وَلِيًّا ﴿٥﴾ يَرِثُنِي وَيَرِثُ مِنْ آلِ يَعْقُوبَ ۖ وَاجْعَلْهُ رَبِّ رَضِيًّا ﴿٦﴾ يَا زَكَرِيَّا إِنَّا نُبَشِّرُكَ بِغُلَامٍ اسْمُهُ يَحْيَىٰ لَمْ نَجْعَل لَّهُ مِن قَبْلُ سَمِيًّا

[This is] a mention of the mercy of your Lord to His servant Zechariah. When he called to his Lord a private supplication. He said, "My Lord, indeed my bones have weakened, and my head has filled with white, and never have I been in my supplication to You, my Lord, unhappy. And indeed, I fear the successors after me, and my wife has been barren, so give me from Yourself an heir. Who will inherit me and inherit from the family of Jacob. And make him, my Lord, pleasing [to You]." [He was told], "O Zechariah, indeed We give you good tidings of a boy whose name will be John. We have not assigned to any before [this] name." [19]

Thereupon king Negus, along with the clergy of his realm, were moved to tears that rolled down their cheeks. The king even wet his beard. Then king Negus said: "These words and those which were revealed to Jesus (peace be upon him) are the rays of the light that have radiated from the same lord." The king then turned to the dejected envoys of Quraish, he said: "Never would I give you back these refugees. They are free to worship and to live in my realm as long as they please."

The envoys said that the Prophet (peace and blessings be upon him) and his followers blasphemed Jesus (peace be upon him). The Muslims were summoned again, and asked what they thought of Jesus. Ja'far answered: "We speak about Jesus Christ (peace be upon him) as the Prophet (peace be upon him) taught us. Jesus is the servant of Allah, and His Messenger. His soul and His Word were breathed into Virgin Mary." The king at once remarked: "This is what we believe. Blessed be you, and blessed be your Prophet." The king then turned to his bishops who looked very upset, he said: "You may fret and fume but Jesus (peace be upon him) is nothing more than what Ja'far has said about him."

He then assured Ja'far and the Muslims of full protection. The king gave back the gifts the envoys of Quraish had brought him, and asked them to leave his country. The Muslims lived in Abyssinia (Ethiopia) untouched and unharmed for many years until they returned to Madinah.

Quraish came to realize that the grudge they nursed against the Prophet (peace and blessings be upon him) would not work but within Makkah. However, now they wanted to kill the Prophet (peace be upon him). They approached Abu Talib for the second time and insisted that he must stop his nephew, or they will be in a war with him as well. Abu Talib was very distressed at their threat, but he could not afford to desert his beloved nephew. He sent for the Prophet (peace be upon him) and told him what they had said, and he said: "Spare me and yourself and do not put a burden on me that I cannot bear." Upon this the Messenger of Allah thought that his uncle would no longer support him, so he replied: "O my uncle! By Allah if they put the moon in my left hand and the sun in my right hand on condition that I must abandon Allah's path, I will never. Even if I perish, I would not abandon it."

The Prophet (Peace be upon him) got up, and as he was leaving, his uncle called him back and said: "My nephew, go and preach what you please, for by Allah I will never abandon you."

But seeing that the Messenger of Allah was committed to his call, again Quraish went to Abu Talib. But then they realized that Abu Talib would never abandon his nephew. So again they went to see him, and they took with them a boy, Amarah ibn Al-Waleed ibn Al-Mugheerah, and said: "O Abu Talib! We have brought you a good boy to make use of his mind and strength, and to take him as your son in exchange for your evil nephew, who has abandoned your forefathers' religion, and brought shame to your family. Allow us to kill him and rid every one of his endless headaches and troubles."

However, Abu Talib said: "This is truly an unfair bargain. You give me your son and I give you my nephew to kill him! By Allah, this is wrong!" Then Al-Mutim ibn Adi, a member of the delegation, interrupted and said: "We have been very fair. We want to rid you of your evil nephew, but we can see that you are determined to refuse our favors."

Abu Talib, turned down all their proposals and he challenged them to do whatever they wanted.

To Kill the Prophet

After all the schemes had failed, Quraish persecuted and inflicted more tortures on the Muslims in a more brutal way. They decided to kill the Messenger of Allah (peace be upon him). However, contrary to their hopes, this consolidated the Call to Islam more. Then Hamzah ibn Abdul-Muttalib and Omar ibn Al-Khattab (May Allah be pleased with them), embraced Islam.

Utaibah ibn Abi Lahab once approached the Messenger of Allah (peace be upon him) and most shamelessly and defiantly bellowed at the Prophet: "I disbelieve in":

"By the star when it descends." [53:1]

Utaibah then said: "I disbelieve in your Quran and in":

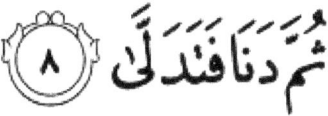

"*Then he [Jibrael (Gabriel)] approached and came closer*" [53:8]

Utaibah ibn Abi Lahab then began to deal harshly with the Prophet (peace be upon him) and laid his evil and violent hand on the Prophet (peace be upon him). He tore the Prophet's shirt and spat at the face of the Prophet, but he missed the Holy face of the Prophet (peace and blessings be upon him). The Prophet (peace be upon him) invoked Allah's wrath on Utaibah and supplicated: "O Allah, the Almighty! Set one of Your dogs on him."

Allah responded to the Prophet's prayer. Utaibah with some of his friends set out for Syria. They slept in Az-Zarqa. A lion approached them. Utaibah remembered the Prophet's supplication. He said: "This lion will surely devour me as Muhammad (peace be upon him) supplicated. He has killed me in Syria while he is in Makkah." The lion then rushed at him like lightning, and snatched Utaibah from amongst his friends and crushed his head.

It is also reported that a wretched idolater Uqbah ibn Abi Mu'ait once crushed the Prophet's neck while the Prophet (peace be upon him) was prostrating himself in prayer until the Prophet's eyes protruded. More such incidents were reported by Ibn Ishaq that show the idolaters hatred of the Messenger of Allah (peace be upon him).

Abu Jahl, the archenemy of the Prophet and Islam, once addressed some of his tribe: "O people of Quraish! Muhammad (peace be upon him) is determined to destroy the religion of our forefathers. He dishonors our way of life, and he abuses our gods. I bear witness to our gods that I will crush Muhammad's head with a big rock while he is in prostration to rid you of him, once and for all. I am not afraid of his sept, Banu Abd Munaf." The terrible and evil audience endorsed his plan and encouraged him to do it quickly.

The next morning, Abu Jahl waited for the Messenger of Allah (peace be upon him) to offer prayer. Quraish sat in their assembly rooms waiting for the death of the Prophet (peace be upon him).

When the Prophet (peace be upon him) prostrated himself, Abu Jahl took a big rock, but as he tried to approach the Prophet (peace and blessings be upon him), he had to withdraw fast. His face was pale as a ghost, and he trembled terribly. Immediately Quraish ran towards him and asked him what has happened. Abu Jahl replied: "When I approached, a male-camel that is very unusual in figure with very fearful canines tried to devour me."

Ibn Ishaq said that the Prophet (peace be upon him), in the context of his comment on the incident, said: "It was Jibril (peace and blessings be upon him). If Abu Jahl had come closer to the Prophet, Jibril had permission from Allah to kill him."

Even so, the tyrants kept trying. Abdullah ibn Amr ibn Al-As said that some people of Quraish were complaining that they had been patient with the Prophet (peace be upon him), who suddenly appeared, then began his usual Tawaaf of the Al-Kabbah. They began to shout and to say sarcastic remarks at him, but the Prophet (peace be upon him) remained silent for two times. On the third, the Prophet stopped and addressed the infidels:

"O people of Quraish! I swear by Allah in Whose Hand is my soul, that you will one day be slaughtered to the last man." As soon as the Prophet (peace be upon him) said 'slaughter,' they all stopped laughing and tried to soothe his anger.

Urwa ibn Az-Zubair said that he asked Abdullah ibn Amr ibn Al-As to tell him of the worst thing that the pagans did to the Prophet (peace be upon him). He said that while the Prophet (peace be upon him) was once praying, Uqbah ibn Al-Muait came and put his garment around the Prophet's neck and strangled the Prophet (peace be upon him) with all this might. Abu Bakr quickly caught him and pushed him away from the Prophet and said: "Do you want to kill a man just because he says, Allah is my Lord?"

Hamzah Ibn Abdul-Muttalib

In the 6th year of Prophethoold, Hamzah ibn Abdul-Muttalib embraced Islam. One day the Prophet (peace and blessing be upon him) was sitting on the hillock of Safa when Abu Jahl happened to pass by and insulted Islam. The Prophet (peace be upon him) kept silent. Abu Jahl took a big rock and cracked the Prophet's head, which began to bleed heavily. Abu Jahl then went to join the Quraishites in their assembly. Shortly after that, Hamzah, while returning from a hunting journey, passed by the same path. His bow was hanging from his shoulder. A slave-girl belonging to Abdullah ibn Jada'an, who had seen the attack, told Hamzah the whole story.

On hearing that, Hamzah was very upset and hurried to Al-Kabbah and there, in the Holy Sanctuary, he found Abu Jahl sitting with Quraishites. Hamzah rushed upon him and struck his bow upon Abu Jahl's head violently and said: "Ah! You have been abusing Muhammad (peace and blessings be upon him). I too follow Muhammad's religion and I profess what he preaches."

Many men rushed to Abu Jahl's help, but Abu Jahl sent them away and said: "Let Abu Ummarah alone, I did abuse his nephew shamelessly." At first, Hamzah's conversion derived initially from the pride of a man who would not accept others humiliating his relatives, but later he was a great strength to Islam.

Omar Ibn Al-Khattab

Three days later after Hamzah became a Muslim, Omar Ibn Al-Khattab became a Muslim, in Dhul-Hijjah, the sixth year of Prophethood. Omar was a man of daring courage. He was feared and respected. The Prophet (peace and be upon him) once raised his hands in prayer and said: "O Allah! Give strength to Islam through the man that you love more: Abu Jahl ibn Hisham or Omar ibn Al-Khattab"

When we examine the several versions that speak of Omar's conversion, we can see various contradictory emotions. On the one hand, he always highly honored the traditions of his people. He liked wine orgies. But on the other hand, he greatly admired the resilience of the Messenger of Allah (peace be upon him) and his relentless dedication to his faith.

These two extreme aspects of Omar's soul created some skepticism in his mind and made him at times believe that Islam is better without him. He experienced fits of outrage followed by fatigue. So his conversion is very interesting.

One day, Omar ibn Al-Khattab headed for the Holy Sanctuary where he heard the Prophet (peace be upon him) offering prayer. He overheard him reciting Surat Al-Haqqah (The Reality, 69).

بِسْمِ اللَّهِ الرَّحْمَنِ الرَّحِيمِ

ٱلْحَاقَّةُ ﴿١﴾ مَا ٱلْحَاقَّةُ ﴿٢﴾ وَمَا أَدْرَاكَ مَا ٱلْحَاقَّةُ ﴿٣﴾ كَذَّبَتْ ثَمُودُ وَعَادٌ بِٱلْقَارِعَةِ ﴿٤﴾ فَأَمَّا ثَمُودُ فَأُهْلِكُوا بِٱلطَّاغِيَةِ ﴿٥﴾ وَأَمَّا عَادٌ فَأُهْلِكُوا بِرِيحٍ صَرْصَرٍ عَاتِيَةٍ ﴿٦﴾ سَخَّرَهَا عَلَيْهِمْ سَبْعَ لَيَالٍ وَثَمَانِيَةَ أَيَّامٍ حُسُومًا فَتَرَى ٱلْقَوْمَ فِيهَا صَرْعَىٰ كَأَنَّهُمْ أَعْجَازُ نَخْلٍ خَاوِيَةٍ ﴿٧﴾ فَهَلْ تَرَىٰ لَهُم مِّنۢ بَاقِيَةٍ ﴿٨﴾

The Inevitable Reality. What is the Inevitable Reality? And what can make you know what is the Inevitable Reality? Thamud and Ad denied the Calamity.

113

So as for Thamud, they were destroyed by a storm of thunder and lightning. And as for Ad, they were destroyed by a violent wind. Which Allah imposed upon them for seven nights and eight days in succession, so you would see the people therein fallen as if they were hollow trunks of palm trees. Then do you see of them any remains? [69:1-8]

The Words of Allah grabbed his heart. They penetrated the innermost cells of his soul. He said that it felt that the words came from a higher power, and he began to question his people's allegations that the man-composed poetry. The Prophet (peace be upon him) went on to recite:

إِنَّهُ لَقَوْلُ رَسُولٍ كَرِيمٍ ۝ وَمَا هُوَ بِقَوْلِ شَاعِرٍ قَلِيلًا مَّا تُؤْمِنُونَ ۝ وَلَا بِقَوْلِ كَاهِنٍ قَلِيلًا مَّا تَذَكَّرُونَ ۝ تَنزِيلٌ مِّن رَّبِّ ٱلْعَٰلَمِينَ ۝

This indeed, the Quran is the word of a noble Messenger. And it is not the word of a poet, or the word of a soothsayer; little do they know. This is the Revelation sent down from the Lord of the Alamin (the Creator of the Universe, mankind, jinn, and all that exists). [69:40-43]

As the Messenger of Allah (peace and blessings be upon him) recited, Islam permeated Omar's heart. But the dark layer of pre-Islamic bigotry and the blind pride in his forefathers overshadowed the essence of the great Truth that began to penetrate its way reluctantly into his soul. He, therefore, continued in his atrocities towards the Prophet and Islam. His sharp temper and extreme hate of the Prophet (peace be upon him) led him one time to leave his house, sword in hand, with the intention of killing the Messenger of Allah (peace and blessings be upon him).

Nuaim ibn Abdullah, a friend, met him on the way accidentally. What had caused so much anger in him and on whom was the fury to burst, he asked. Omar replied angrily: "To destroy the man Muhammad, this traitor, who has shattered the unity of Quraish, and picked holes in our religion, dishonored our wise men, and cursed our gods." Nuaim said: "Omar, I am positive that your soul has deceived you. Do you think that Banu Abd Munaf would let you live if you kill Muhammad (peace be upon him)? Take care of your own family first that betrayed us, and set them right."

Omar asked angrily: "Which of the folk of my house?" Nuaim replied: "Your sister and brother-in-law have embraced Islam and abandoned our religion."

Omar angrily directed his footsteps to his sister's house. As he drew near, he heard the voice of Khabbab ibn Aratt, who was reading Surat Ṭaha (Ta-Ha, 20) to both of them.

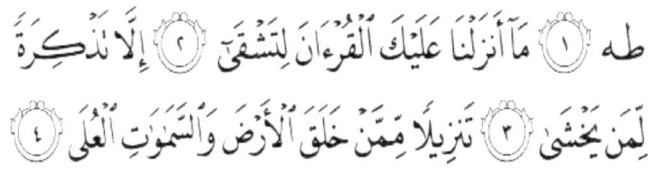

Ta, Ha. [These letters are one of the miracles of the Quran, and none but Allah (Alone) knows their meanings.] We have not sent down the Quran unto you (O Muhammad) to cause you distress.
But only as a Reminder to those who fear (Allah). A revelation from Allah Who has created the earth and heavens. [20:1-4]

Khabbab heard the noise of his footsteps and he quickly hid in the closet. Fatimah, Omar's sister, took hold of the parchment leaf and she hid it. But Omar had already heard his voice reading Surat Ṭaha.

Omar said angrily: "What was that sound that I heard?" His sister and her husband replied" "You heard nothing." "Nay," he said, swearing violently. Omar continued: "I just heard that you have apostatized." He then plunged towards his brother-in-law and hit him violently. Fatimah rushed to rescue him. Immediately, Omar struck her upon her head. Fatimah and her husband then cried aloud: "Yes, we are Muslims, and we believe in Allah and His Messenger (peace be upon him), so do whatever you want."

However, when Omar saw the face of his sister covered with so much blood, he was softened and said: "Let me see what you were reading, so that I may see what Muhammad has brought." But Fatimah said: "O brother, you are unclean, none but the pure may touch it. Please go and wash first." He did so, and took the page and read Surat Ta-Ha until he reached:

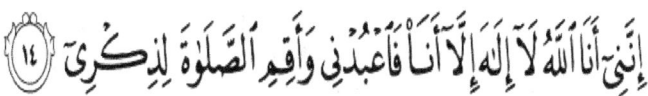

Indeed, I am Allah. There is no deity except Me, so worship Me and establish prayer for My remembrance. [20:14]

Omar was entranced with Ta-Ha. "How beautiful it is, and how graceful! Please guide me to Muhammad," said he. When Khabbab heard this, he said: "O Omar, I hope that Allah has answered the prayer of His Messenger (peace be upon him), for I heard him pray: 'O Allah! Strengthen Islam through either Omar ibn Al-Khattab or Abu Jahl ibn Hisham.'"

Omar then left for a house in Safa where the Messenger of Allah (peace be upon him) was having a secret meeting with his Companions. Omar reached the door with the sword swinging by his arm. He knocked. The Companions turned to see who it was. One of them said: "It is Omar with his sword." Hamzah, dismissing the fears of his friends, said: "Let Omar in. As a friend he is welcome here. But as an enemy, he will have his head cut off with his own sword."

The Prophet (peace be upon him) asked his Companions to open the door. In came Omar. Prophet Muhammad (peace upon him) asked him the reason for his visit. He said: "I come to you in order to believe in Allah and his Messenger and that which he has sent down to you."

Filled with so much delight, the Prophet (peace be upon him) together with his Companions, cried aloud: 'Allahu Akbar' (Allah is Great).

Omar's conversion was a true triumph for Islam. So great was the effect of this on the believers, who were worshiping Allah in secret within four walls, now worshiped openly in the Holy Sanctuary itself. This raised their spirits so high, but dread and uneasiness began to seize Quraish.

Ibn Ishaq reported on the authority of Omar (may Allah be pleased with him): "When I embraced Islam, I remembered the enemy of the Prophet (peace be upon him), i.e., Abu Jahl. So I set out, and I knocked at his door. When he came out, I told him that I had embraced Islam. He slammed the door in my face repulsively, and denounced my actions as shameful and my face as ugly."

Omar's conversion created a great deal of anger. Many people denounced him as an apostate. However, he never wavered in Faith, on the contrary, he persisted in his position even when they wanted to kill him. The polytheists of Quraish marched towards Omar's house in order to kill him.

Abdullah ibn Omar narrated (May Allah be pleased with him): "While Omar was at home, Al-As ibn Wa'il As-Sahmy Abu Amr, came. Al-As was from the tribe of Bani Sahm who were our allies during the pre-Islamic period of ignorance. Al-As said to Omar: 'What is wrong?' He said: 'Your people said they will kill me.' Al-As said: 'Nobody will ever touch you after I have given protection.' So Al-As went out and met his people. He said: 'Where are you going?' They replied: 'We want Omar. He has embraced Islam.' Al-As said: 'Anyone that will touch him will answer to me.' So the people retreated."

Omar embracing Islam had a remarkable impact on the Muslims living in Makkah. Mujahid, on the authority of Ibn Al-Abbas (May Allah be pleased with him) reported that he had asked Omar why he had been given the label of Al-Farouq (the one who distinguishes between right and wrong). He replied: After I had embraced Islam, I asked the Prophet (peace be upon him): 'Are we not on the right path here and Hereafter?' The Prophet (peace be upon him) replied: 'Of course you are! I swear by Allah in Whose Hand is my soul, you are right in this world and in the hereafter.'

Therefore, I asked the Prophet (peace be upon him): 'Why we then had to conduct underground activism. I swear by Allah Who has sent you with the Truth, that we will proclaim your noble cause publicly. We then went out in two groups, Hamzah leading one group, and I the other group. We headed towards Makkah. When the polytheists of Quraish saw us, their faces became pale and got incredibly dejected. On that very occasion, the Messenger of Allah (peace be upon him) gave me the label of Al-Farouq.'

Ibn Masud (May Allah be pleased with him) reported that they (the Muslims) had never been able to perform their prayers inside the Holy Sanctuary except when Omar embraced Islam.

Suhaib ibn Sinan (May Allah be pleased with him) said: "It was only after Omar's embraced Islam, that we began to state our Call, and circumambulate the Sacred House freely. We even had the courage to retaliate against anyone that tried to harm us." In the same context, Ibn Masud said: "Muslims were strengthened a lot since Omar embraced Islam."

Quraish Negotiates

Shortly after the conversion of Hamzah and Omar ibn Al-Khattab (May Allah be pleased with them), Quraish realized that it was no use dispensing out torture. So they began to direct their campaign to a different course. The leaders of Quraish gathered at Al-Kabbah, and Utbah ibn Rabi'a, a chief among them, offered to approach the Messenger of Allah (peace be upon him) and contract a bargain with him. They agreed to give him whatever wealth that he wanted, on condition that he no longer proclaim his new faith. The polytheists endorsed the proposal. Utbah addressed the Prophet (peace be upon him) with the following words:

"No other man of Arabia has brought so great a disaster to a nation, as you have done. You have abused our religion and gods and created strife amongst us. You have left no stone unturned to destroy the relations with us. If you are doing all this for wealth, we will give you greater riches than any Quraishite has ever possessed. And we will make you our top chief. If you are under the power of an evil spirit, and you cannot shake off its load, then we will call a skillful physician to cure you."

"Have you said everything?" asked the Messenger of Allah (peace be upon him). And upon hearing that all had been said, the Prophet began with the Quran, Surat Fuşşilat (Explained in Detail, 41):

$$\text{حمٓ ۝ تَنزِيلٌ مِّنَ ٱلرَّحْمَٰنِ ٱلرَّحِيمِ ۝ كِتَٰبٌ فُصِّلَتْ ءَايَٰتُهُۥ قُرْءَانًا عَرَبِيًّا لِّقَوْمٍ يَعْلَمُونَ ۝ بَشِيرًا وَنَذِيرًا فَأَعْرَضَ أَكْثَرُهُمْ فَهُمْ لَا يَسْمَعُونَ ۝}$$

Ha-Mim. [These letters are one of the wonders of the Quran. None but Allah (Alone) knows their meanings.] This is a revelation from the Entirely Merciful. A Book whose verses have been detailed, an Arabic Quran for a people who know. As a giver of good tidings and a warner; but most of them turn away, so they do not hear. [41:1-4]

The Prophet (peace be upon him) recited the Chapter while Utbah sat and listened attentively. When the Messenger of Allah (peace be upon him) reached the verse that required prostration, the Messenger of Allah (peace be upon him) immediately prostrated himself.

After that, the Messenger of Allah (peace be upon him) turned to Utbah and said: "Well Abu Al-Waleed! I have just given you my reply. You are now free to do whatever you please."

Utbah returned to his people to apprise them of the Prophet's answer. When his compatriots saw him, they swore that he had returned to them with an expression unlike the one he had before meeting the Messenger of Allah (peace be upon him).

He told them what had happened, and the reply that he received, and he added the following: "I have never heard words such as those that Muhammad (peace be upon him) recited. They absolutely relate neither to witchcraft nor poetry. And they do not derive from soothsaying. O people of Quraish! Grant this man full freedom to pursue his purpose, in which case you could safely detach yourselves from him completely. I swear to you that his words carry a supreme Message from Allah. Should another Arab tribe rid you of him, then they will spare you the headache, on the other hand if he succeeds, then you will bask in his kingship and share him his power."

His words of course fell on deaf ears, and did not appeal at all to them. They jeered at Utbah and claimed that Muhammad (peace and blessings be upon him) had bewitched him. In another version of the same event, it was reported that Utbah attentively listened to the Messenger of Allah (peace and blessings be upon him) until he began to recite Allah's Words:

إِذْ جَاءَتْهُمُ ٱلرُّسُلُ مِنْ بَيْنِ أَيْدِيهِمْ وَمِنْ خَلْفِهِمْ أَلَّا تَعْبُدُوٓاْ إِلَّا ٱللَّهَ قَالُواْ لَوْ شَاءَ رَبُّنَا لَأَنزَلَ مَلَٰٓئِكَةً فَإِنَّا بِمَآ أُرْسِلْتُم بِهِۦ كَٰفِرُونَ ۝ فَأَمَّا عَادٌ فَٱسْتَكْبَرُواْ فِى ٱلْأَرْضِ بِغَيْرِ ٱلْحَقِّ وَقَالُواْ مَنْ أَشَدُّ مِنَّا قُوَّةً أَوَلَمْ يَرَوْاْ أَنَّ ٱللَّهَ ٱلَّذِى خَلَقَهُمْ هُوَ أَشَدُّ مِنْهُمْ قُوَّةً وَكَانُواْ بِـَٔايَٰتِنَا يَجْحَدُونَ

"But if they turn away, then say, "I have warned you of a thunderbolt like the thunderbolt that struck Aad and Thamud. When the Messengers came to them, from before them and behind them (saying): 'Worship none but Allah'. They said: If our Lord had so willed, He would surely have sent down the angels. So indeed! We disbelieve in that with which you have been sent." [41:13-14]

It was related that here Utbah stood up panicked and stunned. Utbah placed his hand on the Prophet's mouth beseeching him to stop. He then said: "I beg you in the Name of Allah and uterine ties to stop immediately before the calamity should befall Quraish." He then quickly returned to his people and informed them of what he had heard.

Abu Talib

Abu Talib feared someone might hurt his nephew. He thought about the previous series of incidents including Abu Jahl's hitting the Prophet (peace be upon him) with the rock, the barter affair of Amarah ibn Al-Waleed, Uqbah's attempt to choke the Messenger of Allah (peace be upon him), and finally Omar's intention to kill the Prophet before conversion. The wise man understood that all of these clearly were a plot to kill the Prophet (peace be upon him). In the event of such a thing, Abu Talib deeply understood that neither Hamzah nor Omar would be of any help, socially powerful though they were.

Abu Talib was right. The polytheists were planning to kill the Messenger of Allah (peace and blessing be upon him). They had banded together to put their plan into action. Therefore, Abu Talib assembled all of his kinsfolk of Bani Al-Muttalib, sons of Abd Munaf, and Bani Hashim, and he urged them to defend his nephew. All of them, whether disbelievers or believers, answered positively except his brother Abu Lahab, who sided with the idolaters.

Migration to Madinah

From the Migration to Abyssinia to the Migration to Madinah, many important events took place. Abu Talib, the uncle of the Prophet (peace be upon him), died in the 10th year of the Prophet's mission. During his life, Abu Talib was a strong defender of his nephew. Quraish could not harm Prophet Muhammad. However, when Abu Talib died, Quraish increased the abuse. Hence, Abu Talib's death was a source of deep grief for the Prophet (peace be upon him). The Prophet loved his uncle very much, and wanted him to embrace Islam before death, but Abu Talib refused. He loved his tribe more than Allah, and he thought it would be a cause of his people speaking ill of him.

The Prophet's wife, Khadijah, died in the same year. She had eased the worries of the Prophet (peace be upon him) and the grief he felt at the persecution of Quraish. When Khadijah died, he grieved deeply for her. The year in which Abu Talib and Khadijah died is known as the Year of Grief.

Without the protection of his uncle, Abu Talib, in Makkah, Prophet Muhammad (peace be upon him) needed to reach out and seek support beyond Makkah. He (peace be upon him) wanted to spread the message of Islam to the people of Taif. He trekked from Makkah to Taif to invite the people to the belief in One God.

The Prophet (peace be upon him) met with the chiefs of the major tribe in Taif, Thaqeef tribe. He (peace be upon him) told them about Islam, worshipping only Allah, and leaving idol worshipping. They rejected his message and insulted him. And they unleashed the children of their tribe to throw stones at him and drive him out of their town. With people jeering at him as his ankles bled, he ran out, finding shelter in an empty orchard.

Alone, bleeding, and tired, he (peace be upon him) sat on a rock and prayed. The supplication he (peace be upon him) said at Taif should be memorized by everyone and repeated every time we are in a difficult situation or have been wronged or when calamity strikes.

اَللّٰهُمَّ اِلَيْكَ اَشْكُو ضَعْفَ قُوَّتِى وَقِلَّةَ حِيْلَتِى وَهَوَانِى عَلَى النَّاسِ يَا اَرْحَمَ الرَّاحِمِيْنَ اَنْتَ رَبُّ الْمُسْتَضْعَفِيْنَ وَاَنْتَ رَبِّى اِلٰى مَنْ تَكِلْنِى اِلٰى بَعِيْدٍ يَتَجَهَّمُنِى اَمْ اِلٰى عَدُوٍّ مَلَّكْتَهُ اَمْرِىْ اِنْ لَمْ يَكُنْ بِكَ عَلَىَّ غَضَبٌ فَلَا اُبَالِىْ وَلٰكِنَّ عَافِيَتَكَ هِىَ اَوْسَعُ لِىْ اَعُوْذُ بِنُوْرِ وَجْهِكَ الَّذِىْ اَشْرَقَتْ لَهُ الظُّلُمَاتُ وَصَلُحَ عَلَيْهِ اَمْرُ الدُّنْيَا وَالْاٰخِرَةِ مِنْ اَنْ تُنْزِلَ بِىْ غَضَبَكَ اَوْ يَحِلَّ عَلَىَّ سَخَطَكَ لَكَ الْعُتْبٰى حَتّٰى تَرْضٰى وَلَا حَوْلَ وَلَا قُوَّةَ اِلَّا بِكَ

"O Allah, to You do I complain of my weakness, little resource and lowliness before men. O Most Merciful of those who show mercy, You are the Lord of the weak and You are my Lord. To whom will You leave me? To a far-off stranger who will mistreat me? Or to an enemy to whom You have granted power over me?

If You are not angry with me, then I care not, but Your favor is better for me. I seek refuge in the Light of Your Countenance by which the darkness is illumined and the things of this world and the next are set aright, lest Your anger descend upon me, or Your wrath light upon me. It is You Whom we beseech until You are well pleased. There is no power, and no strength except in You."

At that moment, Angel Jibril came to Prophet Muhammad (peace be upon him) and told him that if he wished, Allah will order an angel to collapse the two mountains surrounding the people of Taif and crush them.

But Prophet Muhammad (peace be upon him) opted for mercy. The Prophet was not overcome with rage or hate. Instead of seeking revenge against the people of Taif, he said to Angel Jibril:

"I rather hope that Allah, the Merciful, will raise from among their descendants people who will worship Allah the One, and will not ascribe partners to Him."

When Prophet Muhammad (peace be upon him) sat on the rock, raising his hands to Allah, the two owners of the orchard saw him and so they sent their slave with a bunch of grapes to give to the Prophet (peace be upon him).

The slave's name was Addas and he was a young Christian man. When Addas gave the Prophet the grapes, he heard the Prophet say, "In the name of Allah," before he ate. Addas was surprised and curious because he never heard anyone say such words before. The Prophet asked Addas where he was from and Addas answered that he was from Nineveh.

The Prophet (peace be upon him) said, "The land of Jonah the Just, son of Matta."

The young man was bewildered that this man, Muhammad, knew of Prophet Jonah. After informing the Prophet that he was a Christian, Addas then asked the Prophet who he was and how he had such knowledge.

The Prophet (peace be upon him) said, "Jonah is my brother. He was a prophet and I am a prophet."

Addas was amazed; he knew that this man indeed had to be a prophet. Addas kissed the Prophet's head and hands and he immediately accepted Islam. So, the Prophet's mission to Taif was not totally unfruitful. One man, Addas, had whole heartedly embraced Islam after meeting and speaking with the Prophet (peace be upon him).

Al-Isra and Al-Miraaj

The journey that Prophet (peace be upon him) took in a single night from Makkah to Jerusalem and then an ascension to the heavens. There are some differences of opinion among the scholars as to when it occurred, but for certain it happened before the Hijrah, in the 10th year of the Prophet's mission or sometimes later.

The correct view of most scholars, is that it happened in a single night, when the Prophet (peace and blessings be upon him) was awake. It happened to him in body and soul. He was taken by night from Al-Masjid al-Haraam from Makkah to Al-Masjid al-Aqsa in Jerusalem.

After the death of his uncle Abu Talib, the Prophet's life was very difficult. His life was between two extremes: gradual successes and more persecutions, but glimpses of encouraging lights were looming on the horizon, the event of the Prophet's Night Journey to Jerusalem and then Ascension into the spheres of the heavens. As for its exact date, the majority of scholars is in favor of a date between 12 to 16 months before the migration to Madinah.

سُبْحَٰنَ ٱلَّذِىٓ أَسْرَىٰ بِعَبْدِهِۦ لَيْلًا مِّنَ ٱلْمَسْجِدِ ٱلْحَرَامِ إِلَى ٱلْمَسْجِدِ ٱلْأَقْصَا ٱلَّذِى بَٰرَكْنَا حَوْلَهُۥ لِنُرِيَهُۥ مِنْ ءَايَٰتِنَآ إِنَّهُۥ هُوَ ٱلسَّمِيعُ ٱلْبَصِيرُ ۝١

Glorified (and Exalted) be He (Allah) [above all that (evil) they associate with Him] Who took His slave (Muhammad peace be upon him) for a journey by night from Al-Masjid-al-Haram (at Makkah) to the farthest mosque (in Jerusalem), al-Aqsa, the neighborhood whereof We have blessed, in order that We might show him (Muhammad peace be upon him) of Our Ayat (proofs, evidences, lessons, signs, etc.). Verily, He is the All-Hearer, the All-Seer. [17:1]

Prophet Muhammad was taken in body from the Masjid of Allah in Makkah to the Masjid in Jerusalem on a great stallion called Al-Buraq in the company of the archangel Jibril.

When they landed and tied the horse to the gate of the Masjid, the Prophet (peace be upon him) led **all** the Prophets in prayer. After that, Angel Jibril took the Prophet to the heavens on the same horse.

When they reached the **1st** heaven Jibril asked the guardian angel to open the gate. It was opened and he saw Prophet Adam (peace be upon him), the father of mankind. The Messenger of Allah (peace be upon him) saluted Prophet Adam. Adam welcomed him and expressed his faith in Prophet Muhammad's mission. The Prophet saw the souls of the wretched on his left, and the souls of the martyrs on his right.

The Prophet (peace be upon him) then ascended to the **2nd** heaven, Jibril asked for opening the gate and there he saw and saluted Prophet Isa (Jesus son of Mariam) and Prophet Yahya (John ibn Zakariya) (peace be upon them).

They returned the salutation, welcomed him and expressed their faith in his mission. Then they ascended to the **3rd** heaven where they saw Prophet Yusuf (Joseph) he saluted him. Prophet Yusuf returned the salutation and he expressed faith in his mission. Then they reached the **4th** heaven where he saluted Prophet Idris (Enoch) (peace be upon him). Idris returned the salutation and expressed faith in his mission. Then they ascended to the **5th** heaven where he saw and saluted Prophet Harun (Aaron) (peace be upon him), the brother of Prophet Musa. Prophet Harun returned the salutation and expressed faith in his mission. In the **6th** heaven he saw and saluted Prophet Musa (Moses). Prophet Musa returned the salutation and expressed faith in his mission. When the Messenger of Allah (peace and blessings be upon him) was leaving, Prophet Musa began weeping. The Messenger of Allah (peace be upon him) asked about the reason. Prophet Musa answered that he was weeping because now he has witnessed a man sent after him as a Messenger (Prophet Muhammad) who was able to lift more of his people to the Garden of Paradise than he himself did.

Prophet Muhammad (peace be upon him) then reached the 7th heaven and saw Prophet Ibrahim (Abraham) (peace be upon him). The Messenger of Allah saluted Prophet Ibrahim, and Prophet Ibrahim returned the salutation and expressed faith in his mission.

Then the Messenger of Allah was taken to **Sidrat-al-Muntaha** (the remotest lote tree) and was shown Al-Bait-al-Mamur [(the much frequented house). This Masjid is like the Sacred House (Kabbah) encompassed daily by 70,000 angels. Those angels who once encompassed it will never have their turn again till the day of Resurrection.

The Prophet (peace be upon him) then was presented to the **Divine Presence** and the Messenger of Allah experienced the thrill of witnessing the Divine Glory and Manifestation at the closest possible proximity. There Allah, the One and Only, the Almighty, revealed unto His servant that which He revealed, and commanded 50 daily prayers.

On his return, the Prophet (peace be upon him) spoke to Prophet Musa (peace be upon him) that his followers had been enjoined to pray 50 times a day. Prophet Musa addressing the Prophet (peace be upon him) said: "Your followers will not be able to perform so many prayers per day. Please go back to your Lord and beg Him for a lower in number."

The Prophet (peace be upon him) turned to Jibril as if holding counsel with him. Jibril (peace be upon him) nodded, "Yes, if you wish," and ascended with him to the Presence of the Lord once again. Allah, Glory is only to Him, reduced the number to 10. He then descended and reported that to Prophet Musa, who again urged the Prophet to ask for a lower number of prayers. The Prophet (peace be upon him) once again asked his Lord to reduce the number of prayers. He went back again and again until they were reduced to five prayers. Prophet Musa asked him to beg the Lord for a lower number, but the Prophet (peace and blessing be upon him) said: "I feel ashamed to repeatedly ask my Lord for a reduction in prayers. I accept His Command and resign to His Will."

When Messenger of Allah (Peace and blessings be upon him) was leaving, a Caller was heard saying: "I have imposed My Ordinance and lessened the burden of My servants."

Many scholars unsure if the Prophet saw Allah with his eye. However, Ibn Abbas said that the word Ru'ya as mentioned in the Holy Quran implies the observation with the help of the eye. In Surat An-Najm (The Star, 53) it says:

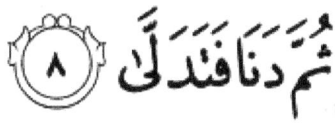

"*Then he [Jibrael (Gabriel)] approached and came closer*" [53:8]

Here (he) refers to archangel Jibril, and this context is entirely different from that in Isra and Miraaj, where '*the approach*' means that of the Lord, Glory is to Him.

Some important incidents occurred in the 'Night Journey':

#1. Jibril extracted the Prophet's heart and washed it with the water of Zamzam.

#2. Two gold vessels were brought to the Prophet (peace be upon him). There was wine in one, while the other was full of milk. The Prophet was asked to choose. He selected the milk and drank it.

Jibril (peace be upon him) said: "You were guided on Al-Fitrah. If you had selected the wine, your nation would have gone astray." The Prophet instinctively made a choice for the good.

It is not easy to render the term "*Fitrah*" into the English language. It represents the original disposition or nature with which a baby comes with when born into this world, as contrasted to the qualities and inclinations acquired during a lifetime. It refers to the spiritual inclination inherent in humans in their unspoiled state.

#3. The Prophet (peace be upon him) said that he saw two manifest rivers, the Euphrates and the Nile, and two hidden rivers. It appears as though that the two manifest rivers, the Euphrates and the Nile symbolically describe the land that the Prophet's Message will settle in, and will be passed on from one generation to next.

#4. The Prophet had the opportunity to see Malik, the guardian of the Hellfire, and he had an unhappy, frowning face. Therein, the Prophet (peace be upon him) saw the Hell tenants, of whom were those people who steal the property of the orphans. They have flews like those of camels, eating red-hot coals and then issuing out of their backs. The Prophet also saw those people that took usury. They had huge bellies that were too big to be able to move around. They will be crushed by the people of Pharaoh when they are admitted into the Hellfire. In the same abode, Prophet Muhammad also saw the sinners, the adulterers, and they were offered rotten tasty meats and fatty ones, but they always selected the rotten meats. Hellfire was filled with women. And the promiscuous and the naked women of this life were hanging from their breasts and burning in fire.

#5. The 'Night Journey' also raised a lot of stir among the people. The Prophet (peace be upon him) told them that he saw the camels of Makkan merchants on their journeys. The Prophet guided them to some of their lost camels and animals that went astray. He told them that he had drank some of their water while they slept and left the container covered.

The polytheists, however, found it a great opportunity to taunt the Muslims and their creed. They pestered the Prophet (peace and blessings be upon him) with many questions such as the description of the Masjid in Jerusalem, where he had never been there before. Prophet Muhammad's answers were most accurate even about Jerusalem. The Prophet (peace be upon him) even gave them information and news about their caravans and camels, but they accepted nothing but disbelief.

The believers, however, understood that Allah, Who created the heavens and the earth, is indeed Powerful enough to take the Prophet (peace be upon him) beyond the heavens. However, the disbelievers went to see Abu Bakr to ask about the event. Abu Bakr replied: "Yes, I certainly believe the Messenger of Allah (peace be upon him)." It was on this reply that Abu Bakr received the title of *As-Siddiq* (the verifier of the truth). The most eloquent and justification of the 'Night Journey' is expressed by Allah: *"Exalted is He who took His Servant by night from al-Masjid al-Haram to al-Masjid al- Aqsa, whose surroundings We have blessed, to show him of Our signs. Indeed, He is the Hearing, the Seeing."* [17:1].

Allah showed many of the Prophets His signs:

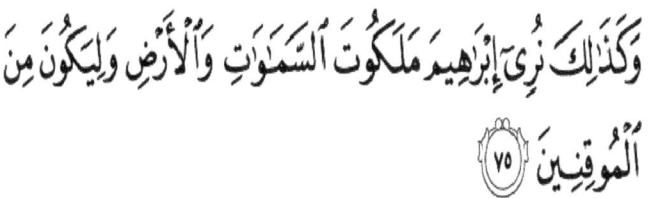

"And thus did We show Abraham the realm of the heavens and the earth that he would be among the certain [in faith]." [6:75]

To Moses, Allah said:

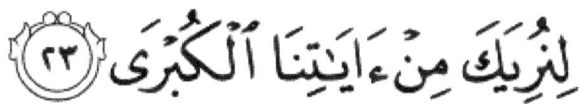

"In order that We may show thee our Greater Signs." [20:23]

The Aqabh Pledge

On the occasion of the pilgrimage, twelve disciples came to embrace Islam and to accept the Prophet (peace be upon him). The men comprised 5 of the 6 that had met the Prophet (peace be upon him) the year before, the 6th man that did not come was Jabir ibn Abdullah ibn Reyab. Many of the men were from *Aws* and *Khazraj*.

From Aws:

#1. Uwaim ibn Sa'idah
#2. Abul Haitham ibn At-Taihan

From Khazraj:

#3. Muadh ibn Al-Harith
#4. Dhakwan ibn Abd Al-Qais
#5. Ubadah ibn As-Samit
#6. Yazeed ibn Thalabah
#7. Al-Abbas ibn Ubadah ibn Nadalah

They affirmed their faith in the Prophet (peace be upon him) and swore that they will only worship Allah alone. They also said that they will not steal nor will they commit adultery, nor kill any children, and will not slander anyone.

Once they had taken the pledge, Prophet Muhammad (peace be upon him) said: "He who carries this out, Allah will reward him, and he who neglects anything and is plagued, it may prove redemption for him in the afterlife. If his sin remains hidden in this world from the eyes of the men and no pain comes from it, then his affair is with Allah alone. Allah may forgive him or He may not."

Envoy to Madinah

After the Pledge, the Messenger of Allah (peace be upon him) sent to Madinah Musb ibn Umair Al-Abdari (may Allah be pleased with him). He was sent as an ambassador to teach the people there the principles of Islam, and to also make attempts at spreading Islam to those who still professed polytheism. Asad ibn Zurarah hosted him in Madinah. Islam spread rapidly from tribe to tribe, and from house to house.

One day Assad and Musab traveled to the habitations of Bani Zafar and Bani Abd Al-Ashhal. When they went into the grounds of Bani Zafar, both sat near a well speaking with some new converts.

Usaid ibn Hudair and Sa'd ibn Mu'adh, chiefs of the two tribes heard about this meeting. Usaid approached the Muslims armed with his spear, but Sa'd excused himself because Assad was his maternal cousin. Usaid was cursing loudly, and he accused Assad and Musab of deceiving his people, and he ordered that they stop. Musab very calmly invited Usaid to sit, and said to him: "If you are pleased with our talk, you can accept it, however, if you should dislike anything, you could freely immunize yourself about what you hate." Usaid replied: "That sounds fair." Usaid pierced his spear in the sand, and he listened to some verses of the Noble Quran. As Musab and Assad read the Quran, his face became very radiant. He instantly asked Musab and Assad about the actions pertinent to embracing Islam. They asked Usaid to wash, clean his garment, bear witness to the Truth and then perform two Rak'at prayer. Usaid responded positively and he did exactly what he was told to do. He then said there was a man (Sa'd ibn Mu'adh) whose people would kill him if he followed Islam. He then left to see Sa'd and his people. Usaid then managed to provide the two men with an opportunity to talk with Sa'd privately.

The previous scene with Usaid recurred again, and so Sa'd embraced Islam, and he quickly told his people swearing that he would never talk to any of them until they had believed in Allah, and in His Prophet (peace be upon him). Before that night arrived, all of his people embraced Islam with the exception to one man, Al-Usairim, who hung back until the Battle of Uhud. He embraced Islam and fought the polytheists bravely but was killed before observing any prostration in the way of prayer. Prophet Muhammad (peace be and blessings be upon him) said: "Al-Usairim has done little but his reward is so great."

Musab lived in Madinah carrying out his mission diligently till all the houses of Al-Ansaar (the future helpers) had accepted Islam. However, one family stood against Islam. They were under the spell of the poet Qais ibn Al-Aslat, who managed to hold them back from Islam until the year 5 A.H.

Shortly before the pilgrimage season, i.e. the 13th year of the Prophet's Message, Musab returned to Makkah and brought with him the great news about Madinah.

During the pilgrimage season, over 70 converts from Madinah came to perform the rituals of pilgrimage in Makkah. They also came to protect the Prophet (peace be upon him). Before coming to Makkah they conducted clandestine contacts with the Messenger of Allah (peace be upon him) and they agreed to meet at night in mid Tashreeq Days (11th, 12th and 13th days of Dhul Hijja).

Ka'b ibn Malik Al-Ansari, a leader of the Ansaar (Helpers), gave an account of the historic meeting that changed the entire course of the struggle between Islam and paganism. Ka'b said:

"We set out for pilgrimage and we were accompanied by a notable of ours called Abdullah ibn Amr ibn Haram, who was still a polytheist. We revealed to him our intention of meeting Prophet Muhammad (peace be upon him) and we encouraged him to give up polytheism than serving as wood for the Hellfire in the Hereafter. He very promptly embraced Islam and so he came with us to the meeting. That night we slept with our people in our camps. But after a third of the night had passed, we began to leave very stealthily and met in a hillock nearby."

"There were 73 men and Asma bint Amr from Bani Salamah, and Nusaibah bint Ka'b from the Najjars. We waited for the Prophet (peace be upon him) till he came in the company of his uncle Al-Abbas ibn Abdul Muttalib who (though he had not embraced Islam) ordered us not to take his nephew away from the protection of his family unless we were truly prepared to defend the Messenger of Allah (peace be upon him) even at the risk of our lives."

Ka'b said: "We have heard your words, and now O Messenger of Allah (peace be upon you), take from us any pledge that you want concerning your Lord and your Message."

The Messenger of Allah (peace be upon him) preached the Message of Allah, and the pledge was taken. Imam Ahmad, on the authority of Jabir, gave the following facts about the meeting:

The Ansaar (Helpers) asked the Prophet (peace be upon him) about the principles over which they would take a pledge. The Prophet (peace be upon him) said:

#1. To obey and to listen in all situations.
#2. To spend in plenty as well in scarcity.

#3. To do good and forbid evil.
#4. In Allah's service, fear only Allah.
#5. To defend the Prophet always.

If you observe these principles, Paradise is yours.

On the authority of Jabir ibn Abdullah ibn Reyab, who said: "When we started to pay allegiance to the Messenger of Allah (peace be upon him), As'ad ibn Zurarah gave the following speech: 'Take it easy people of Yathrib! We have covered that long distance because everyone believe that Muhammad (peace be upon him) is the Messenger of Allah. Following him means that we must leave the pagans even at the risk of our life. However, if you should stay on this path, then your great reward is placed in the Hand of Allah, but if you are caught in fear, then I warn you to give it up now, then you would be more excusable by Allah.'"

With respect to the two women came, the pledge was taken orally, for the Prophet (peace be upon him) had never touched or shook the hand of a foreign lady. The Prophet (peace be upon him) then asked the group to appoint twelve delegates to preach Islam to their people in Madinah.

The delegates elected were nine from Al-Khazraj and three were from Al-Aws. These 12 men were sworn to supervise the affairs of their people just as the Disciples of Jesus did in the first century, and the Prophet (peace be upon him) would act as surety over all the Muslims.

The news of these secret meetings with the Madinese leaked out. Without delay Quraish understood that a treaty of this kind is bound impact their lives and their wealth. The next day, a large delegation from Quraish set out for the camp of the Madinese to protest. They addressed the Madinese as such: "O people of Khazraj, we have heard that you have come here to sign a treaty with this man Muhammad and to lead him out of Makkah. By Allah, we do not want to fight you."

The polytheists that knew nothing about the pledge, began to swear by Allah, and answered in good faith that there was no truth to such news. Abdullah ibn Ubai ibn Salul, a Madinese polytheist, said that his people would never initiate any contract unless he gave them clear orders. The Madinese Muslims, however, remained silent neither confirming nor negating.

Quraish were very convinced and so they went back home. However, they began to study the smallest details, and to track the tiniest clues until it was established that the secret pledge was real, but that was after the Madinese pilgrims had left Makkah. In a fit of rage they chased the Madinese, but they only caught Sa'd ibn Ubadah. They tortured him severely. He was later rescued by Harith ibn Harb ibn Omaiya and Al-Mut'im ibn Adi with whom he had trade relations. So this is the story of the 2nd Aqabah Pledge, later known as the Great Aqabah Pledge.

Lessons learned

Grief for the loss of a relative, Abu Talib, who was protecting the Prophet (peace be upon him), and protecting the call to truth even though he did not believe in it, and for the loss of his believing wife Khadijah, is a natural result of sincere devotion to the call and of sincerity towards the wife whose sacrifice and support were exemplary. When Abu Talib died, the Prophet (peace be upon him) said: "May Allah forgive you and have mercy upon you. I will keep praying for forgiveness for you until Allah forbids me to do so."

The Muslims followed the example of their Prophet (peace be upon him) and prayed for forgiveness for their own deceased mushrik (non-believers) family members, until Allah revealed the words:

مَا كَانَ لِلنَّبِيِّ وَٱلَّذِينَ ءَامَنُوٓاْ أَن يَسۡتَغۡفِرُواْ لِلۡمُشۡرِكِينَ وَلَوۡ كَانُوٓاْ أُوْلِي قُرۡبَىٰ مِنۢ بَعۡدِ مَا تَبَيَّنَ لَهُمۡ أَنَّهُمۡ أَصۡحَٰبُ ٱلۡجَحِيمِ ۝

"It is not proper for the Prophet and those who believe to ask Allah's forgiveness for the Mushriken, even though they be of kin, after it has become clear to them that they are the dwellers of the Fire [because they died in a state of disbelief]." (Quran: 9:113)

So Prophet Muhammad (peace be upon him) stopped praying for forgiveness for his uncle Abu Talib, and all Muslims stopped praying for their deceased relatives. The Messenger of Allah (peace be upon him) continued for the rest of his life to mention the virtues of his wife Khadijah. And he continued to pray for mercy for her, and to honor her friends, so much so that his wife, Aishah, felt jealous of Khadeejah even though Khadijah was dead.

The Messenger of Allah praised Khadijah a lot. Bukhari narrated that Aa'ishah said:

"I never felt as jealous of any of anyone as I did of Khadijah, although I never saw her. But Prophet Muhammd (peace be upon him) mentioned her a great deal. Once I said to him: 'It is as if there is no one in this world but Khadijah,' and the Prophet said: 'She was like that and like that (mentioning good things about her), and I had children from her.'"

The fact that the Prophet went to At-Taif after the people of Makkah had turned away from him, and after during his grief and the loss of Khadijah, indicates that the Prophet (peace be upon him) was determined that the call to Allah must continue and that he had not given up hope that the people would respond. So he looked for new territory for his call after the barriers had gone up in Makkah.

The fact that the At-Taif incited their own children and others against the Prophet (peace be upon him) indicates that the nature of evil is the same all over the world, which is to use the foolish to attack those who advocate good.

The flowing of blood from the body of the Prophet (peace be upon him), when he was a noble and kind man, is the greatest example of the harm and persecution that the daa'iyah may face for the sake of Allah.

The beautiful prayer of the Prophet in the garden uttering those immortal words and lines, is confirmation of the truth of his mission and his determination to continue his efforts, no matter what difficulties lay in his path. It demonstrates that the Prophet's only concern was the pleasure of Allah, and that he did not care about the approval of leaders or of the simple-minded common folk.

"If You are not angry with me, I care not."

This also demonstrates that the Prophet (peace be upon him) was seeking strength from Allah by turning to Him and seeking strength from Him when the persecution grew so intense. And it illustrates the fact that the daa'iyah's primary fear must always be of the wrath and anger of Allah, not the wrath and anger of anyone else.

And the miracle of the Isra and Miraaj teaches us so many things, of which we will mention just 3 for now:

Why Masjid al-Aqsa? This shows us that Al-Masjid al-Aqsa (the farthest Mosque from Makkah), and the land around it, Palestine, is beloved by Allah. Moreover, the fact that Allah chose to take him to Jerusalem first, to lead his fellow Prophets in prayer, endorses the fact that Islam is a message for mankind, not for the Arabs alone. So defending Palestine means defending Islam itself, so all of mankind must undertake to defend it.

Moreover, the fact that prayer was enjoined on the night of the Isra and Miraaj points to the reason why prayer is enjoined. It is as if Allah is telling His believing slaves: 'If the ascent of your Messenger's body and soul into the heavens was a miracle, then you can ascend five times a day as your hearts and souls ascend to Me.'

The Hijrah to Madinah

Quraish learned that some people from Yathrib (Madinah) had become Muslims, therefore they intensified their abuse of the believers in Makkah. So the Prophet (peace be upon him) commanded them to migrate to Madinah. They migrated in secret, however, Omar ibn Al-Khattāb announced to the mushrikeen of Quraish that he was leaving, and said to them: "Whoever wants his mother to grieve him, let him catch up with me tomorrow in the bottom of this valley." But none had the courage to follow him.

When Quraish found out that the Muslims were being honored and protected in Madinah, they met together in the Daar an-Nadwah to plan to kill the Messenger (peace be upon him) himself. They all agreed to choose strong young men from each tribe, then they would all kill the Prophet (peace be upon him) together. In this way the responsibility would be shared among all the tribes and so Banu Manaaf would not be able to fight all of them.

And they would have to accept the diyah (blood money). The young men who were charged with the killing of the Messenger (peace be upon him) waited near his door on the night of the Hijrah to kill him.

However, the Messenger (peace be upon him) was not alone that night. Ali (RA) was with the Prophet. The Prophet (peace be upon him) told Ali to return many items that the people of Quraish had entrusted to him for safekeeping to their owners. The Prophet left his house without his would-be assassins seeing him, and he went to the house of Abu Bakr (RA), who had already prepared two mounts for himself and for the Messenger (peace be upon him). Abu Bakr had hired 'Abdullah ibn Urayqit ad-Diyali, who was a mushrik (a non-believer - practicing idolatry or polytheism), to act as their guide. Abu Bakr told him to avoid the usual route to Madinah and to follow another route that the kuffaar of Quraish did not know.

The Messenger of Allah (peace be upon him) and his Companion Abu Bakr set out on Thursday 1st of Rabee' al-Awwal. At that time, the Prophet was fifty-three years old. No one knew about his Hijrah except for Ali (RA) and the family of Abu Bakr. Aa'ishah and Asma, the daughters of Abu Bakr, prepared food for the journey. Asma tore a piece from her nitaaq (waist-wrapper) and used it to tie up the vessel of food, hence she was given the nickname of Dhaat an-Nitaaqay (she of the two waist-wrappers). They set out with the guide in the direction of Yemen, until they reached the cave of Thawr, in which they stayed for 3 nights, and 'Abdullah ibn Abi Bakr stayed with them. He was an intelligent young man, and was very quick at learning things. He would leave the Prophet and his father before dawn, and then spend the mornings with Quraish in Makkah as if he had slept among them. Each evening he would go to cave and tell them about any news.

Quraish was very angry when the Messenger escaped assassination, so they tried to follow him, but they followed the usual routes, and so they did not find him. However, later they tried the road towards Yemen, and stood at the mouth of the cave of Thawr. One of them said, "Perhaps he and his companion are in this cave," but the others replied by saying, "Do you not see that a spider has woven its webs over the mouth of the cave, and there are birds nesting there, which shows that no one has entered this cave for a long time." Abu Bakr could see their feet when they were standing at the mouth of the cave, and he feared for the life of the Messenger.

The Prophet (peace be upon him) said to him: "By Allah, O'Messenger of Allah, if one of them looks down at his feet he will see us." The Messenger put his mind at rest by saying:

«يَا أَبَا بَكْرٍ، مَا ظَنُّكَ بِاثْنَيْنِ اللّهُ ثَالِثُهُمَا»

"O'Abu Bakr, what do you think of two when Allah is the third one with them?"

Quraish sent word to all the tribes encouraging them to look for the Messenger and his Companion, and to kill them or capture them. They offered a huge reward to anyone that would capture or kill them. Suraaqah ibn Ja'sham wanted that prize, so he decided to keep looking for them.

After the search for the Messenger of Allah (peace be upon him) and his Companions was called off, they came out of the cave with their guide and headed towards the coast, i.e., the coast of the Red Sea.

However, after they had traveled a long distance, Suraaqah caught up with them, but when he get closer, his horse's feet sank into the sand, and he could not go on. He tried three times to make his horse move towards the Messenger, but it refused. At that point, he became sure that the one in front of him was a noble Messenger, so he asked the Messenger to promise him something if he supported him. The Messenger promised to let him wear the two armbands of Khosrow (the last king of the Sasanian Empire). Suraaqah returned to Makkah, and pretended that he had not found anyone.

The Messenger and his Companion reached Madinah on the 12th day of Rabee ' al-Awwal, after the people of the city had waited for a long time, going out each morning to the heights overlooking the city, and not coming back until the sun became hot at noon. When they saw him, they rejoiced greatly, and the little girls began to sing:

"Tala'a al-badru 'alayna ... The full moon has risen upon us from the valley of Al-Wadda, We must be grateful so long as the caller calls us to Allah. O'you who have been sent among us, you have come with a command that must be obeyed."

When the Messenger of Allah (peace be upon him) reached Quba, a village two miles to the south of Madinah, there he laid the foundations for the first mosque. The Prophet (peace be upon him) stayed there for four days, then on Friday morning, he went on to Madinah. The time for Jumu'ah (Friday) prayer came when he was visiting Banu Saalim ibn Awf, so he built a mosque there. This is where the first Jumu'ah prayer in Islam were held, and the first khutbah (sermon) in Islam was delivered.

The Prophet (peace be upon him) then went on to Madinah, and the first thing he did when he arrived, he choose the place where his she-camel sat down to be his masjid (mosque). The land belonged to two orphans among the Ansaar. He wanted to negotiate the price with them, but they said: "No, we will give it to you, O Messenger of Allah."

But the Prophet (peace be upon him) insisted on buying the land from them for ten dinars of gold, which he paid from the wealth of Abu Bakr. Then he urged the Muslims to join him in building the mosque, and everyone hastened to build it. The Prophet (peace be upon him) carried bricks with them until the mosque was completed. The Masjid's walls were made of bricks and its roof made of palm leaves resting on palm trunks.

The Prophet (peace be upon him) then established brotherhood between the Muhaajireen (Emigrants Muslims) and the Ansaar. The Prophet gave each Ansaari a brother from among the Muslim Muhaajireen. Each Ansaari took his Muhaajir brother to his house and offered to share with him everything that he had in his house.

Then the Messenger of Allah (peace be upon him) wrote an agreement between the Muhaajireen and the Ansaar, in which he made a friendly agreement with the Jews and protected them in their religion and property. Ibn Hishaam quotes this document in detail in his Seerah. The document sets out the principles on which the first Muslim state was established. The agreements contains principles of humanity, social justice, and religious tolerance and cooperation in the interest of society.

Below we will list the general principles that this historical document included:

- The Muslim ummah must always be united and undivided.

- The members of the ummah are equal in rights.

- The ummah should stand firm against sin and transgression.

- The ummah should reach an agreement on how to deal with the enemies, and no believer should make any peace treaty without consulting the other believers.

- The society is to be based on the best, the most correct, and strongest system.

- Anyone who rebel against the state and its public systems should be fought and not supported.

- Those who want to live with the Muslims in a cooperative and peaceful manner must always be protected, and must never be oppressed or harmed.

- Non-Muslims must always have the right to their own religion and their wealth. They should never be forced to embrace Islam, and their wealth should never be taken from them.

- Non-Muslims must contribute to the expenses of the state just as Muslims.

- Non-Muslims must cooperate with the Muslims in defending the state. They must contribute to the state's defense budget so long as it is in a state of war.

- The state must help those (non-Muslims) who are oppressed, just as it must help every Muslim who is the victim of oppression and aggression.

- The Muslims and others must always refrain from protecting and helping the enemies of the state and those who help them.

- If the interests of the Ummah are best helped by a peace treaty, then all Muslims and non-Muslims alike, must support and accept that peace treaty.

- No person is to be punished for the sin of another, and the offender only harms himself and his family.

- Freedom of movement must not be restricted within the state and also to areas outside, and must be protected by the state.

- No sinner or wrongdoer must be given protection.

- The society must be based on a foundation of cooperation, righteousness, and piety, and never in sin and transgression.

These principles were supported and protected by the people's belief in Allah, and their awareness that Allah sees and hears everything, and that Allah takes care of those who are honest and sincere, and by the head of the Ummah represented by Muhammad (peace be upon him).

The lessons that one learns from this chapter:

If the strong believers are certain of their strength, they must never hide what they are doing. Do it openly and never pay any attention to the enemies.

This is what Omar ibn Al-Khattāb (RA) did when he migrated. He announced to the mushrikeen that he was leaving, and said to them: "Whoever wants his mother to grieve him, let him catch up with me tomorrow in the bottom of this valley." But none had the courage to follow him.

This shows that a position of strength frightens the enemies of Allah, because if they had wanted to gang up and kill Omar, they could undoubtedly have done so. However, Omar's strong attitude cast fear into their hearts, so each of them feared that his mother would be bereft of him. The followers of evil fear for their lives and are anxious to preserve their life always.

When the followers of evil and falsehood despair of stopping the call to truth and Allah, and when the brave believers escape from their clutches and find a place where they can be safe and happy, the kuffar try to kill the Messenger. They think if they kill the Messenger, they will silence the call to truth.

This is how the evil enemies of truth and reform in every age think, and we have seen and witnessed this in our own times.

The believers who are honest and sincere towards the call for reform and change are prepared to sacrifice their lives for their leader, because if the leader is safe, then the call is safe, but if he is killed, then the call will weaken.

What Ali (RA) did on the night of the Hijrah, sleeping in the Prophet's bed to pretend he was the Prophet, meant that he was willing to sacrifice his own life to save the Messenger of Allah (peace be upon him).

The swords of the men of Quraish would have come down hard on Ali's head, because he had made it easy for the Messenger of Allah to escape. But Ali (RA) did not worry about that. He was happy to protect the Messenger of Allah (peace be upon him).

The fact that the mushrikoon (no-believers) had left items for safekeeping with the Messenger of Allah (peace be upon him), even though they were fighting him and determined to kill him, shows that the enemies of reform are certain in their hearts that the Messenger is true and honest. They knew that the Prophet was better than them in his conduct and attitude and had a purer in heart. However, their blindness, stubbornness and determination to cling to their misguided ways is what makes them plot to kill him.

The attitude of Asma and Aishah, the daughters of Abu Bakr, during the Hijrah shows that reform movements always need women, for they are soft-hearted, more tolerant, more motivated, and better at heart. If a woman knows that something is true and honest, she will not care about any difficulties involved in spreading the message and helping. Women have a glowing history of fighting for the sake of Allah at the time of the Messenger (peace be upon him). Women played a major role in raising the children of the Sahaabah and then the Taabieen with great morals and manners. Women are strong in their faith, and they know that Allah is always there to comfort them.

The fact that the mushrikoon were unable to see the Messenger of Allah (peace be upon him) and his Companion while they were in the cave of Thawr, and how a spider had built its web and a bird was nesting at the mouth of the cave, represent a deeply moving story of how Allah cares for His Messengers (peace be upon him).

Out of mercy towards His slaves, Allah would never allow His Messenger (peace be upon him) to fall into the hands of the mushrikeen. Please always remember that Allah will take care of His sincere slaves at times of crisis and hardship, and He will save them at times of difficulty. Allah will often blind those who lie in wait to harm them. There is nothing in the story of how the Prophet and his Companion were saved after they were surrounded by the mushrikeen in the cave of Thawr except confirmation of the words of Allah:

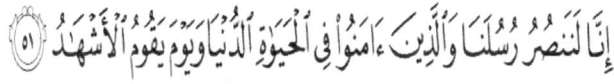

"Indeed We will support Our messengers and those who believe during the life of this world and on the Day when the witnesses will stand." [Al-Quran 40:51]

Abu Bakr's (RA) fear that the mushrikoon might see them in the cave, is an excellent example of how the sincere followers must be with their leader when they are surrounded by danger.

Abu Bakr was not worried about his own life; if that were the case, he would not have never accompanied the Messenger of Allah (peace be upon him). Rather, he feared for the life of the Messenger of Allah (peace be upon him) and for the future of Islam if the Messenger (peace be upon him) fell into the hands of the mushrikeen.

The Prophet's answer, reassuring Abu Bakr with the words: "O'Abu Bakr, what do you think of two when Allah is the third one with them?" is an example of the most sincere trust in Allah. This is a clear sign of the truthfulness of the Messenger's claim to Prophethood. He was certain that Allah will not forsake him at that moment.

Do you see such comfort in the heart of those who falsely claim to be prophets? In such circumstances there is a clear difference between those who truthfully call for reform and those who merely claim to do so in their own personal interests. The heart of the former is always overflowing with faith in Allah and confidence that Allah will support him, whereas the latter collapse at times of fear and struggle.

We can see the fear in Suraaqah, when he caught up with the Messenger (peace be upon him), and he was unable to reach the Prophet. We also can see another sign of the Prophethood of the Messenger (peace be upon him). For the legs of Suraaqah's horse sank into the sand when it tried to reach the Messenger (peace be upon him), until Suraaqah dismounted and turned the horse's face towards Makkah. But when he tried to turn it back towards the Messenger (peace be upon him), the horse became helpless again.

The fact that the Messenger of Allah (peace be upon him) promised Suraaqah the armbands of Khosrow is another miracle. A man who is leaving Makkah would not know that he will one day conquer Persia and seize the treasure of Khosrow, unless he was a Prophet sent by Allah.

The promise of the Messenger (peace be upon him) was fulfilled. Suraaqah asked Omar ibn al-Khartaab to fulfil the Prophet's promise to him when he saw the armbands of Khosrow among the war-booty.

Omar put them on Suraaqah in the presence of a group of the Sahaabah, and said, "Praise be to Allah, Who has divested Khosrow of his armbands and given them to the Bedouin Suraaqah ibn Ja'sham to wear." Thus, the miracles came one after another, to increase the faith of the believers and to reassure those among the People of the Book who were uncertain that the Prophet was indeed a Messenger of Allah (peace be upon him).

We can see the joy of the believers and the Ansaar, at the safe arrival of the Messenger of Allah (peace be upon him). The attitude of the Jews of Madinah was such that they shared the people's joy. The joy of the believers at meeting the Prophet (peace be upon him) comes as no surprise, because he is the one who led them from darkness into light.

From the events of the Hijrah we can see that whenever the Prophet (peace be upon him) stopped in a village, the first thing he did was to establish a mosque.

He established the mosque of Quba when he stayed there for 4 days, and the Prophet built a mosque halfway between Quba' and Madinah when the time for Jumu'ah prayer came, in (the lands of) Banu Saalim ibn Awf, at the bottom of Wadi Ranoona.

And when the Prophet (peace be upon him) reached Madinah, the first thing that he did was to build a mosque there. This points to the importance of the Masajid (Mosques) in Islam. Prayer purifies the hearts, and improve one's attitude and strengthen the ties.

Prayers in congregation are a strong manifestation of unity among Muslims, their common aims and their cooperation in righteousness and piety. Certainly, the mosque plays a very important social and spiritual role, for the Masajid unifies the people's ranks, purifies their souls, and awakens their minds and hearts.

Another unique feature of the Masjid in Islam is that every week there comes from it the word of truth, resounding from the mouth of the khateeb (preacher), denouncing sin and evil, and enjoining good, calling the people to goodness or rousing them from negligence.

The document in which the Messenger of Allah established brotherhood between the Muhaajireen and the Ansaar, and cooperation between Muslims and others, shows that Islam is based on social justice, and that the basis of relationships between the Muslims and others must always be peace so long as the latter choose peace. Thus an Islamic state, no matter where it is and in what era it is founded, must be based on the soundest and most just of laws.

Following are some Quranic verses and a hadith that reflects the Islamic view about "Hope."

﴿ومن يتّقِ اللَّهَ يجعل له مخرجا ويرزقه من حيث لا يحتسب﴾

"...And whosoever fears Allah...He will make a way for him to get out (from every difficulty). And He will provide him from (sources) he never could imagine." (Quran: 65:2-3)

فَإِنَّ مَعَ الْعُسْرِ يُسْرًا

"...After a difficulty, Allah will soon grant relief." (Quran: 65:7)

Allah promises us that after every difficulty is relief. We must never lose hope that our situation will improve.

The Battles of the Prophet

Barely had the Prophet (peace be upon him) settled in Madinah when the battles began between him and Quraish, including their allies among other tribes. It is the convention among historians to call every battle between the Muslims and the mushrikeen, at which the Prophet (peace be upon him) himself was at the battle, a ghazwah (military expedition), and every skirmish, at which the Prophet (peace be upon him) was not present, a sariyah (raiding party). The number of battles at which the Prophet (peace be upon him) was present was 26, and the number of raiding parties was 38. We will discuss only the most famous battles, the number of which is 11.

1. The Battle of Badr

The Battle of Badr took place on the 17th of Ramadaan 2 AH. The reason for the battle was that the Prophet (peace be upon him) had gone out with his Companions to intercept a Quraish caravan that was returning to Makkah from Syria. The caravan was led by Abu Sufyaan. Abu Sufyaan hired Damdam ibn Amr Al-Ghifari to go to Makkah and to get help from Quraish. Amr rode fast and reached Makkah in anger. He stood dramatically before Al-Kabah, cut off the ears and nose of the poor camel that he was riding, then he tore off his own shirt from front and behind, and cried: "O Quraish! Your merchandise is being intercepted by Muhammad and his companions."

Quraish sent troops to protect the caravan. They sent out roughly 1,000 fighters, including 600 men in armor, and over 100 horsemen in armor in addition to the infantry who wore armor. There were also 700 camels, and singers beating drums and singing songs insulting the Muslims.

Badr

17 Ramadan 2AH
March 17 624 CE

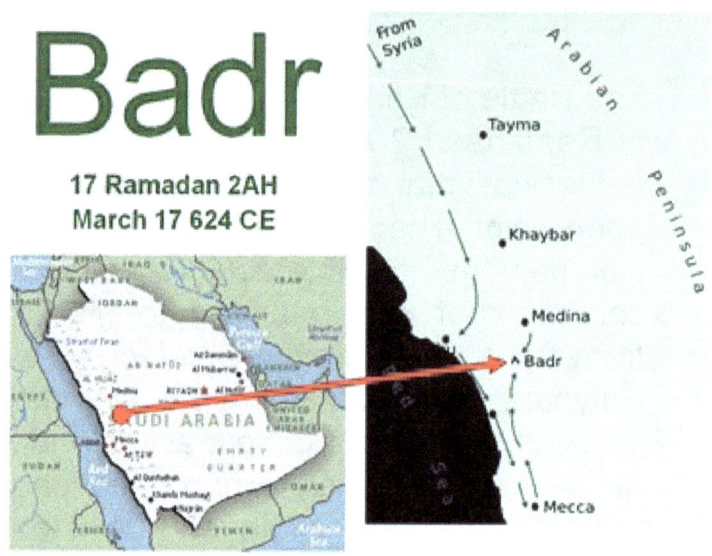

The Prophet's army were approximately 315 men, about 84 Emigrants, 60 from Aws, and 170 from Khazraj. They were not adequately prepared nor well-equipped. They had only 2 horses and about 70 camels. Two or three men rode on each camel for a while then walked on foot. The Prophet (peace be upon him) himself, Ali, and Murthid ibn Abi Murthid Al-Ghanawi had one camel.

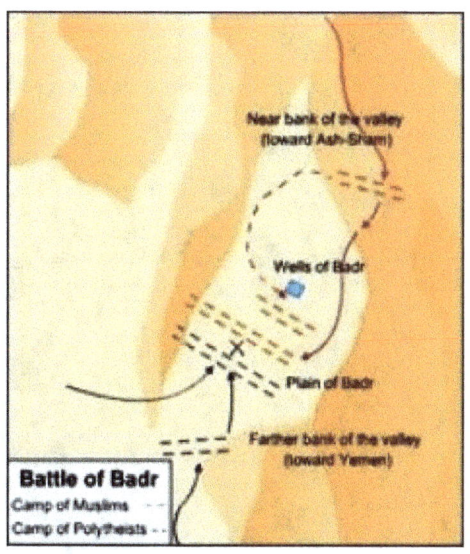

Quraish moved very quickly northward to Badr. But on their way, they received a message from Abu Sufyaan telling them to go back to Makkah because the caravan had escaped the Prophet's army.

Abu Sufyaan led his caravan off the main road, and moved towards the Red Sea. So he slipped past the Madinese ambush, where the Prophet's army was waiting.

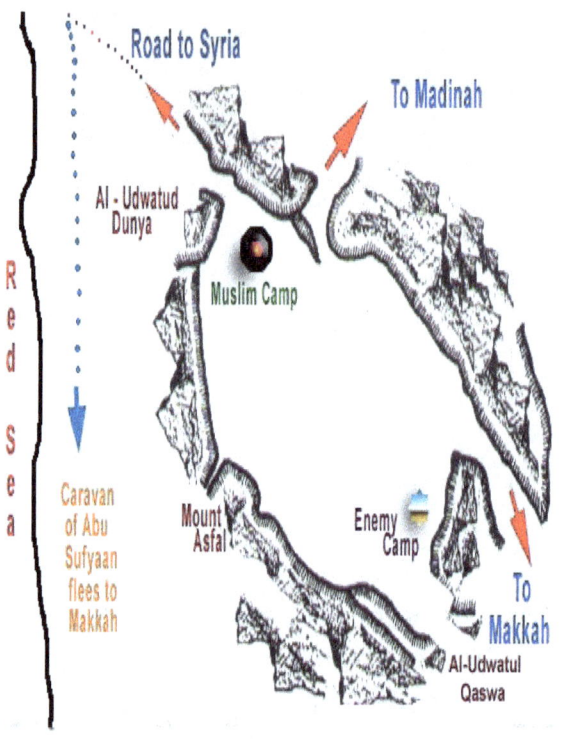

However, Abu Jahl's threats made them stop from returning to Makkah. So Quraish proceeded to Badr. They wanted to punish the Prophet and to prevent the Muslims from intercepting their caravans in the future. Quraish approached Badr and positioned themselves beyond a sand dune at Al-Udwat Al-Quswa.

The Prophet's scouts reported to the Prophet (peace be upon him) that a bloody encounter with the Quraish was unavoidable. The Prophet (peace be upon him) was afraid that the pagan Makkans would march on and destroy Madinah. A move of such nature would surely damage the dignity of all Muslims.

Some Muslims feared the battle and their courage began to waver. About this said in the Quran:

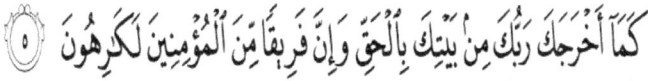

As your Lord caused you (O Muhammad) to go out from your home with the truth, and verily, a party among the believers disliked it;

The Messenger of Allah (peace be upon him) explained to his men about the gravity of the situation and asked for their advice. Abu Bakr (RA) assured the Prophet (peace be upon him) that they would follow through and be obedient to Allah and his Prophet.

Omar stood up and supported the views expressed by his friend. Then Al-Miqdad ibn Amr stood up and said: "O Messenger of Allah! Proceed where Allah directs you to, for we are all with you. We will never say as the Children of Israel said to Moses (peace be upon him):

"Go you and your Lord and fight and we will stay here."

The Messenger of Allah (peace be upon him) was very impressed with the loyalty of his companions. So he said to them: "Forward then, for Allah has promised me one of the two things: capturing the caravan or strife in the cause of Allah against the polytheists), and by Allah, I saw the enemy dead on the ground."

The Prophet (peace be upon him) wanted to stop at the nearest spring of Badr. But Al-Hubab ibn Mundhir asked: "Has Allah inspired you to choose this very spot or is it a tactical of war?

This place is no best; let us go and encamp on the nearest water well, and then destroy all the other wells so that they will be deprived of the water."

The Prophet (peace be upon him) approved of his plan. Then Sa'd ibn Mu'adh proposed that a tent be built for the Prophet (Peace be upon him) to function as headquarters and to provide protection for the Prophet (peace be upon him). A squad of men was also chosen under the leadership of Sa'd ibn Mu'adh, in order to defend the Prophet (Peace be upon him) in his headquarters.

The Messenger of Allah (peace be upon him) spent the whole night in prayer and supplication.

The Muslim army, tired from their long march, enjoyed some sleep, a mark of the Divine favor and of the state of their undisturbed minds.

إِذْ يُغَشِّيكُمُ النُّعَاسَ أَمَنَةً مِّنْهُ وَيُنَزِّلُ عَلَيْكُم مِّنَ ٱلسَّمَآءِ مَآءً لِّيُطَهِّرَكُم بِهِۦ وَيُذْهِبَ عَنكُمْ رِجْزَ ٱلشَّيْطَٰنِ وَلِيَرْبِطَ عَلَىٰ قُلُوبِكُمْ وَيُثَبِّتَ بِهِ ٱلْأَقْدَامَ ۝

(Remember) when He covered you with a slumber as a security from Him, and He caused water (rain) to descend on you from the sky, to clean you thereby and to remove from you the Rijz (whispering, evil-suggestions, etc.) of Shaitan (Satan), and to strengthen your hearts, and make your feet firm thereby.

In the morning, the Messenger of Allah (peace be upon him) called his men to offer the prayers and urged all to fight in the way of Allah. As the sun rose over the desert, Prophet Muhammad (peace be upon him) drew up his small army, and he pointed with an arrow to arrange the ranks.

Quraish positioned their forces opposite the Muslim lines. A few of them approached to draw water from the wells of Badr, but they were killed, except one man, Hakeem ibn Hizam, who later became a devoted Muslim. When the two armies approached closer and were visible to each other, the Messenger of Allah (peace be upon him) began supplicating Allah:

"O Allah! The proud and arrogant Quraysh are already here disobeying you and belying Your Messenger. O Allah! I am waiting for Your victory which You have promised me. I beseech You Allah to defeat them (the enemies)."

The Prophet (peace be upon him) also gave strict orders that his men must not start fighting until he told them and to use their arrows sparingly, and never resort to sword unless the enemies are close. On the other hand Abu Jahl to prayed to Allah: "Our Lord, whichever of the two parties was less kind to his relatives, and brought us what we do not know, then destroy him tomorrow." Allah has mentioned regarding the supplication of Abu Jahl in Quran:

إِنْ تَسْتَفْتِحُوا فَقَدْ جَاءَكُمُ الْفَتْحُ وَإِنْ تَنْتَهُوا فَهُوَ خَيْرٌ لَكُمْ وَإِنْ تَعُودُوا نَعُدْ وَلَنْ تُغْنِيَ عَنْكُمْ فِئَتُكُمْ شَيْئًا وَلَوْ كَثُرَتْ وَأَنَّ اللَّهَ مَعَ الْمُؤْمِنِينَ

8:19 (O disbelievers) if you ask for a judgement, now has the judgement come unto you; and if you cease (to do wrong), it will be better for you, and if you return (to the attack), so shall We return, and your forces will be of no avail to you, however numerous they be; and verily, Allah is with the believers.

Ibn Kathir explained this verse as: "*Allah says to the disbelievers, if you ask for a judgment (between truth and falsehood) and a decision between you and your believing enemies, and you got what you asked for.*"

The first disbeliever to start the fire of the battle, and to be the first killed, was Al-Aswad ibn 'Abdul Asad Al-Makhzumi. He was a fierce bad-tempered idolater. He stepped out swearing that he would drink from the water basin of the Muslims, otherwise, he will destroy it or die for it. He fought with Hamzah ibn 'Abdul Muttalib. Hamzah struck his leg with his sword and finished him off inside the basin.

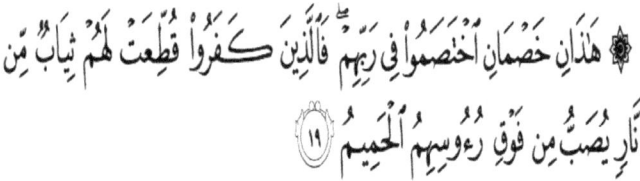

"These two opponents (believers and disbelievers) dispute with each other about their Lord." [22:19]

These Quranic verses were revealed in connection with men of Faith who confess their Lord and seek to carry out His Will (the Prophet's followers at Badr Battle), and men who deny their Lord and defy Him (Quraish).

The duels were followed by more duels and the Makkans suffered heavy losses. They were too much enraged and fell upon the Muslims to eliminate them once and for all. The Prophet and his companions, calling upon Allah for assistance, were made to hold to their positions, and they inflicted heavy losses on Quraish. Immediate was the response from Allah, He sent down angels from the heavens for the help of His Messenger (peace be upon him) and his companions. The Noble Quran observes:

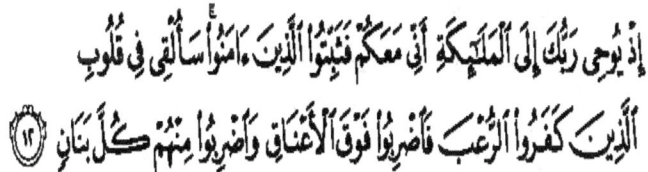

"Verily, I am with you, so keep firm those who have believed. I will cast terror into the hearts of those who have disbelieved, so strike them over the necks, and smite over all their fingers and toes.

Allah, the All-Mighty, said:

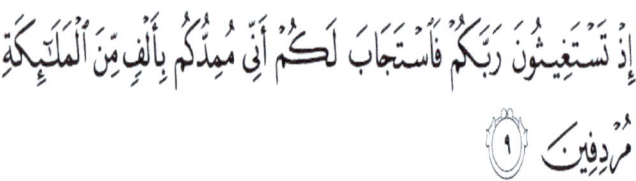

"I will help you with a thousand of the angels each behind the other (following one another) in succession."

Verses 123-124 of Surah Al-I-Imran

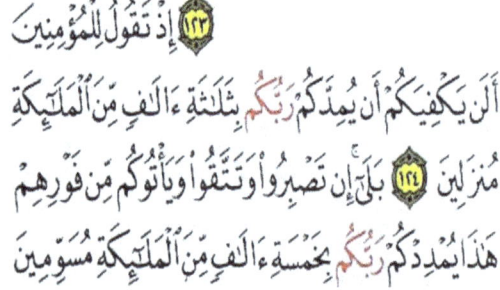

"Allah had helped you at Badr, when you were a contemptible little force: Then fear Allah in order to Show your gratitude. When you did say to the believers: Does it not suffice you that your Creator should help you with three thousand angels sent down."

The Prophet (Peace be upon him), while he went back to his tent, he dozed off a little and then raised his head joyfully crying: "O'Abu Bakr, glad tidings are there for you: Allah's victory has approached, by Allah, I can see Jibril on his stallion in the thick of a sandstorm."

At the instance of Jibril, the Messenger of Allah (peace be upon him) took a handful of sand, and he threw it at the enemy and said: "Confusion seize their faces!"

As he flung the dust, a violent sandstorm blew like furnace blast into the eyes of the enemies. With respect to this, Allah says:

فَلَمْ تَقْتُلُوهُمْ وَلَٰكِنَّ ٱللَّهَ قَتَلَهُمْ وَمَا رَمَيْتَ إِذْ رَمَيْتَ وَلَٰكِنَّ ٱللَّهَ رَمَىٰ وَلِيُبْلِىَ ٱلْمُؤْمِنِينَ مِنْهُ بَلَاءً حَسَنًا إِنَّ ٱللَّهَ سَمِيعٌ عَلِيمٌ ۝

You killed them not, but Allah killed them. And you (Muhammad) threw not when you did throw but Allah threw, that He might test the believers by a fair trial from Him. Verily, Allah is All-Hearer, All-Knower.

The spirit the Prophet (peace be upon him) infused into his men was clearly witnessed by the courage of Umair, a boy of 16, who flung away some dates he was eating crying out: "These dates are holding me back from Paradise." He then plunged into the thick of the battle and died fighting bravely. But a large number of the polytheists were killed and the others began to waver.

The records of Hadith speak very eloquently of the fact that the angels did appear on that day and helped the Muslims. Ibn Abbas said: "During the battle, a Muslim was chasing a disbeliever, and he heard over him the swashing of a whip and the voice of the rider saying: 'Go ahead Haizum'. He glanced at the polytheist who was now on the ground and on his back. The Helper came to the Prophet (peace be upon him) and related that event to him. The Messenger of Allah (peace be upon him) replied: *'You have told the truth. This was the help from Allah."*

Satan (Iblis), in the shape of Suraqah ibn Malik ibn Ju'sham Al-Mudlaji, on seeing angels helping the Muslims, and Quraish rapidly losing, made a very fast retreat despite the polytheists' pleas to stay on. He ran off and jumped into the sea.

The ranks of Quraish began to give way. The Muslim army followed them, slaying or taking captive all that fell. Retreat soon turned into humiliating rout; and they ran in haste, casting away their armor and swords.

The tyrant Abu Jahl, on seeing the heavy losses, tried to stop the tidal wave of the Islamic victory by nerving the polytheists and cheering them on by all means available and pleading with them by Al-Lat and Uzza and all symbols of paganism to stand firm in place and fight, but to no avail. Abu Jahl then began to realize the reality of his arrogance. He was deserted and left by himself on his horse waiting for death at the hand of two courageous boys.

Abdur-Rahman ibn Awf told the following interesting story in this regard: I was in the battle fighting Quraish when two young boys asked me show us Abu Jahl. I asked about their intention, to which they replied, we want to kill him. I acceded to their heartfelt pleas and pointed directly at their target. They both rushed swiftly him, and without any hesitation slashed him simultaneously with their swords and finished him off. They hurried back to the Messenger of Allah (peace be upon him).

The Messenger of Allah (peace be upon him) asked if they had wiped the blood off their swords and they answered no they have not. He then examined their swords and said yes both had killed him. When the battle concluded, Abu Jahl's spoils were given to Mu'adh ibn Amr ibn Al-Jumuh, because the other young boy, Mu'awwadh ibn Al-Afra was later killed in the same battle.

When the Prophet (peace be upon him) ordered that the corpses of the polytheists be placed into an empty well, Abu Hudhaifah ibn Utbah was very sad to see his dead father, who fought on the side of the polytheists. The Prophet (peace be upon him) saw that and asked him about it. Hudhaifah said that he wished he had been guided to the path of Islam. The Prophet (peace be upon him) whispered something to him to comfort him.

On the third day, the Prophet (peace be upon him) went out to look at the slain polytheists. He stood over the bodies of 24 leaders of Quraish, and called them by their name: "It would have been much better for you if you had obeyed Allah and His Messenger? Behold, we have found that our Lord's promise came true; did you find that the promises of your Lord came true?"

Omar ibn Al-Khattab said: "O Messenger of Allah! Why you speak to dead bodies that have no souls in them?" The Messenger of Allah (peace be upon him) answered: "By Him in Whose hand is my soul! You do not hear me better what I am saying than they do."

The polytheists received a very heavy defeat, and some fled away in great disorder in the valleys and hills heading for Makkah. They were too panicked and too ashamed to see their own families and people.

Ibn Ishaq related that the first messenger of bad tidings was Al-Haisaman ibn Abdullah Al-Khuza'i. He narrated to Quraish how their leaders were killed. Quraish did not believe him and thought that he was crazy, but very quickly the news was confirmed by another messenger and so a state of incredible confusion overwhelmed Quraish. Abu Sufyaan ibn Al-Harith gave Abu Lahab (the polytheist uncle of the Prophet) a full account of the battle and the disgraceful defeat they sustained, and he emphasized the role that the angels played in bringing about their tragic end.

Abu Lahab could not control himself and vented his feelings of anger by beating Abu Rafi', a Muslim, but was quiet on his conversion, for repeating the role of the angels. Umm Al-Fadl, a Muslim woman, greatly angered by Abu Lahab's actions, struck him with a log and injured his head.

Seven days later, Abu Lahab died of an ulcer and was left for 3 days unburied. His sons fearing shame, drove their father to a pit and keeping their distance, flung stones and sand at him.

The defeat was a matter of great grief and shame for Quraish. In almost every house there were grief and tears for the dead and the prisoners. They were burning with humiliation and they were very thirsty for some kind of revenge. Wailing and crying however were strictly forbidden fearing that the Muslims would rejoice at their pain.

The News of the Victory Reaches Madinah

Two messengers, Zaid ibn Harithah and Abdullah ibn Rawahah were sent to Madinah, to deliver the glad tidings of victory to the Muslims there.

Due to diverse ethnic groups and political structure of Madinah there were many different respective reactions.

Newsmongers amongst the hypocrites spread the news that the Messenger of Allah (peace be upon him) had been killed because Zaid ibn Harithah was riding the Prophet's she-camel, Al-Qaswa. However, both messengers informed everyone the happy news of the victory, and also provided the exact course of the battle in order to establish the sense of comfort deep in their hearts. Then their chiefs went out of Madinah to wait and to receive the Messenger of Allah (peace and blessings be upon him).

Usamah ibn Zaid said that they got the news of the victory shortly after the wife of Uthman ibn Affan, Ruqaiyah, the Messenger's daughter had been buried.

She had been very ill and the Prophet (peace and blessings be upon him) had asked Uthman to stay in Madinah and to look after her.

Before leaving the landscape of the battle, arguments concerning the spoils of the battle arose amongst the warriors. When the arguments grew louder, the Prophet (peace and blessings be upon him) postponed the matter until the Revelation was sent down to him.

Ubadah bin As-Samit related that they went out with the Prophet (peace and blessing be upon him) and they witnessed the battle of Badr with him. The battle began and Allah, the Mighty, defeated the enemy quickly. Some of the warriors pursued the enemy, they were intent on gathering the spoils from the enemy camps, and others were protecting the Prophet (peace and blessings be upon him). Then when sunset came, some of the warriors gathered together, those who had gathered the booty said: "We collected it alone, so no other man has any right to it."

But those who had followed the enemy said: "You do not have more rights to it than we do. We defeated the enemy while you were collecting the booty."

As for the warriors who had been guarding the Messenger of Allah (peace and blessings be upon him), they also said the same regarding the spoils.

Revelation came down that said:

يَسْـَٔلُونَكَ عَنِ ٱلْأَنفَالِ قُلِ ٱلْأَنفَالُ لِلَّهِ وَٱلرَّسُولِ فَٱتَّقُوا۟ ٱللَّهَ وَأَصْلِحُوا۟ ذَاتَ بَيْنِكُمْ وَأَطِيعُوا۟ ٱللَّهَ وَرَسُولَهُۥٓ إِن كُنتُم مُّؤْمِنِينَ ﴿١﴾

They ask you [O Muhammad (Peace be upon him)] about the spoils of war. Say: "The spoils are for Allah and the Messenger." So fear Allah and adjust all matters of difference among you, and obey Allah and His Messenger. [8:1]

Later, on their way back to Madinah, the Prophet (peace be upon him) stopped at a large sand hill, he divided the spoils evenly among the warriors after the Prophet had taken Al-Khums (1/5th), to give to other warriors that prophet had ordered to stay in the Madinah.

The Messenger of Allah (peace and blessings be upon him) now entered Madinah as a man to be counted on. In consequence, more people embraced Islam, which added more power, strength, and moral standing of Islam.

The Messenger of Allah (peace and blessings be upon him) urged that the Muslims treat all prisoners well. The captors even gave the captives their own bread, which was the more valued part of the meal, and they eat the dates.

However, the prisoners were a problem awaiting resolution because it was a new experience in the history of Islam. The Messenger of Allah (peace and blessings be upon him) asked Abu Bakr (RA) and Omar ibn Al-Khattab (RA) as to what he should be done with the prisoners.

Omar recommended killing them. He said: "They are the leaders of the disbelief (Kufr)." However, the Messenger of Allah (peace and blessings be upon him) liked Abu Bakr's proposal.

However, Abu Bakr recommended that he should ransom them and said: "They are after all our own people and relatives, and any ransom money might give us strength against the disbelievers in the future, moreover, Allah might guide them to Islam."

Thereupon the grief on the face of Allah's Messenger vanished. He pardoned them and accepted ransom for their release. The Messenger of Allah (peace and blessings be upon him) later said that a Quranic verse was then sent down:

"Thereafter (is the time) either for generosity or ransom, until the war lays down its burden." [47:4]

The ransom for the prisoners averaged about 700 Dirhams. Another form of ransom took a teaching dimension. For example, most of the Makkans were literate and so if a prisoner could not afford the ransom, he was entrusted with 10 children to teach them reading and writing. Once most children learned to read and write, the instructor (prisoner) would be set free.

Another clan of prisoners were released unransomed because they had no money and they could not read or write. For example, Zainab, the daughter of the Messenger of Allah (peace and blessings be upon him), paid the ransom of her husband Abul-As with her necklace. However, the warriors released her prisoner and returned the necklace, but on condition that Abul-As allow, the Prophet's daughter, Zainab, to migrate to Madinah, and later he did.

In custody, there was also a very eloquent orator. His name was Suhail ibn Amr. Omar (RA) recommended that they pull out his front teeth to prevent him from speaking clearly, but the Messenger of Allah (peace and blessings be upon him) said no for fear Quraish might retaliate in the same manner, and for fear of Allah's wrath on the Day of Resurrection.

Post-Badr Military Activities

Badr was the first battle between the Messenger of Allah (peace and blessings be upon him) and Quraish. It was a critical battle that gained the Muslims an important victory and acknowledged by everyone. It the battle also dealt a heavy blow to the economic interests of the polytheists. Quraish was very angry since the Muslims had achieved that great victory:

"Verily, you will find the strongest among men in enmity to the believers (Muslims) the Jews and Al-Mushrikûn (polytheists, pagans, idolators and disbelievers, etc.)." [5:82]

Ibn Kathir said that this describes the Jewish people, since their disbelief is that of rebellion, defiance, opposing the truth, belittling other people and degrading the scholars. They killed Jesus (peace be upon him) and many of their Prophets and tried to kill the Messenger of Allah several times, as well as, poisoning him. They also incited their likes among the polytheists against the Prophet.

The desert bedouins living in tents that were pitched near the city of Al-Madinah, depended mostly on looting & plundering as a means of living, and so were totally uninterested to this axial question of belief and disbelief. Their worry was from fear of losing their corrupt ways in the event a powerful Muslim state might rise up and put an end to their ways, hence they hated the Muslims and the Messenger of Allah (peace be upon him) in particular.

This later became a military action, the Uhud Invasion. It left a very bad impression on the good name and respect that the Prophet (peace be upon him) was painstakingly working to preserve.

The Messenger of Allah (peace and blessings be upon him) was always on the lookout for any hostile movements. It was very important to him to launch a pre-emptive strike in order to have a reasonable degree of security in that great instability-provoking sea of unrest.

The following is some of the military activities conducted in the post-Badr period:

The Al-Kudr Invasion

The expedition against the Banu Salim tribe, is also known as the Al Kudr Invasion. It happened after the Battle of Badr in the year 2 A.H of the Islamic calendar. The expedition was ordered by the Prophet (peace be upon him) after he received reports that the Banu Salim were planning to invade Madinah. This was the Muslims first interaction with the people of Bahrain. The Prophet (peace be upon him) received reports that some tribes were amassing an army and moving towards Madinah.

The Messenger of Allah (peace be upon him) responded by launching a pre-emptive attack against their base in Al-Kudr, which was their watering place at the time. When the tribe of Banu Salim heard of this, they fled. However, the Prophet (peace be upon him) captured 500 of their camels, and distributed it between his warriors. This invasion took place in Shawwal in the year 2 A.H., 7 days after the Battle of Badr.

An Attempt on the Life of the Messenger of Allah

The defeat at the Battle of Badr was so great that the Makkans were burning with anger over their horrible defeat. They wanted revenge. So two polytheists offered to quench their thirst and to kill the source of their humiliation, i.e. the Messenger of Allah (peace and blessings be upon him).

One day, Omair ibn Wahab Al-Jumahi, a rotten polytheist, and Safwan ibn Omaiyah sat together mourning their losses and remembering their dead. Omair expressed a strong desire to kill the Messenger of Allah (peace and blessings be upon him) and to release his captured son that was held in Madinah. Safwan, also had his own reasons to see the Messenger of Allah (peace and blessings be upon him) dead. Therefore he offered to pardon Omair's debts and to support his family if he helped him with his plan. Omair quickly agreed and asked Safwan to be very on their plan. So he left for Madinah, and took his sword and he applied to it some kind of deadly poison.

Omar ibn Al-Khattab (RA) saw him at the door of the Masjid and he understood quickly that Omair had come for an evil purpose. Omar ibn Al-Khattab (RA) instantly went into the Masjid and told the Messenger of Allah (peace and blessings be upon him).

Omair then entered with his sword and he said "good morning", to which the Messenger of Allah (peace be upon him) replied that Allah had been very gracious and He had taught them that the greeting of the inhabitants of the Paradise: "peace be upon you!"

The Messenger of Allah (peace and blessings be upon him), asked about his object, Omair said that he wanted to see his captured son. The Messenger of Allah (peace and blessings be upon him) asked him to tell his real goal, but Omari remained unyielding and did not divulge the secret plan that he made with Safwan.

However, the Messenger of Allah (peace and blessings be upon him) revealed to Omair his secret mission. Omair became frightened, and incredible fear seized him.

Omair immediately bore witness to Allah and to the Messengership of the Prophet (peace and blessings be upon him). The Prophet (peace and blessings be upon him) was very pleased. He then asked his Companions to teach Omair the principles of Islam, to recite to him the Quran, and to release his son from captivity. Safwan did not know what had happened. He impatiently awaited Omair's return, but he was told that the man had embraced Islam and became a devoted believer. Omair then came back to Makkah and he began to teach his people about Islam.

The Invasion of Bani Qaynuaq

Previously we mentioned the treaty that the Messenger of Allah (peace be upon him) signed with the Jews. The Prophet (peace be upon him) was always very careful to abide by it to the letter, and the Muslims never violated any of its provisions. The Jews, however, could not rid themselves of their ways, and so they tried to create division amongst the Muslims.

For example, Shas ibn Qais, an old Jewish man, a terrible disbeliever, sent a youth of his to sit amongst the Muslims and to remind them of the Bu'ath wars. He ignited their fire by reciting some of their verses, which they used to compose satirizing each other. The youth succeeded. The parties recalled the old days before Islam, and so tribal fanaticism sprang to the front and brought about a state of war.

The Messenger of Allah (peace be upon him) was told of this, and immediately set out to see to the situation. He lectured them about tolerance. He said: "My brothers! Do you still advance pre-Islamic disputes after I have been sent to you. Never turn backward after Allah has guided you to the Straight Path, and He saved you from disbelief, and created friendship between you."

The Muslim tribes quickly realized that it was a plot hatched by their enemies. They quickly embraced each other and went back to their homes. They were satisfied and in full obedience to the Messenger of Allah (peace and blessings be upon him).

Such were the practices of the trouble-makers. For example, if they owed a Muslim money, they would evade their obligations on the basis that he had converted to Islam and so they would allege that the agreement between them was no longer valid. However, if it was the other way, they would never cease to remind them daily to pay back the debt.

Seeing that God granted the Messenger of Allah (peace be upon him) victory, the Jewish tribes were angry. The worst was the tribe of Banu Qainuqa. They lived next to Madinah. They were skilled craftsmen, and were good at blacksmithing, goldsmithery, and making household instruments. That is why swords and knives were available in large quantities within their tribes. They had over 700 warriors, and they were the bravest and stingiest amongst the Jewish community in Arabia. And so they were the first to breach the non-aggression agreement, which they had already signed with the Messenger of Allah (peace be upon him). Their conduct grew very impolite and intolerable. They loved trouble-making, jeering at the Muslims, injuring those who frequented their markets, and even harassing the women.

So the Messenger of Allah (peace and blessings be upon him) asked them to be kind and sensible. He cautioned them against further transgression.

Nevertheless they remained stubborn and paid no attention to the Prophet's warnings. They said: "Don't be deceived on account of defeating Quraish's most inexperienced warriors. If you are looking for a real fight, you will find that we are experts in war."

In this matter, the Words of Allah were sent down:

3:12 Say to those who disbelieve: "You will be defeated and gathered together to Hell, and worst indeed is that place of rest."

> قَدْ كَانَ لَكُمْ ءَايَةٌ فِى فِئَتَيْنِ الْتَقَتَا فِئَةٌ تُقَٰتِلُ فِى سَبِيلِ اللَّهِ وَأُخْرَىٰ كَافِرَةٌ يَرَوْنَهُم مِّثْلَيْهِمْ رَأْىَ الْعَيْنِ وَاللَّهُ يُؤَيِّدُ بِنَصْرِهِۦ مَن يَشَآءُ
>
> **3:13** There has already been a sign for you in the two armies that met. One was fighting in the cause of Allah, and as for the other, in disbelief. They saw them with their own eyes twice their number. And Allah supports with His aid whom He wills.
>
> إِنَّ فِى ذَٰلِكَ لَعِبْرَةً لِّأُوْلِى الْأَبْصَٰرِ
>
> Verily, in this is a lesson for those who understand.

The Messenger of Allah (peace and blessings be upon him) was more patient and he advised the Muslims to wait for what time might reveal. However, Jewish tribe were itching for war. They went too far in their transgressions. One day a Jewish goldsmith assaulted a Muslim woman and he uncovered her private parts. A Muslim man happened to be there and killed the man. The Jews then killed the Muslim man. The man's family called for help and war started.

On Saturday, Shawwal 15th, 2 A.H., the Messenger of Allah (peace be upon him) went out with his soldiers, and Hamzah ibn Abdul laid siege to the Jews' forts for 15 days. Allah cast fear into their minds and hearts, and so they asked the Messenger (peace be upon him) for help.

At this point, Abdullah ibn Ubai ibn Salul, a Madinese polytheist, started his hypocritical role and began to negotiate for them. The Prophet (peace be upon him) negotiated with this man as being a Muslim. Abdullah had faked conversion into Islam. Banu Qainuqa handed over money and war materials to the Messenger of Allah (peace be upon him). The Prophet set aside one fifth and distributed the rest to his warriors. After that they were banished out of all Arabia to Azrua in Syria.

The As-Sawiq Invasion Dhul-Hijjah 2 A.H.:

Two different hostile actions were being independently directed against the Messenger of Allah (peace be upon him). The plots and were being hatched by Safwan ibn Omaiyah, the hypocrites and

Jews on the one hand, and on the other hand, military hostilities was being prepared by Abu Sufyaan aiming at saving the face of his people, and also trying to show other Arabs that Quraish was still a great military power.

After the battle of Badr, Abu Sufyaan was burning for revenge. He gave a vow that he would never wash off impurity until he had avenged himself on the Prophet (peace be upon him) and his companions. So Abu Sufyaan set out at the head of 200 fighters towards Madinah, but they were not brave enough to attack it in the daylight. Therefore, he resorted to acts of piracy that were done in the night. He infiltrated into Madinah and went to see his old ally, Huyai ibn Akhtab. However, he was a coward and so he did not let him in. Then he went to see Salam ibn Mashkam, chief of Bani Nadeer, a Jewish tribe.

The Jew greeted him very well and gave him all the information that he was seeking. Late at night he sent out a group of his fighters to raid Al-Uraid, a suburb of Madinah. His men destroyed and burnt the palm trees, killed two Muslims, and then ran swiftly back to their lair.

On hearing the news, the Messenger of Allah (peace be upon him) gathered his warriors and set out at their heels, but they could not catch them. However, the Muslims brought back their provisions (Sawiq, a kind of barley porridge), which the polytheists had thrown away in order to lighten their loads and to hasten their escape. This campaign was called the As-Sawiq Invasion. It took place two months after the Battle of Badr.

The Dhi Amr Invasion Muharram, 3 A.H.:

The Prophet's warriors reported that Banu Muharib and Banu Tha'labah were gathering troops to raid the outskirts of Madinah. So the Messenger of Allah (peace and blessings be upon him) at the head of 450 horsemen and footmen went out to handle this invasion.

Uthman ibn Affan was asked to help the affairs of the Muslims in Madinah. When the enemies saw the Messenger of Allah (peace and blessings be upon him) they swiftly dispersed into the mountains and disappeared.

The Muslims stopped at a watering place called "Dhi Amr" for the whole of Safar 3 A.H. The desert bedouins in that area, saw that the Muslims were powerful enough to throw fear into the hearts of their enemies.

Ka'b Ibn Al-Ashraf Killed

Ka'b Ibn Al-Ashraf was the most bitter Jew at the Messenger of Allah (peace and blessings be upon him). He wanted to inflict harm badly on the Messenger of Allah (peace be upon him). He was the most zealous advocate of waging war against the Prophet (peace be upon him). He belonged to Tai' tribe but his mother belonged to Banu Nadeer. He was a very wealthy man known for his handsome features, and he was a poet living in luxury in his fort near Madinah at the rear of Banu Nadeer's habitations.

On hearing the news about the Battle of Badr, he got terribly upset and swore that he would prefer death if the news was true. When the news was confirmed he wrote many poems satirizing the Prophet (peace be upon him), and he eulogized Quraish and he enticed them to fight the Messenger of Allah (peace be upon him).

Moreover, he went to Makkah where he began to trigger the fire of war, and to kindle hate against the Muslims. When Abu Sufyaan asked him to which religion he liked the best, the religion of the Makkans or that of Prophet (peace be upon him), he replied that the pagans were far more guided.

In regards to this matter, Allah sent down His Words:

أَلَمْ تَرَ إِلَى الَّذِينَ أُوتُوا نَصِيبًا مِّنَ الْكِتَبِ

3:23 Have you not seen those who have been given a portion of the Scripture!

يُدْعَوْنَ إِلَى كِتَبِ اللَّهِ لِيَحْكُمَ بَيْنَهُمْ ثُمَّ يَتَوَلَّى فَرِيقٌ مِّنْهُمْ وَهُم مُّعْرِضُونَ

They are being invited to the Book of Allah to settle their dispute, then a party of them turned away, and they are averse.

ذَلِكَ بِأَنَّهُمْ قَالُوا لَن تَمَسَّنَا النَّارُ إِلَّا أَيَّامًا مَّعْدُودَتٍ

3:24 This is because they say: "The Fire shall not touch us but for a number of days."

وَغَرَّهُمْ فِى دِينِهِم مَّا كَانُوا يَفْتَرُونَ

And that which they used to invent in their religion has deceived them.

Ka'b ibn Al-Ashraf then returned to Madinah to start a fresh campaign of insults and propaganda. He wrote obscene songs and amatory sonnets to defame the Muslim women.

At this stage, the situation became very unbearable. The insults and the harassment of women became larger. Then Muhammad ibn Maslamah asked the Prophet (peace be upon him)" "Do you wish that I should put an end to him?" He said: "Yes." He said: "Permit me to talk (to him in the way I deem fit)." He said: "Talk (as you like)."

So, Muhammad ibn Maslamah came to Ka'b and said: "This man (i.e. the Prophet (peace be upon him)) wants to collect charity (from us) and this will make life tougher. We have become his followers and we do not like to forsake him. I want that you should give me a loan."

Ka'b said: "What will you mortgage?" Muhammad ibn Maslamah answered: "What do you want?" Ka'b wanted women and children as articles of security against the debt.

Muhammad said: "Should we pledge our own women whereas you are the most handsome of the Arabs; but we can pledge you our weapons." Ka'b agreed. Salkan ibn Salamah, Abu Na'ilah, also went to see Ka'b for the same loan and told him that he would bring him some more companions that also wanted a loan. The plan was done and provided for the presence of both men and weapons. On Rabi Al-Awwal 14th, at night, the year 3 A.H. the men went and called upon Ka'b at night. They invited him to go out and spend a good time in the moonlight. On the way out, Abu Na'ilah said: "I smell the sweet perfume." Ka'b said: "Yes, I have a mistress who is the most perfumed of all the women of Arabia." Abu Na'ilah again said: "Allow me to smell (the scent on your head)". He then held his head and said to his friends: "Finish him." And so they killed him.

When the Jews learned about the death of Ka'b ibn Al-Ashraf, they were scared. They realized that Prophet's companions thereafter would never hesitate to use force when good words and warnings failed. So they remained silent and faked adherence to the covenants.

Zaid ibn Harithah led warriors on the trade routes of Quraish

This was a very successful campaign prior to the Uhud Battle. It took place in Jumada Ath-Thaniyah, in the year 3 A.H.

Summer was fast approaching and it was time for the Makkan's trade caravans to leave for Syria. The people of Quraish heavily depended on trade. So they held a meeting to discuss how to escape the economic blockade.

They decided to go along a trade route across Najd to Iraq, then to Syria.

Safwan ibn Omaiyah was selected to lead the caravan along this new route, and Furat ibn Haiyan was chosen as a guide. However, news of the meeting seeped out through the mouth of Naim ibn Masud Al-Ashja'i under the effect of alcohol (wine). The news flew very fast to Madinah by Sulit ibn An-Numan. The Messenger of Allah (peace and blessings be upon him) immediately rallied 100 horsemen under the leadership of Zaid ibn Harithah Al-Kalbi, and he dispatched them to capture the caravan.

The horsemen caught up with the caravan at Al-Qardah. The polytheists were arrested. However, Safwan and his guards escaped without defending the caravan. The caravan was loaded with silver and wares. The booty was divided equally among the warriors. The caravan's guide, Furat ibn Haiyan, then embraced Islam on his own.

Quraish could not find another trade route. So the economic blockade on Makkah had a great impact on the economy of Quraish.

Quraish was very upset about their economy and life. They had two options: relinquish all symbols of arrogance and make peace with the Prophet (peace be upon him), or start another war to try to destroy warriors of Madinah. Quraish decided on the second alternative. Quraish cried loudly demanding vengeance. This was the start of the battle of Uhud.

The Battle of Uhud

The defeat at the Battle of Badr was an embarrassment which Quraish could not forget. They wanted revenge. The Makkans even forbade crying over their lost people. Quraish began preparations to launch an overall war against the Prophet (peace be upon him) in order to heal their wounded pride. The most eager polytheists desiring to go war were Ikrimah ibn Abu Sufyaan ibn Harb, Abi Jahl, Safwan ibn Omaiyah, and Abdullah ibn Abi Rabi'a. They were determined to crush Prophet (peace be upon him) once and for all.

Quraish sent emissaries to all the tribes to make common cause against the Prophet (peace be upon him). They managed to enlist the support of two strong tribes Tihamah and Kinana and some desert bedouins Ahabish. They decided that the profits of the escaped caravan that was headed by Abu Sufyaan, which amounted to 1000 camels and $50,000 Dinars, should be used to provide equipment to the army.

Allah Quran has alluded to this decision of theirs in the following verses:

> إِنَّ الَّذِينَ كَفَرُوا يُنْفِقُونَ أَمْوَالَهُمْ لِيَصُدُّوا عَنْ سَبِيلِ اللَّهِ فَسَيُنْفِقُونَهَا ثُمَّ تَكُونُ عَلَيْهِمْ حَسْرَةً ثُمَّ يُغْلَبُونَ
>
> 8:36 Verily, those who disbelieve spend their wealth to hinder (men) from the path of Allah, and so will they continue to spend it; but in the end it will become an anguish for them. Then they will be overcome.

They also devised cleaver ways to recruit warriors, like hiring poets to entice the tribes into fighting the Muslims. Safwan ibn Omaiyah enticed Abu Azza, a poet, in return for riches after the war or supporting his daughters if he is killed. This ungrateful man was a prisoner of war after the Battle of Badr in the hands of the Prophet (peace be upon him), but the Prophet was kind enough to release him unransomed provided he would never fight against him again.

Quraish accelerated their preparations for a decisive war with the Prophet (peace be upon him). At the turn of the year, they were ready for war. Quraish also took their women along with to fight if possible. Thus about 3,000 warriors, of whom 700 were soldiers and 200 well-mounted cavalry with 3,000 camels and 15 women marched towards Madinah.

Their leader was Abu Sufyaan ibn Harb. The cavalry leader was Khalid ibn Al-Waleed and assisted by Ikrimah ibn Abi Jahl, and Bani Abd Ad-Dar held their flag.

Al-Abbas ibn Abdul Muttalib closely watched the military movements, and he sent an urgent message to the Messenger of Allah (peace be upon him), who received it while he was in Quba Masjid. Ubai ibn Ka'b read the letter to the Messenger of Allah (peace be upon him. The Prophet (peace be upon him) hurried back home, then summoned a meeting with the Helpers and Emigrants.

Madinah was put on high alert and all men were armed even during prayer in anticipation of the battle. A group of Helpers guarded the Messenger of Allah (peace be upon him) and stayed all night at his door, amongst whom there were Usaid ibn Hudair, Sa'd ibn Mu'adh, and Sa'd ibn Ubadah.

Quraish continued their march along the usual western road. On reaching Al-Abwa, Abu Sufyaan's wife (Hind bint Utbah), told them to dig up the grave of the Prophet's mother, but the leaders refused to do so for fear of the consequences. Quraish then followed Wadi Al-Aqeeq and encamped at a place called Ainain near the Uhud Mountain. That was on Friday, 6th Shawwal, 3 A.H.

The Messenger of Allah (peace and blessings be upon him) said: "I have dreamt of, I implore Allah to be a dream of bounty, cows slaughtered and that there was a groove at the pointed top of my sword, and that I had inserted my hand into an immune armor."

The interpretation of *the slaughtered cows* was that some of the Prophet's men will be killed, and *the groove at the pointed top of his sword* was that a member of his own House would be hurt. As for *the armor* it was Madinah.

The Prophet (peace be upon him), then offered a suggestion that his Companions should not go out of Madinah and that they should position themselves within the city. He was of the opinion that Quraish should be left in the open to exhaust themselves and thus the Muslims would not risk a battle. But if Quraish attacked Madinah, they would be ready to fight them. Abdullah ibn Ubai ibn Salul, the head of the hypocrites, who attended the meeting as a chief of Al-Khazraj, supported the Prophet's idea. He liked the plan because he never intended to fight.

However it was Allah's Will that he should be humiliated and disgraced in public. It was Allah's Will that the curtain which concealed their disbelief should be uncovered. Allah enabled the Prophet (peace be upon him) to see the reality of those snakes.

Thanks to Allah, the Prophet (peace be upon him), saw them who they were in one of the most critical times of their lives.

Some of the honorable Companions of the Prophet, who had missed Al-Jihad in the Battle of Badr, suggested that the Messenger of Allah (peace be upon him) should go out of Madinah, and they urged him to accept their point of view.

One of them said: "O'Messenger of Allah (peace and blessings be upon him), for long time we have been looking forward to this day. We have begged Allah to make such a day near. So thanks to Allah it is time to fight. Please let us go out and fight the enemies lest they might think that we do not dare to fight them."

Hamza ibn Abdul Muttalib, the uncle of the Prophet (peace be upon him), who had already covered the ornaments of his sword with the enemies' blood in Battle of Badr, was ahead of those wanting to fight. So after weighing very carefully the pros and cons of the issue, they decided that the enemy should be resisted outside the city at Uhud.

Ascending the pulpit at the Friday congregational prayer, the Messenger of Allah (peace and blessings be upon him) urged them to fight courageously. The Prophet said: "If you remain steadfast, you will be helped by Allah." Then the Prophet (peace be upon him) commanded his men to make ready for the battle.

The Prophet (peace be upon him) then entered his house accompanied by his two friends Abu Bakr (RA) and Omar (RA). They helped him dress and wear his headcloth. The Prophet armed himself and wore two armours. He wore his sword and went out to meet the people. That were waiting for him impatiently.

Usaid ibn Hudair and Sa'd ibn Mu'adh were upset with the people. They said: "You have pressed the Prophet (peace be upon him) to fight the enemy outside Madinah." They wanted to leave the whole matter to the Messenger of Allah (peace be upon him).

When the Prophet came out, they said: "O'Messenger of Allah, we should have never disagreed with you. You are free to do what you think is best. If you want to stay inside Madinah we will stay with you. Upon this the Prophet (peace be upon him) remarked: "It is not right for a Prophet that once he had put on his armor to take it off, until Allah has decided between him and the enemy."

The Prophet Divides the Army into 3 Division:

1. Al-Ansari-Aws battalion was commanded by Usaid ibn Hudair

2. Al-Muhajireen battalion, under the command of Mus'ab ibn Umair Al-Abdari.

3. Al-Ansari-Khazraj battalion with Al-Hubab ibn Al-Mundhir to lead it.

The army consisted of 1,000 warriors. 100 of them had armor, and another 50 horsemen. He asked Ibn Umm Maktum to lead the people in prayer in Madinah. The Prophet's army moved northwards.

Upon passing along Al-Wada mountain trail, the Prophet (peace be upon him) saw a well-armed battalion, which were separated from the main body of the army.

The Messenger of Allah (Peace be upon him) inquired who they were, and he was told that they were Jews and were allies of Al-Khazraj. They wanted to fight against the idolaters. The Prophet (peace be upon him) asked: "If they have embraced Islam?" "No," they replied. So the Prophet refused admitting them, because he did not want to seek the assistance of disbelievers against the idolaters.

As soon as the Prophet (peace be upon him) reached a location called Ash-Shaikhan, he looked at his army. He then dismissed those whom he considered to be disabled or very young to stand the fight. However, though they were young, the Messenger of Allah (peace be upon him) allowed both Samura ibn Jundub and Rafi ibn Khadaij to join the army. Because the former was very skillful at shooting arrows, and the latter was strong and he wrestled the former and beat him.

As night came, they performed sunset and the evening prayers. Fifty men were chosen to guard the camp. At the end of the night and before it was daybreak, the Messenger of Allah (peace and blessings be upon him) marched further and when they got to Ash-Shawt he observed the dawn prayer.

There the Prophet (peace be upon him) was so close to the enemy that they could see one another. It was there that Abdullah ibn Ubai, the hypocrite, rebelled against the Prophet. One-third of the army (300 hundred men) withdrew with him. He told the Messenger of Allah (peace and blessings be upon him): "We do not know why we shall kill ourselves." He claimed that his withdrawal was a protest against the Prophet (peace be upon him) for refusing his opinion and accepted that of the others. The truth of the matter, he was a coward. When he saw the size of the enemy he became frightened.

Banu Haritha of Al-Aws and Banu Salama of Al-Khazraj were somewhat impressed by the hypocrite's behavior. And both of them were overwhelmed by confusion. They wanted to withdraw, but Allah saved them from that disgrace. Allah said:

> إِذْ هَمَّتْ طَآئِفَتَانِ مِنكُمْ أَن تَفْشَلَا وَاللَّهُ وَلِيُّهُمَا وَعَلَى اللَّهِ فَلْيَتَوَكَّلِ الْمُؤْمِنُونَ
>
> 3:122 When two parties from among you were about to lose heart, but Allah was their Wali (Supporter and Protector). And in Allah should the believers put their trust.

Abdullah ibn Haram, the father of Jabir ibn Abdullah, tried to stop their withdrawal. He followed them and urged them to go back. He said: "Come and fight in the way of Allah or be defenders." They said: "If we had known that you would truly fight, we would have not gone back." Having lost hope of them, he addressed them and said: "May Allah cast you away, you are enemies of Allah. Allah will certainly suffice His Prophet."

Allah said:

> وَلِيَعْلَمَ الَّذِينَ نَافَقُوا وَقِيلَ لَهُمْ تَعَالَوْا قَاتِلُوا فِى سَبِيلِ اللَّهِ أَوِ ادْفَعُوا
>
> 3:167 And that He might test the hypocrites, it was said to them: "Come, fight in the way of Allah or defend yourselves."
>
> قَالُوا لَوْ نَعْلَمُ قِتَالًا لَاتَّبَعْنَاكُمْ
>
> They said: "Had we known that fighting will take place, we would certainly have followed you."
>
> هُمْ لِلْكُفْرِ يَوْمَئِذٍ أَقْرَبُ مِنْهُمْ لِلْإِيمَانِ يَقُولُونَ بِأَفْوَاهِهِم مَّا لَيْسَ فِى قُلُوبِهِمْ
>
> They were that day, nearer to disbelief than to faith, saying with their mouths what was not in their hearts.
>
> وَاللَّهُ أَعْلَمُ بِمَا يَكْتُمُونَ
>
> And Allah has full knowledge of what they conceal.

With the remainder of warriors, the Messenger of Allah (peace and blessings be upon him) moved closer to the enemy. After the rebellion and withdrawal of the hypocrites, the Prophet's army was reduced to only 700 fighters.

The camp of idolaters was situated in such a location, that paths leading to Uhud were blocked by them. So the Messenger of Allah (peace and blessings be upon him) said: "Which man of you can lead us to where the idolaters are, along a short path that does not pass by them?"

Abu Khaithama said: "O'Messenger of Allah (peace and blessings be upon him), I am the man that you need." Then he chose a short path that led to Uhud by passing Harrah Bani Harithah and their farms, leaving the idolaters' army westwards.

On their way they passed by the land of Marba ibn Qaizi, who was a blind hypocrite. When Marba realized that they were the Prophet's army, he began to throw sand at their faces, so they rushed to kill him, but the Prophet (peace be upon him) said: "Do not kill him for he is blind in heart and eyes."

The Prophet (peace be upon him) went along till they climbed down the hillock of Uhud at the slope of the valley. The Prophet (peace be upon him) camped there facing Madinah while their backs were to the hills of Uhud mountain. So the army of the enemy stood a barrier between the Prophet (peace be upon him) and Madinah.

The Prophet (peace be upon him) mobilized his army. He arranged them into two rows to prepare them for fight. He selected 50 strong archers that formed a squad and asked Abdullah ibn Jubair ibn An-Nu'man Al-Ansari Al-Awsi Al-Badri to lead them.

He ordered to them to stay where they were. Not to move. To stay on a mountain (side) at the south bank of Qanat Al-Wadi (a canal of the valley), south east of Muslims camp at about 150 metres from the Islamic army. The Prophet (peace be upon him) clarified further the mission of this squad. He said to their leader: "Drive off the horses from us by arrows, in case they attack us from the rear. Whether we win the battle or lose, stand here and see that we are not attacked from your side."

He added: "Defend our backs! And if you see us slain. Do not come to help us; and if you see winning, do not share us."

In another version by Al-Bukhari, the Prophet (peace be upon him) said: "If you see us snatched into pieces by birds, do not leave this position until I send for you. And if you see defeating them, do not desert your position until I send for you."

The assignments of each post and their responsibilities for the rest of the army were done by the Prophet (Peace be upon him) as follows: On the left he appointed Az-Zubair ibn Al-Awwam, and made Al-Miqdad ibn Al-Aswad his assistant and supporter. On the right wing, he appointed Al-Mundhir ibn Amr.

Az-Zubair's function was to stand in the face of Khalid ibn Al-Waleed's horsemen. The Prophet (peace be upon him) selected the most courageous men to be in the frontline of the army. They were known for their bravery.

It was an ingenious plan. No other leader could have drawn a better plan. Although the Prophet (peace be upon him) came to the site after than the enemy had arrived, he managed to occupy far better positions.

He made the rocky mountainside to be a shield for the army's rear and right flank. He blocked the only vulnerable gap on the side to provide additional protection for the rear as well as the left wing.

For fear of possible defeat, and to prevent his fighters from fleeing, and falling prisoners in the hands of the enemy, the Prophet (peace be upon him) chose a high place for encampment. Moreover their strategic positions would surely cause heavy losses on the polytheists if they tried to approach or occupy his positions.

Moreover, the Prophet (peace be upon him) reduced the enemy to a slim, narrow scope of choice when they were surrounded for encampment in geographically low positions that would give them nothing of the benefits of any possible victory.

Also at the same time they would not be able to escape. To make up for the quantitative lack in fighting men, the Prophet (peace be upon him) selected strong fighters to stand at the front.

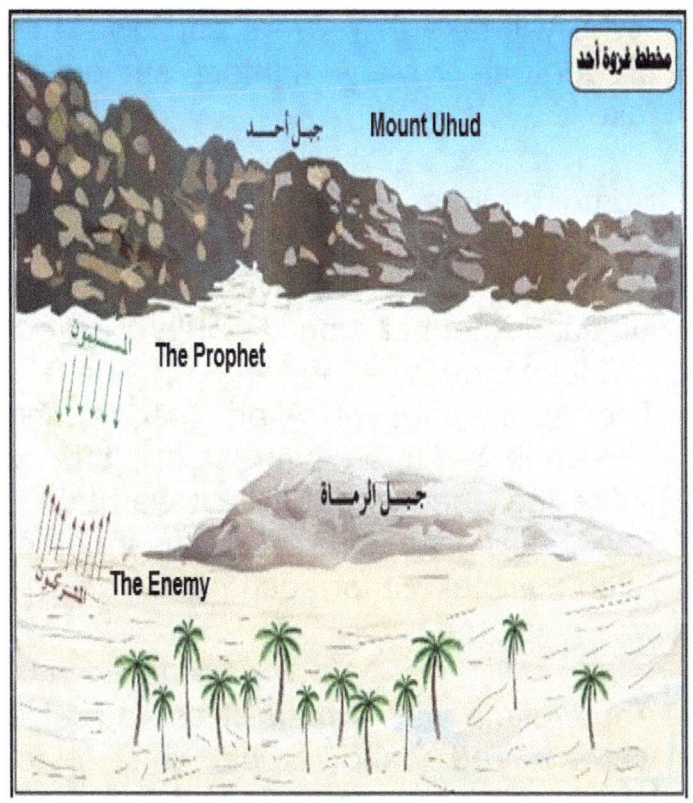

The Prophet (peace be upon him) forbade his fighters to start the fight without having an order from him. The Prophet (peace be upon him) wore two armors, a front one and a back armor.

The Prophet (peace be upon him) told his Companions to fight and urged them to show stamina and steadfastness at fight. To motivate them, the Prophet (peace be upon him) took his sharp sword, and called out unto his Companions and said: "Who will take this sword and give it its proper due?" Many fighters set out to take it.

Some of them were Az-Zubair ibn Al-Awwam, Ali ibn Abi Talib, and Omar ibn Al-Khattab. But it was given to none. Abu Dujana Sammak ibn Kharsha asked: "O'Messenger of Allah, what is its price?" The Messenger of Allah (peace and blessings be upon him) said: "It is to strike the enemy with it till it was bent." So Abu Dujana said: "O'Messenger of Allah I will take it for such price." and he was given the sword.

Abu Dujana was a man of courage. He wore a red band around his head. Whenever he wore the red band, everybody knew that he was determined to fight to death. Therefore as soon as Abu Dujana took the Prophet's sword, he banded his head and began strutting amongst the fighters.

Watching him walk like that, the Prophet (peace be upon him) said: "This is a sort of walking Allah dislikes except in such a situation."

The idolaters used the rows system in the mobilization of their army. The leader of the army was given to Abu Sufyaan Sakhr ibn Harb, and stood in the center position of the army. Khalid ibn Al-Waleed was on the right wing of the army, and Ikrima, the son of Abu Jahl was on the left. Safwan ibn Omaiya led the infantry men. The archers were led by Abdullah ibn Abi Rabia.

Abu Sufyaan reminded his men of what had happened to Quraish in the Battle of Badr when their standard bearer, An-Nadr ibn Al-Harith, was captured. In an attempt to motivate and anger them. He said: "O Bani Abd Ad-Dar! You have been assigned bearers of our standard and you understand that the standard is the first thing the enemy will attack. Should it fall, then we fall down too. Therefore, I say to you, either you promise its safety or leave it for us."

Before the start of the battle, Quraish tried to sow the seeds of discord among the Muslims. Abu Sufyaan sent to the Helpers a message that said: "Let us fight our cousins and do not interfere. If you stand to the side, we will not kill you, because fighting you is not our target." But his attempt proved to be very fruitless. What could such an evil scheme do to men whose faith was as solid as mountains!

The women of Quraishi participated in the battle. They were led by the wife of Abu Sufyaan, Hind bint Utbah. They walked among the rows of the idolaters, played their tambourines and encouraged their men to fight. They inflamed their emotions.

The two parties approached one each other to fight started. The first combatant was the standard-bearer, Talha ibn Abi Talha Al-Abdari. He was one of the bravest men of Quraish fighters. The Muslims nicknamed him 'the ram of the battalion.' He came forth riding his camel and challenged the warriors to a single combat.

Most Muslims refrained from fighting him due to his courage. However, Az-Zubair ibn Al-Awwam moved forward to fight him. He did not give him any chance to fight. He jumped on him like a lion and pulled him down to the ground and killed him with his sword.

The Prophet (peace be upon him) was watching the bravery of the men then said: "Every Messenger of Allah has a disciple, and Az-Zubair is a disciple of mine."

Soon after that the fighting grew fierce. The strain of the battle was centered on the carriers of the standard. After the death of their leader the Ram (Talha ibn Abi Talha), Banu Abd Ad-Dar alternated the mission successively. Talha's brother, Uthman, ran forward and seized the standard which lay by the lifeless body of his brother. Hamzah ibn Abdul Muttalib dealt him a blow that cut his arm and shoulder and exposed his lung.

The standard was raised up again by Abu Sa'd ibn Abi Talha, but quickly Sa'd ibn Abi Waqqas sent a deadly arrow that hit him in the throat and made his tongue hang out breathing his last.

Musafi ibn Talha ibn Abi Talha then lifted up the standard, but was shot with an arrow by Asim ibn Thabit ibn Abi Al-Aqlah. His brother Kilab ibn Talha ibn Abi Talha lifted it up, but Az-Zubair ibn Al-Awwam killed him. Their brother Al-Jallas ibn Talha ibn Abi Talha lifted the banner up but Talha ibn Ubaidu-Allah stabbed him to death.

All those 6 men killed defending the standard, belonged to one house, the house of Abi Talha Abdullah ibn Uthman ibn Abd Ad-Dar. Another man from Bani Abd Ad-Dar, Artat ibn Sharhabeel lifted up the standard but he was killed by Ali ibn Abi Talib.

Then it was Shuraih ibn Qariz who was killed by Quzman. He was a hypocrite who fought for prestige only, not in defense of Islam. Abu Zaid Amr ibn Abd Munaf Al-Abdari lifted up the standard but he was also killed by Quzman. A son of Sharhabeel ibn Hashim Al-Abdari hoisted it and he was also killed by Quzman.

So we see that 10 fighters of Bani Abd Ad-Dar, the standard-bearers, were killed quickly. Seeing that none of Abd Ad-Dars survived to carry the standard, a slave of theirs, Sawab, came to raise it. The slave was braver than his former masters. Sawab went on fighting till his hand was cut off. So he knelt down and held the banner with his chest and neck. He remained there until he was killed. In the meanwhile he did not stop saying: "O Allah, have I been excused?"

After the death of the slave Sawab, the standard fell on the ground, and remained there as there was no brave man to carry it. While battles centered on the standard, bitter fighting was going on the battlefield.

The spirit of Faith overwhelmed the Muslims' ranks. They rushed among the idolaters as a destructive flood that overflowed and knocked down all barriers that stood in its way.

Abu Dujana, wearing his red band, rushed forth fighting with the sword of the Messenger of Allah (peace and blessings be upon him). He was determined to pay its price at all costs. He killed all the idolaters that stood in his way splitting and dispersing their ranks.

There was an evil man among the idolaters whose only target was to finish off the wounded Muslims. During the fight Abu Dujana drew near this man. Abu Dujana implored Allah that this evil man might engage in combat. The idolater struck Abu Dujana, but he escaped it and it pierced into the leather shield. The idolater's sword became stuck in the shield. So Abu Dujana struck and killed him.

Into the thick of the battle, Abu Dujana rushed to kill a person who was inciting the enemy to kill the Muslims, but it was a woman. Abu Dujana spared her saying: 'I respect the Prophet's sword too much to use it on a woman.' The woman was Hind bint Utbah."

Hamzah ibn Abdul Muttalib also displayed wonderful bravery against the overwhelming odds. Heroes dispersed off his way as if they were trees blown away by a hurricane. It was Allah's Will that he was murdered when he was at the top. He was not killed in a face-to-face fight on the battlefield, but he was assassinated in the dark of night, by cowards.

Hamzah's assassin, Wahshi ibn Harb, described how he killed Hamzah. He said: "When Quraish marched to Uhud, Jubair said to me: 'If you kill Hamzah, the uncle of Muhammad, stealthily, I will give you freedom.' So when the two parties fought, I set out seeking only Hamzah. I saw him fighting. He was like a white and black striped camel. No one could stand in his way. I was hiding trying to find an opportunity to spear him, hiding sometimes behind a tree or a rock hoping that he might draw nearer and be within range. I balanced my spear, then I speared him in his stomach. He attempted to kill me but he was overcome by his wound. Then I came to him, and I pulled out my spear and I hid. I killed him to free myself. So when I got back to Makkah, I became a free man."

One of the brave adventurers of that day was Hanzala Al-Ghaseel. Hanzala, who was newly married, and he left his wife's bed for Al-Jihad. He made his way through their ranks till he reached Abu Sufyaan Sakhr ibn Harb and had almost killed him, but he had been ordained to be a martyr. For at that moment, Shaddad ibn Al-Aswad who struck him to death.

The archers squad whom the Messenger of Allah (peace and blessings be upon him) placed on the Archers Mountain, had the advantage over Quraish. The Makkan horsemen that were commanded by Khalid ibn Al-Waleed, and supported by Abu Amir Al-Fasiq, tried to attack the left wing of the Muslim army 3 times, but thanks to the great efforts of the archers, the 3 assaults were stopped.

For a while it looked as if the 3,000 idolaters had been fighting 30,000 Muslims and not merely several hundreds. Ibn Ishaq said: "Then Allah sent down His Help unto the Muslims and verified His Promise to them. They idolaters were evacuated them from their camp. No doubt it was a certain defeat."

Abdullah ibn Az-Zubair related that his father had said: "By Allah, I was watching the servants of Hind bint Utbah and her friends fleeing with their garments gathered up. No one was there to prevent us from capturing them."

In another version by Al-Bara ibn Azib, which is mentioned in Sahih Al-Bukhari: "When we fought them, they fled, and their women could be seen fleeing in the mountains with their legs and anklets showing." We pursued them putting them to sword and collecting the spoils.

The Archers' Fatal Mistake

While the small army of Islam were about to record the second absolute and clear victory over the Makkans, the majority of the archers on the mountainside forgot what the Prophet (peace be upon him) had told them. They committed a fatal mistake that turned the war badly with heavy losses amongst the Muslims. And it almost brought about the murder of the Messenger of Allah (peace and blessing be upon him).

In spite of the strict orders of the Prophet (peace be upon him), and their leader's, 40 archers left their posts, seduced by the too soon roar of victory as well as worldly greed for the spoils of war.

The others, however, 9 in number and Abdullah, their leader, obeyed the Prophet's order and stayed where they were until they were given leave or killed to the last. Still the Muslims were left inadequately defended.

The clever Khalid ibn Al-Waleed saw this golden opportunity and turned swiftly round to the rear of the Muslim army and encompass them. They killed Ibn Jubair and his group, they fell promptly upon the rear of the Muslims. So the polytheists returned once again to counterattack the Muslims.

An idolist woman, called Umra bint Alqama Al-Harithiyah, ran towards their standard, and she picked it up and hoisted it. So the idolaters gathered together around the standard and called out unto one another till they surrounded the Muslims and stoodfast to fight again.

The Prophet (peace be upon him) was then among a small group of fighters, 9 in number at the rear of the army. Khalid and his men took him by utter surprise, and forced him to follow either of two options: Flee for his life and abandon his army to its doomed end, or take action at the risk of his life to rally the ranks of the Muslims again.

The genius of the Messenger of Allah (peace and blessings be upon him), his peerless and matchless courage made him select the second option. He raised his voice and said: "Slaves of Allah." He knew that his voice would be heard by the idolaters before it was heard by the Muslims. Still he called out to his Companions risking his own life. The idolaters recognized him and quickly ran to his position to kill him.

The encompassment of the Muslims revealed 3 kinds of people

The 1st Muslim group were those who were only interested in saving their own life and so they fled.

They left the battlefield and did not care what happened to the others. Some of them fled as far as Madinah, and some went up the mountain. The 2nd Muslim group were those who were brave and returned to the battle. However, they mixed with the idolaters in such a way that they could not recognize one another. As a result, some of them were killed by mistake.

Then Hudhaifah caught sight of his father Al-Yaman about to be killed by other Muslims. So he said: "O servants of Allah! Beware! This is my father. This is my father." Aishah (RA) said: "They did not part with him until he was killed." Hudhaifah then said: "May Allah forgive you." And Urwa said: "By Allah, from that time on Hudhaifah has always been blessed and wealthy until he died." That was because he forgave everyone and refused to take any blood-money for his father's murder but asked that it be spent in charity.

This Muslim group suffered from great confusion. A lot of them got lost and did not know where to go. At this bad time they heard someone calling: "Muhammad is killed." This news made them even more afraid and almost out of sense. Their morale broke down. Some of them stopped fighting, slackened, and threw down their weapons. Others tried to get in touch with Abdullah ibn Ubai, the head of the hypocrites, and to seek his assistance to fetch them a security pledge from Abu Sufyaan.

Anas ibn An-Nadr passed by those people who were shuddering of fear, and asked: "What are you waiting for?" They said: "The Messenger of Allah (peace and blessings be upon him) has been killed."

He replied: "What do you live for after Muhammad (peace be upon him)? Go fight and die for what the Messenger of Allah (peace and blessings be upon him) has died for." Then he said: "O'Allah I apologize for what these people (i.e., the Muslims) did."

Then he moved on until he met Sa'd ibn Mu'adh who asked him: "Where to, Abu Omar?" Anas said: "Ah, how fine the scent of the Paradise is! I smell it here in Uhud." So he went on and fought against the idolaters until he was killed. No one but his sister could recognize his dead body. His body was cut and stabbed by over 80 swords, arrows, and spears. It was by the tip of his finger that she, after the battle, recognized him.

Thabit ibn Ad-Dahdah called unto his people and said: "if Muhammad (peace be upon him) is dead, Allah is Everlasting and He never dies. Fight in defense of your Faith. Allah will help you and so you will be victorious." A group of Helpers joined him and all of them attacked a battalion of Khalid's horsemen. He kept on fighting until he and his friends were killed.

An Emigrant passed by a Helper who was bleeding. He said: "O fellow! Have you heard that Muhammad is dead?" The Helper answered: "If Muhammad (peace be upon him) is dead, then he must have completed the delivery of the Message. So fight in defense of your religion!"

With such bravery and encouragement, the Muslims recovered their spirits, and desisted the idea of surrender or contacting the hypocrite Abdullah ibn Ubai. They fought and attempted to make way to the headquarters, even after the news of the Prophet's death had been falsified. The 3rd group of Muslims were those who cared for nothing except the Prophet (peace be upon him). At the head of them were the great Companions like Abu Bakr, Omar ibn Al-Khattab, Ali ibn Abi Talib and others (May Allah be pleased with them all), who hastened to protect the Prophet (peace be upon him) through unparalleled devotion.

As those groups of Muslims were receiving the blows of the idolaters and resisting rapidly, the fight was heavy around the Messenger of Allah (peace and blessings be upon him), who had only 9 people around him. As soon as the Prophet called out unto the Muslims: "I am the Messenger of Allah (peace be upon him)," the idolaters heard his voice and recognized him. So they turned back and attacked him with all their power before any of his Companions ran to his aid.

A violent raging fight broke out between the 9 Muslims and the inhabitants of hell, the idolaters, during which peerless sort of love, self-sacrifice, bravery and heroism were revealed.

Muslim, on the authority of Anas ibn Malik related that the Prophet (peace be upon him) along with 7 Helpers and 2 Emigrants, were trapped when the idolaters attacked them. The Messenger of Allah (peace and blessings be upon him) then said: "He who pushes back those idolaters, will be housed in Paradise." or "He will be my Companion in Paradise." One of the Helpers stepped forward and fought the idolaters in defense of the Prophet (peace be upon him) until he was killed. Then they attacked the Prophet (peace be upon him) again. The same fight was repeated again and again till all the 7 Helpers were killed. Then the Messenger of Allah (peace and blessings be upon him) then said to his two Companions: "We have not done justice to our Companions."

The last of those 7 Helpers was Amara ibn Yazeed ibn As-Sakan, who kept on fighting until his wounds neutralized him and he fell dead.

After the fall of Ibn Sakan, the Prophet (peace be upon him) remained alone with only 2 Companions: Talha ibn Ubaidullâh and Sa'd ibn Abi Waqqas. That was the most dangerous time for the Prophet (peace be upon him), and it was the golden opportunity for the idolaters who quickly took advantage of it. They concentrated their attack on the Prophet (Peace be upon him) and tried very hard to kill him.

Utbah ibn Abi Waqqas pelted him with rocks. One of the stones fell on his face. His lower right tooth Rubaiya (i.e., the tooth that is between a canine and a front tooth) was injured. His lower lip was wounded. He was also attacked by Abdullah ibn Shihab Az-Zuhri who sliced his forehead. Abdullah ibn Qami'a (Qami'a means 'a humiliated woman), struck him violently on his shoulder with his sword; and that stroke hurt the Messenger of Allah (Peace be upon him) for over a month, but it was not strong enough to break his two armours. He dealt him a heavy blow on his cheek. It was so strong that it penetrated his helmet into his holy cheek.

"Take this stroke from me, I am Ibn Qami'a." He said while striking the Messenger with his sword. The Messenger of Allah (peace and blessings be upon him) replied, while he was wiping the blood flowing on his face: "I implore Allah to humiliate you." (i.e., Aqma'aka Allah).

About that incident, Allah, Glory is to Him, sent down a Quranic verse:

$$\text{لَيْسَ لَكَ مِنَ الْأَمْرِ شَيْءٌ أَوْ يَتُوبَ عَلَيْهِمْ أَوْ يُعَذِّبَهُمْ فَإِنَّهُمْ ظَالِمُونَ}$$

3:128 Not for you is the decision; whether He turns in mercy to (pardon) them or punishes them; verily, they are the wrongdoers.

At-Tabarani related that the Messenger of Allah (peace and blessings be upon him) said: "Allah's Wrath is great on those who besmear the face of His Messenger, O Allah, forgive my people for they have no knowledge."

Talha ibn Ubaidullah, fought so fiercely and bravely, and so although they were only 2, they were able to stop the idolaters short of realizing their aim, killing the Prophet (peace be upon him). They were of the best skillful Arab archers and kept on defending the Messenger of Allah (peace and blessings be upon him) until the idolaters were driven off the Prophet (peace be upon him).

The Messenger of Allah (peace and blessings be upon him) emptied his quiver of arrows and asked Sa'd ibn Abi Waqqas: "Shoot, an arrow Sa'd. May my father and mother be sacrificed for you." The Messenger of Allah (peace be upon him) had never gathered his parents except in the case of Sa'd, a privilege granted to him for his bravery.

In a version by Jabir, related by An-Nasa'I, concerning the attitude of Talha ibn Ubaidullah towards the gathering of idolaters around the Prophet (peace be upon him).

When there were only some Helpers with him, Jabir said: "When the idolaters reached the Prophet, the Messenger of Allah (peace and blessings be upon him) said: 'Who will fight them back?' Talha said: 'I will.'" When all the Helpers were killed, Talha fought as much as the other 7 until his hand was hurt and his fingers were gone. So he said: 'Be they cut off!' The Prophet (peace be upon him) said: 'If you had said: In the Name of Allah, the angels would have raised you up before the people's very eyes.'" Talha had sustained 39 wounds, and his fingers were paralyzed.

If the Prophet's elite Companions had seen the grave situation, they would have rushed to him. Sadly, they got there after the Messenger of Allah (Peace be upon him) had been wounded and 6 of the Helpers killed, and the 7th was staggering with so many wounds and desperately fighting in defense of the Prophet (peace be upon him).

However as soon as they arrived, they quickly surrounded the Messenger (peace and blessings be upon him) with their bodies and weapons and prevented the enemies from reaching him.

The first friend who returned to protect the Prophet (peace be upon him), was his cave-mate Abu Bakr As-Siddiq (May Allah be pleased with him always).

Ibn Hibban's Sahih related that Aishah (May Allah be pleased with her), that Abu Bakr had said: "I was the first to go back and see him. Before him I saw one man fighting to shield him from the enemies. I said to myself: 'I wish he were Talha. Let him be Talha! Let my parents be sacrificed for you!' On the way, I was overtaken by Abu Ubaidah ibn Al-Jarrah, who was then flying as swiftly as a bird. We both rushed to help the Prophet's wounds. There we found Talha suffering from serious wounds. I then saw that two rings of the iron-ringed helmet had penetrated the Prophet's cheek. So I set out to take them out, but Abu Ubaidah begged: 'By Allah, O Abu Bakr, I beseech you, let me do that.'

Fearing to hurt the Prophet (peace be upon him) he started pulling one of the two rings out very carefully with his mouth. Then he also pulled the arrow out by his mouth. His tooth fell. He then he pulled the second ring very carefully with his mouth. The Messenger of Allah (Peace be upon him) said: 'See to your brother. He is worthy of being housed in Paradise.' We approached Talha to cure him but found out that he had had some 10 sword-strokes in his body."

Quickly a group of Muslim heroes gathered around the Prophet (peace be upon him) and they formed a shield to protect him from the idolaters.

The number of idolaters was steadily increasing, and their attacks, increased. The Messenger of Allah (peace and blessings be upon him) fell into one of the holes dug by Abu Amir Al-Fasiq to be used as traps. His knee was hurt. Ali helped him by grasping his hand up. Talha ibn Ubaidullah took him in his lap until he could stand. Nafi ibn Jubair said: I heard an Emigrant say: "I have witnessed the Uhud Battle and saw arrows hurled from all directions at the Messenger of Allah (peace be upon him).

None of them however hit him. Ubedullah ibn Shihab Az-Zuhri said: 'Guide me to Muhammad (peace be upon him)! By Allah, if I did not kill him, I would not hope to live.' Although the Messenger of Allah (peace and blessings be upon him) was next to him, alone, he did not see him."

The Muslims showed unprecedented courage. Abu Dujana stood before the Messenger of Allah (peace and blessings be upon him) and protected him from the arrows by his back. Hatib ibn Balta ran after Utbah ibn Abi Waqqas, who broke the incisor of the Prophet (Peace be upon him), and struck him with the sword, cracked his head and took his mare and sword. Sa'd ibn Abi Waqqas wanted so much to kill his brother Utbah, but he could not, however, Hatib could. Sahl ibn Haneef, a hero archer, who had pledged to die in the cause of Allah, also played a prominent part in the battle. The Prophet (Peace be upon him) also shot arrows. He shot so many arrows that the two ends of his bow were flattened. Qatadah ibn An-Nu'man took it with him after the battle. On that day, his eye was fell down onto his cheek, the Messenger of Allah put it back in its socket and became the better eye and the better of the two eyes.

On that day Abdur Rahman ibn Awf fought till his mouth got broken. He sustained over twenty wounds. His legs were injured and that lamed him.

Malik ibn Sinan, the father of Abi Sa'eed Al-Khudri sucked the blood out of the Prophet's cheek to clean it. The Messenger of Allah (peace and blessings be upon him) said: "Spit it!" But Malik said: "By Allah, I will never spit it". Then ran out and continued to fight. The Prophet (peace be upon him) then said: "Anyone who wants to see a man of the people of Paradise, let him look at Malik." No sooner had he resumed fighting than he was killed in the thick of the battle. Umm Amarah participated in the battle. She encountered Ibn Qami'a in combat, and sustained a wound on her shoulder, but she also struck him with her sword several times but he survived because he was wearing two armors. She went on fighting until her wounds counted twelve. Mus'ab ibn Umair fought so fiercely defending the Messenger of Allah (peace be upon him) against the attacks of Ibn Qami'a and his fellows. He carried the standard with his right hand.

But in the process of fighting, it was cut off, so he picked-up the standard in his left hand till this was also cut-off, so he knelt down and shielded it with his chest and neck. Ibn Qami'a killed him, he mistook him for the Prophet because he resembled him in appearance. Ibn Qami'a shouted 'Muhammad (Peace be upon him) has been killed.'

When Mus'ab was killed, the Messenger of Allah (peace and blessings be upon him) delivered the standard to Ali ibn Abi Talib. Then the Prophet (peace be upon him) made his way to his army. Ka'b ibn Malik saw the Prophet approaching and shouted: "Muslims, be cherished! The Messenger of Allah (Peace be upon him) is alive." Upon hearing the shout, the Muslims raced towards the source of the shout which brought about 30 Companions to protect the Messenger of Allah (peace be upon him). The Messenger of Allah (peace be upon him) wanted to move everyone to the hillocks nearby. But hostilities of the enemy grew fiercer to foil the plan of withdrawal. However, their attempts were fruitless due to the heroic devotion of the lions of Islam.

Uthman ibn Abdullah ibn Al-Mugheerah, one of the enemy horsemen, moved towards the Messenger of Allah (peace and blessings be upon him) while saying: "Either I kill Muhammad or I will be killed." The Messenger of Allah (peace and blessings be upon him) moved forward to stop him but Uthman's horse tripped. So Al-Harith ibn As-Simma struck him and he finished him off. But then another Makkan horseman, Abdullah ibn Jabir, attacked Al-Harith ibn As-Simma, and struck him on the shoulder, and he was carried to the camp suffering from serious wounds. However, that idolater did not escape death, for Abu Dujana, the red banded hero, struck him heavily and cut his head off. During the bitter battle, a desire to sleep overwhelmed the Muslims, that was a tranquility and security from Allah to help His slave Muslims as the Quran spoke in this context.

ثُمَّ أَنزَلَ عَلَيْكُم مِّن بَعْدِ الْغَمِّ أَمَنَةً نُّعَاساً يَغْشَىٰ طَائِفَةً مِّنكُمْ

3:154 Then after the distress, He sent down security for you. Slumber overtook a party of you,

Abu Talhah said: "I was overwhelmed by the desire to sleep on Uhud Day. My sword fell from my hand several times and again and again I picked it up."

The Muslims retreated to the cover of Mountain Uhud. And the rest of the army followed them to that safe position. So the Prophet (Peace be upon him) foiled Khalid ibn Al-Waleed's plan.

Ibn Ishaq said: "When the Prophet (peace be upon him) was moving up the hillock, Ubai ibn Khalaf followed him and said: 'Where is Muhammad? Either I will kill him or I will be killed.' The Companions said: 'O'Messenger of Allah, let us go back and fight him?' But the Prophet Allah (peace be upon him) said: 'Leave him!' So when he drew nearer, the Prophet (peace be upon him) took Al-Harith ibn As-Simma's spear. Then he faced him, and he speared him in his clavicle. The spear hit him so strong that it made him roll off his horse over and over. When he returned to his people, they saw that he had only had a small scratch on his neck.

When the blood became congested he said: "By Allah, Muhammad has killed me. He had already told me when we were in Makkah: 'I will kill you.' By Allah, even if he had spate on me, he would have killed me." The enemy of Allah then died at a place called Sarif, while they were taking him back to Makkah."

When the Prophet (peace be upon him) settled down in his headquarters in the hillock, the enemies of Allah started their last attack upon the Muslims. Ibn Ishaq said: "While the Messenger of Allah (peace and blessings be upon him) was on the way to the hillock, the enemies of Allah ascended the mountain. Khalid ibn Al-Waleed and Abu Sufyaan led the army. So the Prophet (peace be upon him) asked Allah: 'O'Allah, your enemy should not be higher in position or in power than your servants. So the Messenger of Allah (peace and blessings be upon him) said to Sa'd: "Drive them off." "How can I drive them off by myself?" But the Prophet (peace be upon him) repeated the phrase 3 times. Sa'd then took an arrow out of his quiver, shot it and killed one of them. He said: "then I took another one and I shot it at another man.

Then I took a third arrow and killed a third man. Then they climbed down the mountain. I said to myself, 'this must be a blessed arrow.' I put it in my quiver." He kept it with him till he died. His children kept it ever after he died.

That was the last attack made by the enemies of Allah. They returned to their camp and started preparations to go back to Makkah. Many of them involved themselves in mutilating the murdered Muslims, and so did their women. They cut off the noses, the ears, and the genitals of the martyrs. They even opened their bellies. Hind ibn Utbah ripped open the liver of Hamzah and chewed it. She even made from the ears and noses anklets and necklaces.

Sahl said: "By Allah, I know who washed the wounds of the Prophet (peace be upon him). His daughter Fatimah washed it. When Fatimah saw that water increased the flow of blood, Fatimah took a piece of straw, burnt it a little and stuck it to the wound so blood stopped flowing."

Then Abu Sufyaan said: "Omar!" The Prophet (Peace be upon him) said: "Go and see what the matter is." He went there. Abu Sufyaan said: "Today was a vengeance for the Battle of Badr. This for that. War is attended with alternate success." Omar shouted back: "No. They are not the same. Our killed men are housed in Paradise; but yours are in Fire."

Abu Sufyaan asked him: "I beseech you by Allah's Name, tell me the truth: Have we killed Muhammad?" Omar said: "No! And he is listening to your words." He said: "For me, you are more truthful than Ibn Qami'a, and even more reliable. We will meet again at Badr next year." The Messenger of Allah (peace and blessings be upon him) said to one of his men: "Say: 'Yes, it is an appointment.'"

The Messenger of Allah (peace and blessings be upon him) told Ali ibn Abi Talib: "Follow them and see their aim. If they ride camels, this means that they are going back to Makkah, but if they ride horses and lead camels unmounted, they are going to Madinah. By the One, in Whose Hand my soul is, I would fight them again."

Ali said: "I followed them and I saw that they are mounting camels and leaving the horses unmounted. They were going back to Makkah."

After the departure of the Quraish, the Muslims went to see the identity of the killed and the wounded. Zaid ibn Thabit said: "The Messenger of Allah sent me to seek Sa'd ibn Ar-Rabî' and said: "When you see him say: 'peace be upon you from me and ask him how do he feels?'"

Zaid said: "I started wandering about checking the killed then I came across Sa'd when he was dying with over 70 stabs of a sword, a spear and an arrow in his body. So I said: O'Sa'd, the Messenger of Allah sends you his greetings, and says 'peace be upon you, tell me how do you feel?'"

Sa'd said: "And let peace be upon the Messenger of Allah too. Tell him, I smell the scent of Paradise. And please tell the Helpers, my people, 'you shall not be excused before Allah if the Prophet (peace be upon him) is hurt and you are still alive." Then he died.

Then they came across Al-Usairim, Amr ibn Thabit, whom they had urged to embrace Islam but refused. They saw him close to death. They asked him: "What made you come here? Is it to defend your people or because of an inclination to Islam?" He said: "It is certainly an inclination to Islam. I believe in Allah and in His Messenger." And he immediately died. They told the Messenger of Allah (peace and blessings be upon him) about him. Hearing that, he said: 'He is one of the inhabitants of Paradise.'" Although he had not offered one single prayer.

Qazman, who was among the injured, fought heroically. He killed 7 or 8 idolaters. They took him to the habitation of Bani Zufr. The Muslims gave him glad tidings of the Paradise. But he said: "By Allah I have fought out of a zeal to my people. Had it not been for that I would have not fought." When he was in more pain, he committed suicide. The Prophet (peace and blessings be upon him) had said: "He is an inhabitant of Fire."

Contrary to Qazman there was a Jew of Bani Tha'labah among the killed. He said to his people, "By Allah you have already known that it is imperative to support Muhammad." They said: "Today is Saturday." He said: "There is no Saturday for you."

Bani Tha'labah then took his sword and armor and said: "If I die, my property should be put at Muhammad's disposal". He kept on fighting until he was killed. The Messenger of Allah (peace and blessings be upon him) said about him, "Mukhaireeq is the best Jew."

The Messenger of Allah (peace and blessings be upon him) supervised the martyrs' burial and then said: "I bear witness that anyone who is hurt in the way of Allah, Allah will resurrect them with their wound bleeding a liquid which is blood-like in color but musk in scent."

Some of the Companions carried some men killed in the war to Madinah, but the Messenger of Allah (peace and blessings be upon him) ordered that they must be sent back and buried where they died.

He said that they should not be washed but buried as they were but after stripping them off their armors and leather clothes. He buried every 2 or 3 men together in one grave and even join 2 men in one garment while saying: "Who is the more learned of the Quran?" and he would bury him first. He would say: "I bear witness to those on the Day of Resurrection."

They missed the coffin of Hanzalah, they looked for it and found it with water dripping off it. The Messenger of Allah (peace and blessings be upon him) said that the angels were washing him and said: "Ask his wife". They asked her and she said that he had been in a state of ceremonial impurity. That was why Hanzalah was called 'Ghaseel Al-Mala'ikah', the one washed by the angels.

When the Prophet (peace be upon him) saw how his uncle and foster brother, Hamzah, was mutilated, he was extremely sad. When his aunt Safiyah came to see her brother Hamzah, the Prophet ordered her son Az-Zubair to dismiss her in order not to see what happened to Hamzah.

She refused and said: "I was told that they have mutilated him. But so long as it is in the way of Allah, whatever happens to him satisfies us. Allah is Sufficient and I will be patient if Allah wills." She approached, looked at him and supplicated Allah and said: "To Allah we all belong and to Him we will return." and she implored Allah to forgive him. Then the Messenger of Allah (peace and blessings be upon him) ordered that he should be buried with Abdullah ibn Jahsh. He was his nephew and his foster brother.

Ibn Masud said: I have never seen the Prophet (peace be upon him) weep as much as he did for Hamzah ibn Abdul Muttalib. He placed him towards Al-Qiblah, then he sobbed his heart out.

The sight of the martyrs was heart-breaking. Khabbab said: "No shroud long enough was available for Hamzah except a darkish garment. When they covered his head with the garment, it was too short to cover his feet. And if they covered his feet, then his head would be revealed. So they covered his head with the garment and put some plant called 'Al-Idhkhir' on his feet."

Most of the narrations confirmed that 70 Muslims were killed, 65, Helpers; 41 of whom were from Khazraj and 24 from Aws. This, besides 1 Jew and 4 Emigrants.

As for the polytheists, 22 of them were killed, but some versions speak of 37. Allah knows best.

The Uhud Battle was just one phase of military activities between the two parties each of whom earned their legitimate portion of both success and failure. In this sense, this battle could be rightly regarded as an inseparable war. Some Quranic verses were revealed to shed light on the most decisive phases of the battle. Sixty verses relevant to the battle were revealed giving full account of the first phase of the battle:

> وَإِذْ غَدَوْتَ مِنْ أَهْلِكَ تُبَوِّئُ الْمُؤْمِنِينَ مَقَاعِدَ لِلْقِتَالِ وَاللَّهُ سَمِيعٌ عَلِيمٌ
>
> 3:121 And (remember) when you left your household in the morning to post the believers at their stations for the battle (of Uhud). And Allah is All-Hearer, All-Knower.

And to end in a complete commentary on its results and moralities:

> إِنَّمَا نُمْلِى لَهُمْ لِيَزْدَادُوا إِثْمًا وَلَهُمْ عَذَابٌ مُهِينٌ
>
> We postpone the punishment only so that they may increase in sinfulness. And for them is a disgraceful torment.
>
> مَّا كَانَ اللَّهُ لِيَذَرَ الْمُؤْمِنِينَ عَلَى مَا أَنتُمْ عَلَيْهِ حَتَّى يَمِيزَ الْخَبِيثَ مِنَ الطَّيِّبِ
>
> 3:179 Allah will not leave the believers in the state in which you are now, until He distinguishes the wicked from the good.

Ibn Qayyim al-Jawziyya wrote about the battle of Uhud and gave full elucidation of the Divine benefits and the moralities that resulted from it. Some scholars said that the reverse in Uhud resulted from the disregard, on the part of the archers, the explicit commands of the Messenger of Allah (peace and blessings be upon him), and abandoning their location which they were ordered to safeguard to the end. In other words, the success depends upon the obedience to the Prophet (peace be upon him).

As long as they carry out his orders, Allah will help them face all kinds of odds. But when they set aside his commands pursuing of worldly riches, they are bound to come to grief.

Another important issue is that it was often customary for Prophets to be tried with different adversities. Should the Muslims be victorious every time, then many pretenders to Faith will enter Islam, then the clear line of demarcation between true believers and hypocrites will be blurry. If the Muslims were to be defeated each time, the final objective of the Message of Prophets will not be effected. Thus, it is good then to combine failures and successes so that sifting among true Muslims and hypocrites could be seen.

In the aftermath of the battle of Uhud, the hypocrites revealed their true intentions in actions and words. Therefore, the Prophet (peace be upon him) got to see the wicked elements working secretly in his homeland, and so later appropriate actions can be taken.

Another point in this context is that tests and trials are sent by Allah to teach true believers how to be patient in times of adversity. Moreover, martyrdom, the highest rank that a true friend of Allah could occupy, is a passport gift from Allah to give true believers Paradise. So in summary, fighting in the cause of Allah is an excellent opportunity for the true believers to have their sins erased.

The Battle of Uhud had a very bad impact on both the credibility and military standing of the Muslims. Their power and dignity in people's eyes were damaged. The Jews and the hypocrites, and the bedouins hated the Prophet (peace be upon him), and so they wanted to destroy him badly.

Two months after the Battle of Uhud, Banu Asad made arrangements to raid Madinah, and Udal and the Qarah tribes conspired together against the Prophet (peace be upon him) in the month of Safar, 4 A.H. They killed 10 of the Prophet's Companions. Moreover, Banu Amir plotted against the Prophet (peace be upon him), and killed 70 Companions in the battle of Mauna Well.

During that period also, Banu Nadeer plotted to kill the Messenger of Allah (peace be upon him) in Rabi Al-Awwal in 4 A.H. So in Jumada Al-Ula in 4 A.H., Banu Ghatfan wanted to attack Madinah. The Muslims became an attractive target after they lost their military credibility in the Battle of Uhud. However, the Messenger of Allah (peace be upon him) wisely managed to stop all these dangers, and even to redeem the lost dignity of the Muslims, and to gain them fresh glory and noble standing once again. The first thing he did was the Hamra Al-Asad pursuit operation, to retain the Muslim military reputation. The Prophet (peace be upon him) succeeded in recovering his followers' dignity in such a manner that surprised both the Jews and the hypocrites, alike. After that, he dispatched more military errands and missions:

The Abi Salamah Mission
(Muharram 1st, 4 A.H):

The first people to fight the Muslims in the aftermath of Uhud were Banu Asad ibn Khuzaimah. Talhah and Salamah, sons of Khuwailid gathered volunteers to fight the Prophet (peace be upon him). However, the Messenger of Allah (peace be upon him) immediately dispatched 150 warriors headed by Abu Salamah. Abu Salamah took Bani Asad ibn Khuzaimah in their own homeland, and he neutralized them, and he dispersed them and captured their cattle. However, sadly, on his return, Abu Salamah had a bad infection of a previous wound that he sustained in the Battle of Uhud, and he died.

An Errand led by Abdallah ibn Unais

On the 5th day of the same month Muharram, 4 A.H., Khalid ibn Sufyan Al-Hudhali mustered some fighters to raid the Muslim positions. At the request of the Messenger of Allah (peace be upon him), Abdullah ibn Unais went out to stop them. It took him 18 days but successfully fulfilled his task.

He cut the head of the rebels and brought it back to Madinah on Saturday, 7 days before the end of Muharram. The Messenger of Allah (peace be upon him), as a reward, gave Abdullah ibn Unais a log stick saying: "This will function as a sign of recognition for me and you on the Day of Resurrection." Later on his death bed, Abdullah asked that the log be with him in his shroud.

The Event of Ar-Raji

In Safar of the 4th year A.H., some members of the tribes of Qarah and Udal came to Madinah. They asked the Messenger of Allah (peace be upon him) to send some of his Companions to instruct them in religion. The Prophet (peace be upon him) sent 6 of his Companions, but in another version, he sent 10 headed by Murthid ibn Abi Murthid Al-Ghanawi, but according to Al-Bukhari, headed by Asim ibn Thabit, the grandfather of Asim ibn Omar ibn Al-Khattab.

But when they reached a spot called Ar-Raji that is between Jeddah and Rabigh, 100 archers of the Banu Lihyan tribe attacked them. The Muslims quickly took shelter on some high ground, Fudfud. The bedouins told that they would not be killed. But Asim refused to come down, instead he fought them until 6 of his companions and he were killed. Khubaib, Zaid ibn Ad-Dathna, and another man were still alive.

Again the bedouins said that they would not kill them and they accepted. However, when they descended, the bedouins bound them. The third Muslim man scolded them for their insincerity and he tried to fight them, and so they killed him. The other two men, Khubaib and Zaid, had killed some notables of Quraish at Badr, so they were taken and sold in Makkah. Khubaib was detained for some time but then they wanted to crucify him. He was taken from the Holy Sanctuary to At-Tan'im for crucifixion. Khubaib requested a short interval to offer a two-Rak'a prayer.

After the final greeting, Khubaib turned to his executioners, and said: "Had I not been afraid that you would think that I was afraid of death, I would have prayed for a long time." So Khubaib was the first to set the tradition of praying two Rak'a before being executed. He then said: "O'Allah! Count them one by one, exterminate them to the last one."

Khubaib then recited verses of poetry that spoke very eloquently of the atrocities borne by him, and to testify to his Faith in Allah at this hour of grief:

The confederates have gathered their men around me. They have gathered their women and children. I am tied tightly to a lofty trunk. To Allah alone I complain of my sufferings. And for death they have prepared me. Lord of the Throne! Give me strength against their intentions. They have cut my flesh bit by bit, and I have been deprived of water and food. They asked me to choose infidelity, but death is preferable. Tears roll out of my eyes, but it is not fear. By Allah! Death I do not fear. I will never show subservience to the enemy. Bless my broken limbs and torn skin.

Abu Sufyaan then asked him: "On Allah, you do not wish that Muhammad (peace be upon him) were here in your place so we can cut off his head, and that you were with your own family?"

Khubaib answered, "By Allah, I would never wish that Muhammad (peace be upon him) were here in this place that I occupy or that a small thorn could hurt him, and that I were sitting with my own family."

Quraish then ordered Uqbah ibn Al-Harith, whose father had been killed by Khubaib to crucify him. They also appointed someone to guard his dead corpse. But Amr ibn Omaiyah Ad-Damari took the corpse stealthily at night to bury. It was later said that shortly before his death, Khubaib was seen eating a bunch of grapes although there was not even a single piece of date available in Makkah at that time. [It was nothing but sustenance bestowed upon him by Allah].

And Safwan ibn Omaiyah purchased Zaid ibn Ad-Dathna, and killed him as an act of vengeance for his father.

Quraish sent someone to fetch a portion of Asim ibn Thabit body, but to their anger, they could not approach his corpse because a large swarm of hornets had been shielding him against any malicious tampering. Omar ibn Al-Khattab, when heard this piece of news said: "Allah verily protects His believing slave after death just as He does during life."

The Tragedy of Ma'una well

Ma'una Well tragedy was worse than that of The Event of Ar-Raji. It took place in that same month. Abu Bara, Amir ibn Malik came to the Prophet (peace be upon him) in Madinah. The Prophet (peace be upon him) asked him to embrace Islam but Amir neither agreed nor refused. He said: "O Messenger of Allah, if you send some of your Companions to the people of Najd to call them to Islam, I positive that they will accept Islam."

The Messenger of Allah (peace and blessing be upon him) said: "I am afraid the people of Najd will kill them." But Amr said: "I will protect them." Ibn Ishaq said that 40 men were sent to them, but As-Sahih said that they were 70.

Al-Mundhir ibn Amr, one of Bani Sa'ida, headed that group. They were the best and most learned in the Quran and jurisprudence. On their way to Najd they often gathered firewood to buy food for the people of 'Ahl As-Suffah'. They kept on doing that until they arrived at Ma'una Well. Ma'una Well was a well in between Bani Amir, Harrah and Bani Saleem. They stayed there and then sent the Message of the Messenger of Allah (peace and blessings be upon him) with Haram ibn Milhan, the brother of Umm Sulaim to the enemy of Allah Amir ibn At-Tufail.

Amir did not like the kind Message but he ordered his men to spear Haram in the back. When the spear penetrated Haram's body, he saw the blood coming out and he said: "Allahu Akbar! (i.e., Allah is the Greatest) By Lord of Al-Ka'bah I have won!"

Then the enemy of Allah, quickly, called out Bani Amir to fight the rest. But Bani Amir refused because they were under the protection of Abu Bara. So he turned to Bani Saleem for help. The people of Usaiyah, Ri'al and Dhakwan, who were folks of Bani Saleem, answered his call.

The Companions of the Messenger of Allah (peace and blessings be upon him), who were surrounded by idolaters, kept on fighting till they were all killed. The only survivor was Ka'b ibn Zaid ibn An-Najjar. Zaid was carried wounded from among the dead. It was in Al-Khandaq (the trench) Battle that Zaid was killed.

Al-Mundhir ibn Uqbah ibn Amir and Amr ibn Omaiyah Ad-Damari, who were entrusted with the Muslims' animals far from them, saw the birds circling in the air over the dead bodies. Al-Mundhir rushed to share in the fight but he was killed.
And Amr ibn Omaiyah was captured. Amir set him free when he found out that he was of Mudar tribe. However, that was after he had cut his hair. He did that to satisfy a pledge of his mother's to set a slave free.

Returning to the Messenger of Allah (peace be upon him), Amr ibn Omaiyah told the news, which resulted in the murder of 70 of the best believers.

On his way back to Qarqara, Amr ibn Omaiyah rested in the shade of a tree, and there two other men of Bani Kilab and sat with him. But when they slept, Amr killed them to avenge some of his killed companions. But the he found out that they had been given a pledge of protection by the Messenger of Allah (peace and blessings be upon him). He then told the Prophet (peace be upon him) what he had done. The Messenger of Allah (peace and blessings be upon him) said to Amr: "You have killed two men that I had pledged to protect; their blood-money shall be a debt I have to discharge." The Prophet (peace be upon him) then collected their blood-money from the Muslims.

However, the death of these two men was later to trigger the invasion of Bani An-Nadeer. The Messenger of Allah (peace and blessings be upon him) was so deeply sad by this tragedy and that of Ar-Raji that he often used to invoke Allah's wrath against those people and the tribes that killed his Companions. Anas reported that for 30 days the Messenger of Allah (peace and blessings be upon him) supplicated Allah against those who killed his Companions at Ma'una Well. In every dawn prayer he would invoke Allah's wrath against Ri'l, Dhakwan.

Then a new Qur'ânic verse was revealed:

> وَلَا تَحْسَبَنَّ الَّذِينَ قُتِلُوا فِى سَبِيلِ اللَّهِ أَمْوَاتًا بَلْ أَحْيَاءٌ عِندَ رَبِّهِمْ يُرْزَقُونَ
>
> 3:169 Think not of those as dead who are killed in the way of Allah. Nay, they are alive, with their Lord, and they have provision.
>
> فَرِحِينَ بِمَا آتَاهُمُ اللَّهُ مِن فَضْلِهِ وَيَسْتَبْشِرُونَ بِالَّذِينَ لَمْ يَلْحَقُوا بِهِم مِّنْ خَلْفِهِمْ أَلَّا خَوْفٌ عَلَيْهِمْ وَلَا هُمْ يَحْزَنُونَ
>
> 3:170 They rejoice in what Allah has bestowed upon them of His bounty and rejoice for the sake of those who have not yet joined them, but are left behind (not yet martyred) that on them no fear shall come, nor shall they grieve.
>
> يَسْتَبْشِرُونَ بِنِعْمَةٍ مِّنَ اللَّهِ وَفَضْلٍ وَأَنَّ اللَّهَ لَا يُضِيعُ أَجْرَ الْمُؤْمِنِينَ
>
> 3:171 They rejoice in a grace and a bounty from Allah, and that Allah will not waste the reward of the believers.

So the Messenger of Allah (peace be upon him) stopped his invocation.

The Bani An-Nadeer Invasion
(Rabi Al-Awwal, 4 A.H. / Aug. 625 A.D.):

The Prophet (peace be upon him) sought so hard to make peace with the Jewish tribes, but all his attempts failed. As they had betrayed Jesus as Judas had, they hated the Messenger of Allah (peace be upon him) even more. They were always trying to find ways to shed the blood of the Muslims and to undermine the cause of Islam despite all the pledges and covenants they had given to the Messenger of Allah (peace and blessings be upon him). Their behavior swayed between resignation and slackness after the Ka'b ibn Al-Ashraf event. He was the bitter Jew poet that continuously incited his listeners to murder Muslims. So the Jewish tribes wanted to inflict harm badly on the Messenger of Allah (peace be upon him). They first of all declared open hatred and hostility, and they did all sorts of actions to harm the Muslims, but still they wanted to avoid full-scale war.

The Messenger of Allah (peace be upon him) on his part, was very patient with them. However, they went too far in their provocative actions and the attempt on his life.

So the Messenger of Allah (peace be upon him) with some of his companions went to see Banu An-Nadeer to seek their help and to try to make peace once again. However, they asked the Prophet (peace be upon him) and his companions: Abu Bakr, Ali, Omar, and others to sit and wait next to a wall. Then the Jews held a private meeting and conspired to kill the Prophet [peace be upon him).

The wickedest man amongst them, Amr ibn Jahsh, volunteered to climb up the wall and drop a large rock on the Prophet's head. But Salam ibn Mashkam, cautioned them against executing such a crime, predicting that Allah would reveal their plot to His Messenger (peace be upon him), and he also said that such an act would constitute a violation of their treaty with the Muslims.

In fact, the angel Gabriel came down to reveal to the Prophet (peace be upon him) their evil intention. Therefore, with his companions, he went back to the Madinah. On their way, the Prophet (peace be upon him) told his companions of the divine revelation.

The Messenger of Allah (peace and blessings be upon him) asked Muhammad ibn Maslamah to communicate an ultimatum to Banu An-Nadeer that they must leave Madinah within 10 days, otherwise, their heads would be chopped off.

The chief of the hypocrites, Abdullah ibn Ubai, urged the Jews not to listen to the Prophet's words and to stay. He also offered his support with 2,000 of his followers. In this regards, Allah said [59:11]:

$$ اَلَمْ تَرَ إِلَى الَّذِينَ نَافَقُوا يَقُولُونَ لِإِخْوَانِهِمُ الَّذِينَ كَفَرُوا مِنْ أَهْلِ الْكِتَابِ $$

Have you not observed the hypocrites who say to their disbelieving brethren among the People of the Scripture, "

$$ أَبَدًا أَحَدًا فِيكُمْ نُطِيعُ لَئِنْ أُخْرِجْتُمْ لَنَخْرُجَنَّ مَعَكُمْ وَلَا $$

If you are expelled, we indeed will go out with you, and we shall never obey anyone against you;

$$ وَإِنْ قُوتِلْتُمْ لَنَنْصُرَنَّكُمْ $$

and if you are attacked, we shall indeed help you."

$$ وَاللَّهُ يَشْهَدُ إِنَّهُمْ لَكَاذِبُونَ $$

But Allah is Witness that they verily are liars.

So the Jews regained their confidence and now were even determined to fight. Their chief Huyai ibn Akhtab believed the chief of the hypocrites. So he sent to the Prophet (Peace be upon him) saying: "We will not leave Madinah."

Certainly the situation was very awkward. Launching a war against them could be bad in the light of the unfavorable conditions they were going through. Moreover, the hostile environments was growing in power and hatred around them.

The Jews of Bani An-Nadeer were also very strong, and going to war would be attended with unpredictable risks. But on the other hand, the constant state of assassinations and acts of treachery carried out against the Muslims brought about intolerable headaches.

After having weighed the gravity of the situation and the shameful attempt on the life of the Prophet (peace be upon him), the Muslims made the difficult decision of going to war. So when the Prophet (peace be upon him) received the reply of Huyai ibn Akhtab, the Prophet (peace be upon him) and his Companions set out to fight them.

The command was given to Ali ibn Abi Talib. He laid siege to their forts for 6 nights, but in another version, 15 nights. Banu An-Nadeer shot arrows and pelted stones at the Muslims enjoying their strategic advantage that their thick walls and fields of palm trees provided.

Trees are so precious, especially in the desert. The Muslims did not want to cut them, but they were ordered to cut down. In this respect, Allah, the All-Mighty, states in the Quran [59:5]:

What you cut down of the Linah, or you left them standing on their stems, it was by leave of Allah,

and in order that He might disgrace the rebellious.

The Quraizah tribe stayed neutral, and the hypocrite Abdullah ibn Ubai as well as Ghatfan failed to keep their words of support to Banu An-Nadeer. In this regard Allah says [59:16]:

كَمَثَلِ الشَّيْطَانِ إِذْ قَالَ لِلْإِنسَانِ اكْفُرْ

Like Shaytan, when he says to man: "Disbelieve."

فَلَمَّا كَفَرَ قَالَ إِنِّي بَرِيءٌ مِّنكَ إِنِّي أَخَافُ اللَّهَ رَبَّ الْعَالَمِينَ

But when he disbelieves, Shaytan says: "I am free of you, I fear Allah, the Lord of all that exists!"

The siege did not last long. Allah, the All-Mighty, cast fear into their hearts, and so they complied the Prophet's order and left Madinah. The Messenger of Allah (peace and blessings be upon him) allowed them to carry with them whatever their camels could lift.

Their caravan had 600 loaded camels. Their chiefs Huyai ibn Akhtab and Salam ibn Abi Al-Huqaiq went to Khaibar, whereas another party went to Syria. But two of Jews embraced Islam, Yameen ibn Amr and Abu Sa'd ibn Wahab.

Almost all the verses of Surah Al-Hashr

(Chapter 59, The Gathering) describe the banishment of the tribe, and reveal the shameful manners of the hypocrites. The verses manifest the rules relevant to the booty. In this Surah, Allah praises the Helpers and the Emigrants.

In this very Chapter, Allah also tells the believers to be moral and to prepare themselves for the world to come. As this Chapter focuses on Bani An-Nadeer and their banishment, Ibn Abbas used to describe it as An-Nadeer Chapter.

The Najd Operations

With the peaceful triumph over Bani An-Nadeer, the Prophet's control over Madinah was established.

The hypocrites retreated to a state of silence and stopped their conspiracies, at least publicly. Therefore, the Messenger of Allah (peace and blessings be upon him) directed all his resources towards defeating the desert Bedouins that killed his missionaries, and were contemplating an invasion of Madinah. The scouts reported that they have seen the Bedouin troops of Bani Muharib and Tha'labah of Ghatfan around Madinah. The Messenger of Allah (peace and blessings be upon him), wanted to cast fear into their hearts and deter them from committing further violence. The Prophets' operations were carried out repeatedly and produced good results. The hard-hearted Bedouins ran into the mountains.

The Second Invasion of Badr
(Sha'ban 4 A.H., January 626 A.D):

When the Prophet (peace be upon him) destroyed the power of the Arab-desert tribes, the Messenger of Allah (peace and blessings be upon him) wanted to crush his greatest enemy. A year had passed since the Muslims had fought Quraish at the Battle of Uhud. So the Prophet (peace be upon him) set out to Badr accompanied by one 1,500 warriors and 10 mounted horsemen. Ali ibn Abi Talib led the troops. They waited at Badr for the idolaters to come.

Abu Sufyaan's troops comprised 2,000 footmen and 50 horsemen. After some distance form Makkah, they camped at a water place called Mijannah. Being very terrified of the consequences of the battle, Abu Sufyaan tried to dissuade his men from going to war. He told them to return with him to Makkah. His men had the same fears and apprehensions, because they quickly obeyed him without any objections.

The Muslims waited for eight days waiting for their enemy. They took advantage of their stay and sold goods and earned good profit. When the idolaters ran away from the fight, the balance of powers shifted to the Muslims. They regained their dignity, their military reputation, and they managed to impose their will over the entire region.

The Invasion of Doumat Al-Jandal (Rabi' Al-Awwal, 5 A.H):

With the Prophet's return from Badr, peace and security became a reality. The Islamic headquarters, Madinah, had full security. The Messenger of Allah (peace and blessings be upon him) then deemed it fit and appropriate to subdue all hostile elements within Arabia in order to force undisputed recognition out of enemy and friend alike.

A few months later, the Messenger of Allah (peace be upon him) heard that some tribes near Doumat Al-Jandal, on the borders of Syria, were involved in robbery and plundering. It was also reported that they were on their way to raid Madinah.

The Prophet (peace be upon him) set out at the head of 1000 warriors taking with him a man, named Madhkur, from Bani Udhrah, as their guide.

They marched by night and hide by day to take the enemy by surprise. When they drew near their destination, the Prophet (peace be upon him) discovered that the enemy had fled to another place, so they captured their cattle and shepherds. The Prophet (Peace be upon him) stayed in that area for 5 days during which he sent out expeditionary forces to hunt for the enemy but none were found. The Prophet (peace be upon him) returned to Madinah and en route he entered into a peace treaty with Uyainah ibn Hisn. Doumat Al-Jandal is located at about a distance of 15 days march from Madinah and 5 days from Syria.

The Messenger of Allah (peace and blessings be upon him) managed to spread security and peace in the whole area. The hypocrites were silenced for good. One tribe of the Jews was evacuated, while the other tribe continued to fake good neighborliness and adherence to the covenants.

The desert bedouins were also subdued for good. And Quraish were no longer eager on attacking Madinah. This security created excellent circumstances for the Prophet (peace be upon him) to resume his logical course in propagating Islam and communicating the Messages of His Lord.

The Invasion of the Al-Ahzab (the Confederates) (5th year Hijr):

After the Battle of Uhad, peace and tranquility enveloped the turbulent Arabian Peninsula. It began to experience a period of quiet after a year war. However, the Jewish tribes were not happy. After they were exiled to Khaibar, they waited anxiously for the results of the Uhad. So when they heard the news, they prepared themselves to deal a deadly blow to the Muslims as well. However, they were too cowardly to move directly alone, so they laid a terrible plan to achieve their objectives. Many leaders of Bani Nadir visited Makkah. Twenty leaders of the Jews negotiated an unholy alliance with Quraish to attack the Messenger of Allah (peace and blessings be upon him). They promised Quraish full support and backing.

People of Quraish, who had become too weak to challenge the Muslims at Badr again, seized this opportunity to redeem their stained honor. The Jewish leaders then visited other parts of Arabia and managed to inflame the confederates of disbelief against the Messenger of Allah (peace and blessings be upon him), and against his Message, and against the believers.

Kinanah and others from Tihama, in the south, united together with Quraish. They recruited 4,000 men under the leadership of Abu Sufyaan. Then from the east, the tribes of Banu Saleem, Ghatfan, Bani Murrah united as well. They all marched to Madinah and gathered in its vicinity with 10,000 fighters. They outnumbered Muslims. So if they had launched an attack, they would have killed everyone. However, some intelligence officers reported the army's movements. The Messenger of Allah (peace and blessings be upon him) conducted a careful discussion of a plan to defend Madinah. Salman Al-Farisi said: "O'Messenger of Allah! When siege was laid to us in Persia, we dug trenches to defend the city. It was truly an unprecedented wise plan.

The Messenger of Allah (peace and blessings be upon him) hurriedly gave orders to implement it.

So they started to build a trench around Madinah. There was food shortage at the time – you could not get much. But severe hunger, bordering on starvation, could not stop or discourage them.

Sahl ibn Sa'd said: 40 yards was allocated to the company of the Messenger of Allah (peace and blessings be upon him). Some men dug while others evacuated the earth on their backs.

Unable to fight the hunger, it overwhelmed all their senses. Jabir ibn Abdullah, saw that the Prophet (peace and blessings be upon him) starving, slaughtered his last sheep, then cooked some barley and asked the Prophet (peace be upon him) and some Companions to accept his invitation. However, the Prophet (peace be upon him) gathered the 1,000 of people digging the trench and took them with him to Jabir's house. Jabir panicked and was embarrassed. There was not enough food for everyone.

But in a remarkable miracle, they all ate until they were all full and still the shoulder of the sheep and dough that was being baked remained as they were undiminished.

Then a woman brought a handful of dates and gave them to the Prophet (peace be upon him). He took the dates, threw them over his robe and invited everyone to eat. The dates began to increase and increase in number until they dropped over the trim of his robe.

Another preternatural Prophetic signs appeared in the process of trenching. A touch rock was an obstacle in the ditch. The Messenger of Allah (peace and blessings be upon him) took a spade (used to breaking and moving the earth) and struck the rock, it turned into loose rocks. In another version: There stood out a rock too immune for the spades to break up. So the Messenger of Allah (peace and blessings be upon him) took a spade, and struck the rock uttering "in the Name of Allah, the keys of Ash-Sham (Syria) are mine, I swear by Allah, I can see its palaces at the moment."

And on the second strike he said: "Allah is Great, Persia is mine, I swear by Allah, I can see the palace of Madain." And on the third strike, the rock, turned into tiny pieces, he said: "Allah is Great, the keys of Yemen are mine. I can see the gates of Sana."

The northern region of Madinah was the most vulnerable, all other sides are surrounded by palm trees and mountains. The Messenger of Allah (peace and blessings be upon him) knew that the Confederates would strike the weakest side, so they dug the trench on that side. They went on digging the trench for many days. They used to work on it during the day, and go back home in the evening.

When the believers saw the enemies of Allah they said [Ahzab: 22]:

"And when the believers saw the companies, they said, "This is what Allah and His Messenger had promised us, and Allah and His Messenger spoke the truth." And it increased them only in faith and acceptance."

This Ayah is an important principle, to follow the Messenger of Allah (peace and blessings be upon him) in all his words, and deeds, etc. Hence Allah commanded the people to take the Prophet (peace be upon him) as an example on the day of Al-Ahzab, with regard to patience, guarding, striving and waiting for Allah to provide the way out; may the peace and blessings of Allah be upon him forever, until the Day of Judgment.

Allah's Promise of victory was deeply established in their minds. They fixed themselves in Sila Mountain and the trench stood as a barrier between them and the enemies of Allah.

On attempting to attack the Madinah, the enemies of Allah were blocked when they saw the wide trench. So they decided to lay a blockade around Madinah. They tried find a vulnerable spot through which they could enter Madinah. To deter their enemies of Allah from entering, the Muslims shot at them with arrows. The veteran fighters of Quraish were upset by the situation. So they decided that a group of them led by Amr ibn Abd-e-Wudd, Dirar ibn Al-Khattab, and Ikrima ibn Abi Jahl, should try to enter through the trench. They managed to enter and capture a marshy area between the trench and Sila Mountain. Then Amr challenged the Muslims to a fight, and Ali ibn Abi Talib was deputed. After a fierce fight, Ali killed Amr so the others ran away in a state of panic and confusion. A few days, the enemies of Allah tried again but failed due to Muslims heroic confrontation. In the context of the events of the Battle of the Trench, the Messenger of Allah (peace and blessings be upon him) forgot to observe some prayers in their right time.

Jabir (RA) narrated: On the Day of Trench Omar ibn Al-Khattab (RA) cursed at the disbelievers of Quraish and said: "I have not done the afternoon prayer and the sun has set." The Messenger of Allah (Peace be upon him) replied: "I have not offered the prayer too." The Prophet then went and performed ablution, observed the afternoon prayer after the sun had set, then offered the sunset prayer after it."

Since the trench stood between the two parties, no direct engagement took place. It was just confined to arrow hurling. Still the fight claimed the lives of a number of fighters, 6 Muslims and 10 polytheists, and two killed by sword. Sa'd ibn Mu'adh was shot by an arrow that sliced his artery. Knowing that he was going to die, he said: "Oh, Allah, you know nothing is closer to my heart than fighting those disbelievers who belied Your Messenger and banished him from his town. Oh, Allah, you have decreed that we should fight them, so if there is still more fighting, let me live fight them more. If it has settled down, I implore you to ignite it so that I breathe my last in its context."

He completed his supplication asking Allah not to let him die yet until he had had full revenge on Banu Quraiza. In the midst of these difficult circumstances, the chief criminal of Bani Nadir, Huyai, went to Banu Quraiza to incite their Jewish Chief, Ka'b ibn Asad Al-Qurazi, who had a pact with the Messenger of Allah (peace and blessings be upon him) to run to his aid in times of war. Ka'b resisted all of Huyai's temptations, but Huyai was clever enough and so he managed to win Ka'b to his side and to persuade him to break his covenant with the Prophet (peace be upon him).

Banu Quraiza then launched war operations against Madinah, especially the secluded forts that housed the women and children. Safiyah (RA) daughter of Abdul Muttalib said: "A Jew was spotted prowling around outside and there were no men to defend us. So I took a bar of wood and struck the Jew." This event discouraged the Jews from conducting more attacks. They thought that those sites were protected by fighters. However, the Jews went on providing the idolaters with supplies supporting against the Messenger of Allah (peace and blessings be upon him).

On hearing the rumors about Banu Quraiza, the Prophet (peace be upon him) sent four of his companions to investigate. He sent Sa'd ibn Ubada, Sa'd ibn Mu'adh, Abdullah ibn Rawaha, and Khawat ibn Jubair. Unfortunately the four men learned that the news was true. Moreover, the Jews announced openly that no pact of alliance existed any longer with Messenger of Allah (peace and blessings be upon him).

The Messenger of Allah (peace and blessings be upon him) was briefed on this situation. The Muslims backs was now vulnerable to the attacks of Banu Quraiza, and a huge army from the front, while their women and children unprotected standing in between. In this matter, Allah said [Ahzab: 10]:

[Remember] when they came at you from above you and from below you, and when eyes shifted [in fear], and hearts reached the throats and you assumed about Allah [various] assumptions.

The Muslims were helpless. The hypocrites began taunting them about the delusion of ever defeating Caesar, the emperor of the Romans, and Kisra, the emperor of Persia. They began to sow the seeds of defeatism. Here, Allah says [Ahzab: 12]:

And [remember] when the hypocrites and those in whose hearts is disease said, "Allah and His Messenger did not promise us except delusion."

The Messenger of Allah (peace and blessings be upon him) wrapped himself in his robe, then began to meditate. The spirit of hopefulness prevailed over him. He stood up and said: "Allah is great! Allah sends good tidings of victory and support."

He told his men how to protect the women and children. He sent some fighters back to Madinah to guard them. He then took actions to undermine the ranks of the disbelieving confederates. A man from the tribe of Ghatfan called Na'im ibn Mas'ud asked to see the Messenger of Allah (peace and blessings be upon him).

He said that he had embraced Islam secretly and asked the Messenger of Allah to order him do anything that might benefit the Muslims. The man then moved between Quraish, the Jews, and Ghatfan managed to incite them. For example, he went to see the chiefs of Banu Quraiza and told them not to trust Quraish nor help them unless the latter pledged some hostages. Na'im then went to the camp of Quraish and managed to practice a similar trick. He said that the Jews regretted breaching their covenant with Messenger of Allah (peace and blessing be upon him). Moreover, he told them that the Jews maintained regular correspondence with the Prophet (peace be upon him). Na'im then pushed Quraish not to send hostages to the Jews. On a third run, he did the same with the people of Ghatfan.

On Saturday night, Shawwal 5 A.H., both Ghatfan and Quraish sent envoys to the Jews encouraging them to go into war against Muhammad (peace and blessings be upon him). However, the Jews sent a message that said they would not fight on Saturday. Moreover, they said that they needed hostages from them to guarantee their truthfulness.

On receiving the Jews' reply, Ghatfan and Quraish now believed what Na'im's had told them. So they sent a message to the Jews asking them again to go to war and to preclude that condition of hostages. But Na'im's scheme proved very successful, and so a state of distrust prevailed, which reduced their morale to a low degree.

The Messenger of Allah (peace and blessings be upon him) invoked Allah's wrath on the Confederates by supplicating: "Oh, Allah! You are quick in account, we beseech You to defeat the confederates."

Allah immediately answered the supplications and sent rain and cold wearied them, tents were blown down, cooking vessels and other equipage overthrown. In that windy and cold night, the Messenger of Allah (peace and blessings be upon him) sent Hudhaifa ibn Al-Yaman to hunt around for news about the enemy. Hudhaifa saw that they were preparing to leave. They were very upset about their inability to achieve their target.

Allah fulfilled His Promise. He spared the Muslims from fighting a huge army, and Allah supported His slave [Muhammad (peace and blessings be upon him)] and inflicted a heavy blow on the Confederates. The siege of Madinah began in Shawwal and ended in Dhul Qa'dah. So the siege lasted for over a month. It was more a battle of nerves rather than a battle of fighting and losses. No harsh fighting was recorded. However, it was one of the most critical battles in the early history of Islam. It proved that no forces of any size, could ever destroy the true faith (Islam) growing steadily in Madinah. When Allah sent fear and terror into the Confederates hearts, His Messenger (peace and blessings be upon him) was then in a stronger position to confidently declare that thenceforth, Muslims must take the initiative in war and must never wait for the land of Islam to be invaded. The blessed Al-Aqsa then must be defended and liberated. Allah designated Masjid al-Aqsa and its surrounding area as *"blessed".*

Invading Bany Quraiza

Archangel Jibreel (Gabriel) (peace and blessings be upon him) came down on the very day the Messenger of Allah (peace and blessings be upon him) came back to Madinah after battle. Jibreel came while the Prophet (peace be upon him) was washing in Umm Salama's house. Jibreel (peace be upon him) asked that the Prophet should take his sword and head for the habitation of Banu Quraiza. Jibreel said that he with many angels will go ahead to shake their homes and forts to cast fear in their hearts.

The Prophet (peace be upon him), immediately called the athan caller and ordered him to declare war against Banu Quraiza. The Prophet (peace be upon him) asked Ibn Umm Maktum to take care of Madinah, and asked Ali ibn Abi Talib to march with the war banner towards the appointed target. The Messenger of Allah (peace and blessings be upon him) set out at the head of 3,000 infantry men and 30 horsemen of Muhajireen (Emigrants) and Ansar (Helpers).

On their way, the afternoon prayer was due, but some refused to observe it until they had defeated the enemy, while others offered it in its proper time. However, the Messenger of Allah (peace and blessings be upon him) objected to neither.

When they reached Banu Quraiza, the Prophet (peace be upon him) laid tight siege to their forts. Seeing the terrible state they were in, the chief of the Jews Ka'b ibn Asad offered them 3 alternatives: (1) to embrace Islam, thus securing their life, wealth, women and children, and reminded them they had read in their books about the truth of Muhammad's Prophethood, (2) kill their children and women and then challenge the Messenger of Allah (peace and blessings be upon him) and his followers to the sword to either kill the Muslims or be killed, (3) or fight the Prophet (peace be upon him) by surprise on the Jewish Shabbat (Saturday), a day which is mutually understood to witness no fighting. However, none of the alternatives interested them. So Ka'b ibn Asad became angry and said: "You have never been decisive about anything since you were born."

To learn about their fate, they requested that Abu Lubaba be sent to them for advice. On his arrival, asked the women and children to cry desperately. In answer to their questions, he pointed to his throat, meaning it is suicide to fight the Messenger of Allah (peace be upon him). He then immediately understood that he had betrayed the Prophet's trust, so he headed directly for the Masjid in Madinah and tied himself to a wooden tall pole until the Messenger of Allah (peace be upon him) have forgiven him. When the Messenger of Allah (peace be upon him) was informed about it, he said, "I would have begged Allah to forgive him, but because he had tied himself out of his own free will, then it was Allah Who would turn to him in forgiveness."

Banu Quraiza could have endured the siege for a long time because food and water were very plentifully and their forts were greatly fortified, whereas the Muslims were suffering a lot from hunger, cold, and fatigue. Nevertheless, this was a battle of nerves, for Allah had sent fear into Banu Quraiza's hearts, and their morale had collapsed.

So they complied with the Messenger's judgment. The Messenger of Allah (peace and blessings be upon him) ordered that the men arm's be tied so they would not harm anyone. The women and children were not harassed nor harmed. Immediately, Al-Aws tribe intervened and asked the Prophet (peace be upon him) to be compassionate towards Banu Quraiza. Al-Aws tribe recommended that Sa'd ibn Mu'adh, a former ally, be delegated to give verdict about them, and they agreed.

However, Sa'd was not there. He stayed behind in Madinah due to a serious wound he sustained in the Confederates Battle. On his way to the Prophet (peace be upon him), the Jews used to urged him to be kind in his judgment on account of former friendship. Sa'd stayed silent but when they persisted he said: "It is time for me not to be afraid of the blame of the blamers." On hearing his attitude, some of them returned to Madinah waiting for doom.

On arrival, he was told that Banu Quraiza had agreed to accept his verdict. He immediately wondered if his judgment would pass on all people present, the Messenger of Allah (peace be upon him) included, turning his face away in honor of him. The reply was yes.

He decided that many of the able-bodied male persons belonging to the tribe should be killed. The Messenger of Allah (peace be upon him) accepted his judgment saying that Sa'd had ruled by the Command of Allah. After the war with Banu Quraiza had been settled, Sa'd ibn Mu'adh's wish was granted and he gave his last breath. Abu Lubaba stayed tied for six nights in the Masjid. His wife untied him at prayer times. One early morning, Allah the All-Forgiving revealed a verse to the Prophet (Peace be upon him) that Allah had turned to Abu Lubaba with forgiveness.

The Slander Affair

A painful incident happened on the Prophet's return from the expedition against Bani Mustaliq. The Muslim army stopped for a night near Madinah. In this expedition, the Messenger of Allah (peace and blessings be upon him) was accompanied by his wife, Aishah (RA). As it so happened, Aishah went out some distance from the camp to attend to the call of nature. Later she discovered that she had lost her necklace somewhere. The necklace was of no great value, but it belonged to a friend. Aishah went out to search for it. On her return, the army had already marched away with the camel she was riding. She sat down and cried till sleep overpowered her. Safwan ibn Mu'attal, an Emigrant, recognized her, so he brought her on his camel to Madinah. He walked behind the camel.

The hypocrites of Madinah led by Abdullah ibn Ubai ibn Salul, began spreading a malicious tale about Aishah (RA). Unfortunately, even some of the Muslims also became involved in it.

On arrival in Madinah, the Messenger of Allah (peace be upon him) held counsel with his Companions. They pronounced many different opinions that ranged from divorce to retention. Aishah (RA) was unaware of the rumors. She was ill and was confined to bed for a month. On recovering, she heard of the gossip, so she went to her parents seeking the truth. She then burst into tears and she wept to such an extent that she felt her liver was about to rip open. The Messenger of Allah (peace be upon him) visited her. He said: "If you are innocent, Allah will clear you, otherwise, you must beg for His forgiveness." She asked her parents to speak for her, but they had nothing to say.

So she said: "If I tell you I am innocent, you will not believe me, and if I were to admit something that Allah knows I am innocent, you will believe me. Therefore, I will have nothing to say but the words of the father of Prophet Yusuf (Joseph) (peace be upon him):

> وَجَآءُوا عَلَىٰ قَمِيصِهِ بِدَمٍ كَذِبٍ
>
> **12:18** And they brought his shirt stained with false blood.
>
> قَالَ بَلْ سَوَّلَتْ لَكُمْ أَنفُسُكُمْ أَمْرًا فَصَبْرٌ جَمِيلٌ وَاللَّهُ الْمُسْتَعَانُ عَلَىٰ مَا تَصِفُونَ
>
> He said: "Nay, but your own selves have made up a tale. So (for me) patience is most fitting. And it is Allah (Alone) Whose help can be sought against that (lie) which you describe."

So (for me) patience is most fitting. And she turned away and lay down for some rest. At that decisive moment the Revelation came acquitting Aishah (May Allah be pleased with her) of all the slanderous that was fabricated in this concern. Aishah (RA) praised Allah thankfully.

"Verily! Those who brought forth the slander (against 'Aishah (RA)) are a group among you." [24:11]

The three men involved in the slander affair, Hamnah bint Jahsh, Mistah ibn Athatha, and Hassan ibn Thabit were flogged with 80 stripes. As for the main of the slander, Abdullah ibn Ubai, he was not flogged. His punishment will be saved for him in the Hereafter.

The early part of the year 7 A.H. saw the Islamization of 3 important men of Makkah, Khalid ibn Al-Waleed, Amr ibn Al-'As, and Uthman ibn Talhah. On their arrival and entrance into the fold of Islam, the Messenger of Allah (peace and blessings be upon him) said, "Quraish has given us its own blood."

Abu Bakr (RA) Performs Pilgrimage

In the month of Dhul-Qa'dah or in Dhul-Hijjah in 9th of Al-Hijra, the Prophet (peace be upon him) sent Abu Bakr (RA) to lead the Al-Hajj (pilgrimage). Soon after their departure, Revelation came from Allah: Chapter 9 of the Quran, 'Repentance' (Surah Tauba) in which 'freedom from (all) obligations' is proclaimed from Allah with respect to those idolatrous tribes that had shown no respect for the treaty that they had entered into with the Messenger of Allah.

بَرَآءَةٌ مِّنَ اللَّهِ وَرَسُولِهِ إِلَى الَّذِينَ عَاهَدتُّمْ مِّنَ الْمُشْرِكِينَ

9:1 Freedom from (all) obligations (is declared) from Allah and His Messenger to those of the Mushrikin (idolaters), with whom you made a treaty.

فَسِيحُوا فِى الْأَرْضِ أَرْبَعَةَ أَشْهُرٍ وَاعْلَمُوا أَنَّكُمْ غَيْرُ مُعْجِزِي اللَّهِ وَأَنَّ اللَّهَ مُخْزِى الْكَافِرِينَ

9:2 So travel freely (O Mushrikin) for four months (as you will) throughout the land, but know that you cannot escape (from the punishment of) Allah; and Allah will disgrace the disbelievers.

Ali ibn Abi Talib was asked to make this declaration public. Quickly Ali overtook Abu Bakr at Al-Arj. Abu Bakr asked if the Messenger of Allah (peace and blessings be upon him) had put him in command. Ali said that he had been sent to make the proclamation only. The two Companions then continued with the pilgrimage. Towards the end of the pilgrimage, on the day of the ritual sacrifice, Ali stood at Al-Jamrah (a spot at which stones are pelted), and he gave the idolaters 4 months' time to reconsider their position. As for the other idolaters who had abated nothing of the Muslims' rights nor helped anyone against the Prophet (peace be upon him), the terms of the treaty would still run valid until the duration of which expired.

Abu Bakr then sent some Companions to declare publicly that no disbeliever would after that year perform pilgrimage, nor would anyone be allowed to make the Tawaf of the Sacred House undressed. This proclamation removed all aspects of paganism out of Arabia.

Rules that must be obeyed by all Muslims

The Prophet (peace be upon him) said to never commit treachery. And to never hurt or deform the corpse of a dead person nor kill a child. He forbade bearing down hard on others or constraining them. "Pacify", the Prophet said, "and do not disincline".

When it happened that the Prophet (peace be upon him) arrived at the battlefield at night, he would never fight the enemy until morning.

- He absolutely forbade burning or *torturing people or any creature or animal*

- He also absolutely forbade killing children, women, animals or even hitting them.

He also forbade theft and robbery. Moreover, he said that any gains acquired through plundering are forbidden as the flesh of a corpse. *Destruction* of *tillage* and *cutting d*o*wn* of trees are all *forbidden*.

- Never kill a wounded person, and never run after a fleeing one or kill a captive.

- Messengers and envoys must never be harmed or killed. He also stressed to never kill those who made covenants. He even said: "He whoever kills or harms one who is under pledge to a covenant shall never smell Paradise."

The invasion and the conquest of Makkah a decisive battle that destroyed paganism totally. The people as a result of that battle were able to differentiate the truth from the error. Misbelief no longer existed in their life. Sane folks raced to embrace Islam.

Amr ibn Salamah said: "When we were at a water (spring), and when we saw camel riders passing by, we asked them: 'What is this man (i.e., the Prophet)?' They would say, 'He claims that God has revealed so and so.' I often memorized those words as if they had been recited within my heart. The Arabs used to ascribe their Islamization to the conquest.

So when the conquest took place, peoples rushed to declare their Islam. My father was one of the quickest of all my people to embrace Islam. Arriving at his people he said: 'Perform this prayer at such a time, and so and so prayers at such. When it is prayer time, let one of you call athan for the prayer, and retain the most learned of the Quran among you to be the leader (Imam)."

The conquest of Makkah was a great event upon the consolidation of Islam. That influence was absolutely confirmed after the invasion of Tabuk. The huge crowds of people who ran to embrace Islam, and the huge army which included over 10,000 fighters that conquered Makkah, had grown to over 30,000 fighters sharing in the Tabuk invasion. And over 140,000 Muslim pilgrims shared in the Farewell Pilgrimage. The pilgrimage had an enormous number of people saying Labbaik (Lord, here we are worshipping You).

The Farewell Pilgrimage

After completing his Message: 'There is no god but Allah', a new message lit in the heart of the Messenger of Allah (peace and blessings be upon him). It was telling him that his life in the Lower World was about to end. That was clear in his message to Mu'adh whom he had sent to Yemen in the 10th year of Al-Hijra: "O'Mu'adh! You may not see me after this year. You may even pass by this very Masjid of mine and see my grave." Upon hearing this, Mu'adh cried a lot.

Allah's love was so bounteous as to let His Messenger (peace and blessings be upon him) see the fruits of his labor for which he suffered so much during his last 20 years. He spent his last days meeting, at the outskirts of Makkah, with members of different tribes who used to ask him questions about Islam, and in return he used to obtain their testimony that he had delivered the Message.

The Messenger of Allah (peace and blessings be upon him) announced his intention to also proceed with this blessed pilgrimage journey himself.

Thousands of people came to Madinah, all of whom sought guidance and wanted to follow the Prophet (peace be upon him) in the pilgrimage to Al-Hajj. On a Saturday of the last 4 days of Dhul-Qa'dah, the Messenger of Allah (Peace be upon him) began his preparations. He washed and combed his hair, applied some perfume, he wore his garment, then he saddled his camel and set off in the afternoon. The Prophet (peace be upon him) arrived at Dhul-Hulaifa just before the afternoon prayer. He performed wudu and 2 Rak'as and spent the night there.

When it was morning, the Messenger of Allah (peace and blessings be upon him) said to his Companions:

"A messenger, sent by my Lord, came to me at night and said: 'Pray in this blessed valley and say: I intend Umrah combined with pilgrimage."

Before performing the noon prayer, the Prophet (peace be upon him) washed for Ihram (ritual consecration), and Aishah (May Allah be pleased with her) put musk perfume on him with her hand with a Dharira (a plant). He then performed the noon prayer shortened, 2 Rak'as. He then mounted his she-camel 'Al-Qaswa' and said: 'There is no god but Allah'. When he moved into the desert, he praised Allah.

He continued with his journey. It took him 8 days. When he approached Makkah. The Prophet (peace be upon him) spent the night at Dhi Tuwa, and went into Makkah after performing the dawn prayer. He took a bath on Sunday morning, the fourth of Dhul-Hijjah the 10th year of Al-Hijra.

As soon as he entered Al-Haram Masjid, he walked around Al-Ka'bah, and did the Sa'ee between As-Safa and Al-Marwah. He did not finish the Ihram (ritual) because he intended Umrah and then Al-Hajj. He camped on a high place of Makkah at Al-Hajun. As for circumambulation, he did only that of Al-Hajj part.

On the 8th day of Dhul-Hijjah, the Day of Tarwiyah, the Messenger of Allah (peace be upon him) performed all prayers at Mina. After Dawn prayer, he left Mina until he reached Arafah. There was a tent built for the Prophet at Namirah. The Messenger of Allah (peace be upon him) sat inside the tent until sunset. He asked that Al-Qaswa, his she-camel be saddled. The Prophet then went down the valley where approximately 144,000 people gathered. There the Messenger of Allah (peace be upon him) stood up and delivered the following speech:

"O'people! Listen to what I say. I do not know if I will ever meet you again at this place after this year. It is not lawful for you to shed the blood of each another, or to take (steal) the fortunes of one another. They are as unlawful (Haram) as shedding blood on this day, and in such a Haram month, and in such a sanctified city as this sacred city (Makkah and the areas around it)."

"Witness! All practices and ways of paganism and ignorance are now under my feet. And the blood and revenge of the Days of Ignorance (pre-Islamic days) are now settled. The first claim on blood I stop is that of Ibn Rabi'a ibn Harith who was nursed in the tribe of Sa'd and whom Hudhail killed. Taking interest on money is totally haram (forbidden) in Islam."

"O'people! Fear Allah regarding women. You have married them on the security of Allah, and made them lawful unto you by Words of Allah! It is obligatory upon them to honor the marital rights, and not to commit acts of impropriety. If they do, then you have authority to discipline them, yet never severely. If your wife refrains from impropriety and is faithful to you, then you must clothe, love, and feed them appropriately."

"Verily, I have left with you the Book of Allah and the Sunnah (The Traditions) of His Messenger which if you hold onto always, you shall never be lost again."

"O'people, I will not be succeeded by a Prophet and you will not be succeeded by any other nation. So worship your Lord, pray the five prayers, fast Ramadan, and pay the Zakat (poor-due) willingly."

"I recommend that you to do the pilgrimage (if you can) to the Sacred House of Allah, obey those who are in charge of you, you will then be awarded Paradise."

"If you are asked about me, what would you say?"

They replied: "We bear witness that you have delivered the Message and discharged your ministry."

"O'Allah, Be a witness!"

The Prophet then raised his fore skywards and then moved it down towards people while saying ("O'Allah, Bear witness") 3 times.

As soon as the Messenger of Allah (peace and blessings be upon him) had finished delivering his speech, the following Quranic verse was revealed to him [5:3]:

اليَوْمَ أَكْمَلْتُ لَكُمْ دِينَكُمْ وَأَتْمَمْتُ عَلَيْكُمْ نِعْمَتِي وَرَضِيتُ لَكُمُ الْأِسْلَامَ دِينًا

This day, I have perfected your religion for you, completed My favor upon you, and have chosen for you Islam as your religion.

Upon hearing this verse, Omar cried. "What makes you cry?" The Messenger of Allah (peace and blessings be upon him) was asked. Omar answered: "Nothing succeeds perfection but imperfection."

Bilal then called the athan for prayer and then he made the second call. The Messenger of Allah (peace be upon him) performed both of the noon and the afternoon prayers separately, with no prayers in between.

The Messenger of Allah (peace be upon him) then mounted his she-camel Al-Qaswa, and approached the location of the vigil. He directed his face towards Al-Qiblah, and kept on standing until sunset when the sky's yellow color vanished a little and the disc of the sun set down. The Messenger of Allah (peace and blessings be upon him) then moved towards Muzdalifa, where he prayed the sunset prayer and the evening prayer.

The Messenger of Allah (peace and blessings be upon him) did not entertain the Glory of Allah between the 2 prayers. Then the Prophet (peace be upon him) slept till it was dawn prayer time. The Prophet (peace be upon him) performed the prayer with one first call and one second call at about daybreak. He mounted his Al-Qaswa, and went towards Al-Mashar Al-Haram. The Prophet (peace be upon him) faced Al-Qiblah and supplicated "Allah is the Greatest. There is no god but Allah." The Prophet stayed there until it was morning and before the sun rose high in the sky, he went to Mina. He walked to big Jamrah.

The Prophet pelted seven pebbles at it and said: "Allah is the Greatest" each time. They were very small pebbles thrown from the bottom of the valley.

Later the Prophet (peace and blessings be upon him) road his she-camel and returned to the House. The Prophet prayed the noon prayer at Makkah, and there he saw the children of Abdul Muttalib giving drinking water to the people at the Zamzam Well.

"Draw up water, children of Abdul Muttalib, I would draw up the water with you too, but I am afraid the people would appropriate this honor after me." The children handed him a container of water and the Prophet (peace be upon him) drank to his fill.

At high time morning of the 10th of Dhul-Hijjah, the Messenger of Allah (peace and blessings be upon him) delivered another speech. While the Prophet was riding a grey mule. Ali conveyed his message to the people. The Prophet (peace be upon him) repeated many of the statements that was said the day before.

The Messenger of Allah (peace and blessings be upon him) said: "Time has grown alike in state and form to the time when Allah created the earth and the heavens. A year is 12 months. Four of them are Sacred Months (Hurum). And 3 of the 4 months are successive.

They are Dhul-Qadah, Dhul-Hijjah, and Al-Muharram. The 4th month is Rajab Mudar, and is between Jumada and Shaban."

"What is this month?" the Prophet asked. The people answered: "Allah and His Messenger know best." He kept silent for a while. "Is it not Dhul-Hijjah?" He asked. "Yes. It is." The people answered.

Then the Prophet (peace be upon him) asked, "What is this town called?" The people said: "Allah and His Messenger know best." He was silent again for a while. The people thought he would give it another name. "Is it not Al-Baldah? (The town)" He asked. "Yes. It is." The people answered.

Then he said: "Shedding the blood of each other and taking (stealing) one another's provisions (unwillingly) are all wrong (Haram). It is unlawful to violate this. They must all be as sacred to one another as this sacred day, and in this sacred month, and in this sacred town."

"You will all be resurrected (after death) to your Lord. And there you will be accounted for all your deeds. So never turn into people who go astray and hurt or kill one another."

"Have I not delivered the Message?" The people answers: "Yes you have." "O Allah! Bear witness!"

"Let none of you inflict an evil thing upon his/her parents. For Satan has given up hope to being worshipped in this country of yours, but he will be obeyed at your committing small bad things. Satan will be happy with such things."

The Prophet (peace be upon him) spent At-Tashreeq Days, the 11th, 12th and 13th of Dhul-Hijjah, in Mina teaching, praying and remembering Allah. On some days, he delivered speeches as well.

On the 13th of Dhul-Hijjah, the Messenger of Allah (peace and blessings be upon him) stayed at a high place of a mountain side at Bani Kinanah from Al-Abtah. He spent the day and night there. The Prophet (peace be upon him) performed the noon, the afternoon, the sunset, and the evening prayers. He slept for a short time, then he left for the Ka'bah. At Ka'bah he did the Farewell Circumambulation (Tawaf Al-Wada), and asked his Companions to do the same. And upon the accomplishment of his religious duties, he left for Madinah.

The Final Expeditions

The Byzantine State denied Muslims the right to live. Their arrogance made them kill anyone who embraced Islam. The Messenger of Allah (peace and blessings be upon him) mobilized a great army in Safar in the 11th year of Al-Hijra. The Prophet (peace be upon him) gave the command to Osamah ibn Zaid ibn Haritha. He ordered him to have the horses tread on the lands bordering Palestine. The goal was to frighten the Byzantines and to put confidence into the hearts of Muslims who lived at the borders of the Byzantines.

Giving the leadership command to Osamah upset some folks. Osamah was too young, and so many people hesitated to joining his expedition. However, the Messenger of Allah (peace and blessings be upon him) addressed the people and said: "No wonder now you challenge his leadership, for you have already challenged the leadership of his father. By Allah! His father was one of the most beloved people to me and his son is one of the most beloved to me after his father."

After this, the people quickly joined his army. The number of fighters in his army was so enormous. But rumors about the Prophet's health delayed the expedition in order for them to know what Allah had willed for His Messenger (peace and blessings be upon him). Sadly the Prophet (peace he upon him) was not alive during the time of the expedition. Allah willed it be the first expedition sent during the caliphate of Abu Bakr (RA).

The Journey to Allah

When Islam grew complete and the new faith dominated Arabia, the Messenger of Allah (peace and blessings be upon him) started to develop some symptoms that showed he was about to leave this world.

The people saw things though his statements and deeds. For example:

- In Ramadan in the 10th year of Al-Hijra, the Messenger of Allah (peace and blessings be upon him) secluded himself for 20 days in contrast to 10 day during the previous years.

- The Archangel, Jibreel (Gabriel) (peace be upon him), reviewed the Quran twice with the Prophet (peace be upon him).

- The Prophet's words during the Farewell Pilgrimage (Al-Wida). For example, "I do not know if I will meet you at this place once again after this year."

- The revelation of Surah An-Nasr amid At-Tashreeq Days.

بِسْمِ اللَّهِ الرَّحْمَٰنِ الرَّحِيمِ

In the Name of Allah, the Most Gracious, the Most Merciful.

إِذَا جَاءَ نَصْرُ اللَّهِ وَالْفَتْحُ

When there comes the help of Allah and the Conquest.

وَرَأَيْتَ النَّاسَ يَدْخُلُونَ فِي دِينِ اللَّهِ أَفْوَاجًا

And you see that the people enter Allah's religion in crowds.

فَسَبِّحْ بِحَمْدِ رَبِّكَ وَاسْتَغْفِرْهُ إِنَّهُ كَانَ تَوَّابًا

So, glorify the praises of your Lord, and ask His forgiveness. Verily, He is the One Who accepts the repentance and Who forgives.

"When إِذَا جَاءَ نَصْرُ اللَّهِ وَالْفَتْحُ (When there comes the help of Allah and the Conquest.) was revealed, the Messenger of Allah said نُعِيَتْ إِلَيَّ نَفْسِي My death has been announced to me. And indeed he died during that year."

So when Surah An-Nasr was sent down on him, the Prophet (peace be upon him) knew that it was the parting time, and that Surah was a message of his approaching death.

- And on the early days of Safar in the 11th year of Al-Hijra, the Messenger of Allah (peace and blessings be upon him) went out to Uhud, and he did a farewell prayer to the martyrs. The Prophet's Companionions saw that he was saying goodbye to both the dead and the living as well. The Messenger of Allah (peace and blessings be upon him) then ascended the pulpit and said:

    "I am to precede you and I have been made witness to you. By Allah! You will see me at the 'Fountain' shortly. By Allah! I do not fear that you will forget Allah and turning polytheists after me. However, I do fear for you the love of worldly riches that might entice you to strike one another's neck."

- One day, at midnight, the Prophet (peace be upon him) went to Al-Baqee cemetery. He prayed and asked Allah to forgive the martyrs. The Prophet said: "Peace be upon you tomb-dwellers.

May that morning that dawns on you be better than that which dawn upon the living. Difficulties are coming to them like cloudy lumps of a dark night. And the last one is bringing more evil than the first." The Prophet (peace be upon him) then comforted them and said: "We will follow you very soon."

The start of the illness

On Monday the 29th of Safar in the 11th year of Al-Hijra, the Messenger of Allah (peace and blessings be upon him) participated in funeral rites in Al-Baqee. Then on the way back, the Prophet (peace be upon him) had a headache, and his temperature rose high that the heat from his head was felt over his headband.

Still the Prophet (peace be upon him) led the prayer for 11 days though he was very weak and ill. The total number of his sick days were about 14 days.

The last week

When the Prophet (peace be upon him) grew more ill, he asked his wives: "Where shall I stay tomorrow?" All understood what the Prophet wanted. So they told him to stay wherever he wanted. So he walked to Aishah's room while leaning on Al-Fadl ibn Al-Abbas and Ali ibn Abi Talib. He dragged his feet slowly until he came into her room. And in that room he spent the last week of his life.

During that week, Aishah used to recite Al-Mu'awwidhat (Chapters 113 (Falaq) and 114 (Nas) of the Quran), and also other supplications which the Prophet had taught her.

Five tough Days before death

On Wednesday, 5 days before the Prophet (peace be upon him) died, his temperature rose very high showing the difficulty of his illness. The Prophet (peace be upon him) fainted and experienced lots of pain. Still the Prophet (peace be upon him) said: "Pour out on me 7 Qirab (water skin pots) to go out to meet the people and to talk to them."

They seated him near a container that was used for washing, and they poured out water on him until he said: "That is enough."

Then he felt better to enter the Masjid. He entered and sat on the pulpit and said to the people: "The curse of Allah fell upon the Jews and the Christians because they made their Prophets' graves places of worship."

"Do not make my grave a worshipped idol!"

Then the Prophet (peace be upon him) asked the people to repay any injuries he might have ever caused them: "Anyone I have ever lashed his back, I give him my back. And anyone I have ever harmed his honor, I offer them my honor so that he may avenge himself."

The Messenger of Allah (peace and blessings be upon him), hen descended and did the noon prayer. Then he returned to the pulpit and sat. A man then said: "You owe me 3 Dirhams." The Prophet (peace be upon him) said: "Fadl, pay him what I owe him."

The Prophet (peace be upon him) then said: "Be good to Al-Ansar (the Helpers). They are our family and with them we found shelter. You must fully acknowledge and appreciate the favor that they have shown upon us, and you must overlook their faults."

"Allah, the Great, has given a slave of His the opportunity to make a choice between whatever he desires in this world, but he has opted for the latter."

Upon hearing this, Abu Bakr cried and said: 'We sacrifice our fathers and mothers for your sake.' The people wondered why Abu Bakr said that.

People said: 'Look at that old man! The Messenger of Allah (peace and blessings be upon him) says about a slave of Allah who was given the choice between the best fortunes of this world and the bounty of Allah in the Hereafter, but Abu Bakr says: We sacrifice our fathers and mothers for your sake!'

It was later on that the people realized what he meant. The Messenger of Allah (peace and blessings be upon him) was the slave told to choose.

Then the Prophet (Peace be upon him) said: "The person that I feel the most secure in his company is Abu Bakr. If I were to make friendship with any other one than Allah, Abu Bakr would be friend of mine. For him I feel the brotherhood of Islam. No gate would be kept open in the Masjid except that of Abu Bakr's."

Four days before his death

On Thursday, 4 days before his death, the Messenger of Allah (peace and blessings be upon him) said: "I want you to write something so that you will never fall into error."

Upon hearing this, Omar ibn Al-Khattab said: "The Messenger of Allah (peace and blessings be upon him) is suffering from severe pain and you have the Quran with you. The Book of Allah is sufficient unto you." However, others wanted the writing to be made. When the Prophet (Peace be upon him) heard them arguing about this, he ordered them to go away and leave him alone.

The Messenger of Allah (Peace and blessings be upon him) recommended that Christians, Jews, and polytheists should be expelled out of Arabia. He also recommended that delegations must be honored in a way similar to the one he used to do. As for the third recommendation, the narrator had forgotten it. However, it could have been to be faithful to the Quran and the Sunnah.

In spite of the severity of his illness, the Messenger of Allah (peace and blessings be upon him) led all the prayers until that Thursday, 4 days before he died. On that day the Prophet led the sunset prayer and recited [Mursalat (77:1)]: "By the winds (or angels or the Messengers of Allah) sent forth one after another."

In the evening he grew much more tired that he could not enter the Masjid. Aishah said: The Prophet (peace be upon him) asked: "Have the people done the prayer?" "No. They have not. They are waiting for you."

The Prophet (peace be upon him) said: "Put some water in the washing pot." We did as he asked. So he washed then as he stood up, he fainted. Then when he came round, he asked again "Have the people prayed?" Then the same sequence of events took place again for the 2nd and the 3rd. So he sent to Abu Bakr to lead the prayer. Abu Bakr led 17 prayers in the lifetime of the Prophet (peace be upon him).

Aishah asked the Prophet (peace be upon him) to let another person than her father, Abu Bakr, to lead the prayers lest the people get tired of him, but the Prophet (peace be upon him) refused and said: "You (women) are like the women that tried to tempt Joseph (Yusuf) into immorality. Send my request to Abu Bakr to lead the prayer again."

A day or two days before death

On Saturday, the Prophet (Peace be upon him) felt better. So he went out leaning on two men to lead the noon prayer. Abu Bakr, who was about to lead withdrew quickly when he saw the Prophet (peace be upon him) coming. However, the Messenger of Allah (peace and blessings be upon him) gave him a sign to stay, then he said: "Seat me next to him." So they seated him on the left hand side of Abu Bakr. The Messenger of Allah (peace be upon him) led the prayer, but Abu Bakr followed him loudly at every 'Allahu Akbar'. The Prophet (peace be upon him) said: "So the people may hear."

A day before his death

On Sunday, a day before he died, the Messenger of Allah (peace and blessings be upon him) set his servants free, paid as a charity the last 7 Dinars he owned in this life, and he gave his weapons as a present to the people. When night fell Aishah borrowed some oil from her neighbor to light the oil-lantern. Even the Prophet's armor was mortgaged as a security with a Jew for 30 Sa' (an ancient unit of volume, equal to 2 to 4 liters) of barley.

The last day alive

While the people were performing the dawn prayer on Monday, which was led by Abu Bakr, they were happy to see the Messenger of Allah (peace and blessings be upon him) raising the curtain of Aishah's room. He looked at them. They were aligned properly and so he smiled cheerfully. Seeing him, Abu Bakr was happy and he quickly withdrew to join the lines and to let the Prophet lead the prayer. Abu Bakr thought that the Prophet (peace be upon him) wanted to pray with them.

However, the Prophet (peace be upon him) made a gesture to continue their prayer, and he went back into his room and drew down the curtain.

The Messenger of Allah (peace and blessings be upon him) did not live for the next prayer time.

When it was daytime, the Messenger of Allah (peace be upon him) called his daughter, Fatimah, and said something to her in a secret voice that made her cry. Then he said something else to her which made her laugh.

Aishah asked Fatimah after the Prophet's death, as to her weeping and then laughing to which Fatimah said: "The first time he said to me that he would not recover from his illness and so I wept. Then he said that I would be the first of his family to join him, so I laughed."

The Messenger of Allah (peace and blessings be upon him), gave his daughter glad tidings that she would become the lady of all women of the world. Fatimah witnessed the great pain that her father was feeling.

So Fatimah said: "What great pain my father is in!" To these words, the Messenger of Allah (peace and blessings be upon him) told her that he not suffer any more when today is over."

He asked that his grandchildren, Al-Hasan and Al-Husain, be brought to him. He kissed them and said that they be looked after well. He then asked to see his wives. They were brought to him. He told them to remember Allah. Then pain grew so much severe that the trace of poison he had at Khaibar came to light.

The Khaibar story. After the battle of Khaibar the Prophet (peace be upon him) was invited to eat some food. A Jewish woman had cooked a poisoned sheep for them. The first companion to eat the food died. Then Prophet (peace be upon him) who had already taken a bite warned his companions that the sheep has told him it is poisoned so stop eating.

The Messenger of Allah (peace be upon him) then said: Take your hands away (from the food). The Messenger of Allah (peace be upon him) then asked the Jews: "Have you poisoned this sheep?"

They said, "Yes." He asked: "What made you do so?" They said, "We wanted to know if you were a liar in which case we would get rid of you, and if you are a prophet then the poison would not harm you."

The Prophet (peace be upon him) was so much in pain that he said to Aishah: "I still feel the pain of that food that I tasted at Khaibar. I feel as if death is approaching." He ordered the people to perform the prayers and be attentive to slaves. He repeated it several times.

The Prophet breathes his last

When the pains of death started, Aishah leant the Prophet against her. Aishah used to say: One of Allah's gifts upon me is that the Messenger of Allah (peace and blessings be upon him) died in my room, while I am still alive. He died between my neck and chest while he was leaning against me. And Allah has mixed his saliva with mine at his death.

Abdur Rahman, the son of Abu Bakr, came into the room with a Siwak (the root of a desert plant used for brushing teeth) in his hand. Aishah saw that the Prophet (peace be upon him) was looking at the Siwak, so Aishah asked: "Would you like me to take it for you?" The Prophet (peace be upon him) nodded in agreement. As the Siwak was too hard for him, Aishah asked: "Shall I soften it for you?" The Prophet (peace be upon him) nodded in agreement. So Aishah softened with her mouth and he passed it between his teeth.

As soon as the Prophet (peace be upon him) had finished his Siwak brushing, he raised his finger up, looked upwards to the ceiling and moved his lips. So Aishah listened to him.

The Messenger of Allah (peace and blessings be upon him) said: "With those on whom You have bestowed Your Grace with the Prophets and the Truthful ones (As-Siddeeqeen), the martyrs and the good doers. Forgive me and have mercy upon me. The most exalted Companionship on high. To Allah we turn and to Him we turn back for help and our last abode."

The death event took place at high morning time on Monday, the 12th of Rabi Al-Awwal, in the 11th year of Al-Hijrah. He was 63 years and 4 days old when he died.

The Prophet's passing was soon known by everyone in Madinah. Great grief spread to all areas.

Anas said: "I have never saw a day brighter than that day on which the Messenger of Allah (peace and blessings be upon him) came to us, and I have never saw a more darker day than that one on which the Messenger of Allah (peace and blessings be upon him) died on."

Omar, felt so much pain that he almost fainted. He addressed the people: "Some of the hypocrites said that the Messenger of Allah (peace be upon him) had died. He did not die, but he returned to his Lord as Moses ibn Imran did. He stayed away for 40 nights, but then he returned though they said he had been dead. By Allah, the Messenger of Allah (peace and blessings be upon him) will come back and he will cut off the legs and hands of those who claim his death."

Abu Bakr left his house and came to the Masjid. He entered his daughter's, Aishah's, abode, and he went directly to where the Messenger of Allah (Peace be upon him) was.

The Messenger of Allah (peace and blessings be upon him) was covered with a Yemeni mantle. Abu Bakr uncovered the Prophet's face and tended down, kissed him and cried. Then Abu Bakr said: "I sacrifice my mother and father for your sake. Allah, verily, will not cause you to die again. You have just experienced the death that Allah had ordained on earth."

Then Abu Bakr went out and heard Omar talking to the people. Abu Bakr said: "Omar be seated." Omar refused to do so. Abu Bakr then said: "He who worships Muhammad (peace and blessings be upon him), Muhammad is dead now. But he who worships Allah, He is the Ever Living and He never dies.

Allah says:

> وَمَا مُحَمَّدٌ إِلاَّ رَسُولٌ قَدْ خَلَتْ مِن قَبْلِهِ الرُّسُلُ
>
> 3:144 Muhammad is no more than a Messenger, and indeed Messengers have passed away before him.
>
> أَفَإِنْ مَاتَ أَوْ قُتِلَ انقَلَبْتُمْ عَلَى أَعْقَابِكُمْ
>
> If he dies or is killed, will you then turn back on your heels!
>
> وَمَن يَنقَلِبْ عَلَىٰ عَقِبَيْهِ فَلَن يَضُرَّ اللَّهَ شَيْئًا وَسَيَجْزِي اللَّهُ الشَّاكِرِينَ
>
> And he who turns back on his heels, not the least harm will he do to Allah; and Allah will reward the grateful.
>
> وَمَا كَانَ لِنَفْسٍ أَنْ تَمُوتَ إِلاَّ بِإِذْنِ اللَّهِ كِتَابًا مُّؤَجَّلاً
>
> 3:145 And no person can ever die except by Allah's leave and at an appointed term.

Ibn Abbas said: "By Allah, it truly sounded as if the people had never heard those verses until Abu Bakr recited them as a reminder. So people started reciting them until there was no person who did not recite them."

Ibn Al-Musaiyab said that Omar had said: "By Allah, as soon as I heard Abu Bakr recite those Quranic verses, I fell to the ground. And only then did I grasp that Muhammad (peace and blessings be upon him) had truly died."

Burial and Farewell

Debate about who would succeed the Messenger of Allah (Peace and blessings be upon him) broke out even before having the Prophet's body prepared for burial. Lots of arguments took place between the Emigrants and Helpers. Finally they understood what the Prophet (peace be upon him) wanted. So they acknowledged Abu Bakr (May Allah be pleased with him) as a caliph. People were so busy arguing that it was the dawn of Tuesday, and yet the Prophet's blessed body (peace and blessings be upon him) was still on his bed covered with a garment.

On Tuesday, the Prophet's body was washed with his clothes on. He was washed by Al-Abbas, Ali, Qathm and Al-Fadl (the two sons of Al-Abbas), Shaqran, the Messenger's freed slave, Aws ibn Khauli and Osamah ibn Zaid. Al-Abbas, Qathm and Al-Fadl turned his body around, whereas Shaqran and Osamah poured water. Ali washed the Prophet (peace be upon him) and Aws leant the Prophet against his chest.

They shrouded the Messenger of Allah (peace and blessings be upon him) in 3 white Sahooli cotton cloth. A disagreement then arose with regard to the burial place. Abu Bakr said: "I heard the Messenger of Allah (peace and blessings be upon him) say: 'The Prophets were buried where they died.' Therefore, Abu Talhah moved the bed on which the Prophet died, then he dug underneath and made the Prophet's tomb.

Before the burial, people entered the room 10 by 10. They prayed for the Prophet (peace and blessings be upon him). The first to pray for the Prophet were people of his clan. After that, the Emigrants, then the Helpers. The women prayed for him after men. And the very young were the last to pray.

This process took all day Tuesday and Wednesday night (the night before Wednesday morning). Aishah said: "They did not know that the Prophet (peace and blessings be upon him) was being buried until they heard the sound of tools digging the ground that Wednesday night."

The Prophet's Household
(Peace and Blessings be Upon Them)

- Khadijah Bint Khuwailid: In Makkah (prior to Hijr), his wife Khadijah. He was 25 years old and she was 40 years old when they got married. Khadijah was the first woman he married. Khadijah was the only wife he had until she died. He had both sons and daughters with her. However, the sons died and did not live long. The Prophet's daughters were Zainab, Ruqaiya, Umm Kulthum and Fatimah.

- Zainab married her maternal cousin Abu Al-As ibn Al-Rabi before Al-Hijra.

- Ruqaiya and Umm Kulthum were married to Uthman ibn Affan (RA). Uthman married Umm Kulthum after the death of her sister Ruqaiya.

- Fatimah was married to Ali ibn Abi Talib during the period between Badr and Uhud battles.

- The daughters and sons that Fatimah and Ali had were Zainab and Umm Kulthum, Al-Hasan and Al-Husain.

It is well-known that the Messenger of Allah (peace and blessings be upon him) was exceptionally authorized by Allah to have more than 4 wives for humanitarian reasons (after the death of their husbands). The wives that he married were 13. Nine of the wives outlived him.

- Two wives died during the Prophet's lifetime: Khadijah and the Mother of the poor (Umm Al-Masakeen).

- Zainab bint Khuzaima and two other wives, the Prophet (peace be upon him) did not consummate his marriage.

- Sawdah bint Zama: the Prophet (peace be upon him) married her in Shawwal, in the 10th year of his Prophethood, after the death of Khadijah. Prior to that, Sawdah was married to her cousin As-Sakran ibn Amr.

- Aishah bint Abu Bakr: The Prophet (peace be upon him) married her in the 11th year of his Prophethood, 2 years and 5 months before Al-Hijra. The Prophet (peace be upon him) did not consummate the marriage with her until she had attained puberty, seven months after Al-Hijra, and that was in Madinah. She was the only virgin he married. She was the most beloved wife to him. Aishah was the most learned in jurisprudence.

Life was different during the Prophet's time. People had a very difficult life. Women matured much earlier back then. Aisha started menstruating and went through puberty at age 9. Life was very difficult. This was not unusual at all during those times. Most children died at a very early age. People had only a few fruit dates to eat. Most died even without ever seeing or tasting bread. And most of the Prophet's children died at an early age.

Aishah was a very religious person. She was one to remember and take account of the way he lived and how he dealt with things. She very much loved the Prophet (peace be upon him), as you have read earlier.

- Hafsah bint Omar ibn Al-Khattab: She was Aiyim (i.e. husbandless). Her previous husband was Khunais ibn Hudhafa As-Sahmi during the period of the Badr and Uhud battles. The Prophet (peace be upon him) married her in the 3rd year of Al-Hijra.

- Zainab bint Khuzaimah: Zainab was from Bani Hilal ibn Amir ibn Sa'sa'a. Zainab other name was Umm Al-Masakeen, because of her kindness towards them. She was the wife of Abdullah ibn Jahsh, who did at Uhud. Zainab was married to the Prophet (peace be upon him) in the 4th year of Al-Hijra. However, she died 3 months after her marriage to the Messenger of Allah (peace and blessings be upon him).

- Umm Salamah Hind bint Abi Omaiyah: She was the wife of Abu Salamah. He died in Jumada Al-Akhir during the 4th year of Al-Hijra. The Messenger of Allah (peace and blessings be upon him) married her in Shawwal during that year.

-
- Zainab bint Jahsh ibn Riyab: She was from Bani Asad ibn Khuzaimah. Zainab was the Prophet's paternal cousin. Zainab was married to Zaid ibn Haritha. He was then considered son (adopted) of the Prophet (peace and blessings be upon him). However, Zaid divorced her

About Zainab, Allah sent down verses of Al-Ahzab Chapter that discussed the adoption of children in detail. The Prophet (peace be upon him) married Zainab in Dhul-Qa'dah, the 5th year of Al-Hijra.

Adopted children must carry their own names since children need to know their origins. Adopted children cannot legally inherit under Islamic law. However, if the child is an orphan and has no support, then the reward from Allah is so much. The Prophet (peace be on him) said: "I, and the **one** who raises an orphan (a child without a father), will be with me in Paradise."

- Juwairiyah bint Al-Harith: Al-Harith was the head of Bani Al-Mustaliq of Khuza'ah. Juwairiyah fell to the Muslims from Bani Al-Mustaliq. Thabit ibn Qais ibn Shammas made her a covenant to set her free later. The Messenger of Allah (peace and blessings be upon him) married her in Sha'ban in the 6th year of Al-Hijra.

- Maimunah bint Al-Harith: Maimunah was the daughter of Al-Harith. She was the sister of Umm Al-Fadl Lubabah bint Al-Harith. The Prophet (peace and blessings be upon him) married Maimunah after the Compensatory Umrah. That was in Dhul-Qa'dah in the 7th year of Al-Hijra.

- Umm Habibah (Ramlah): The daughter of Abu Sufyaan. Ramlah was married to Ubaidullah ibn Jahsh. Ramlah migrated with Ubaidullah to Abyssinia, Ethiopia. When Ubaidullah became a Christian, Ramlah stoodfast to her religion and refused to convert. When Ubaidullah died in Abyssinia (Ethiopia), the Messenger of Allah (Peace be upon him) sent Amr ibn Omaiyah Ad-Damri with a letter to Negus, the king, and he asked him for Umm Habibah's hand. That was in Muharram, in the 7th year of Al-Hijra. Negus agreed and sent her to the Prophet (peace and blessings be upon him) in the 7th year of Al-Hijra.

The two wives that the Messenger of Allah (peace be upon him) did not consummate marriage with were, one from Kindah (the one called Al-Jauniyah) and the other from Bani Kilab.

Through marriage, the Prophet (peace be upon him) established a great friendship with both Abu Bakr and Omar. Also getting his daughter Fatimah married to Ali ibn Abi Talib, and the marriage of his two daughters, Ruqaiyah and Umm Kulthum to Uthman, show clearly that the Prophet aimed at confirming the friendship among these 4 men.

Also there was a tradition among Arabs to honor the in-law relations. Hostility and fights against family would bring shame and disgrace.

Umm Salamah was from Bani Makhzum, the tribe of Abu Jahl and Khalid ibn Al-Waleed. Umm Salamah marriage to the Prophet (peace be upon him) produced good results. For example, Khalid's indecisive attitude at Uhud was partly due to the Prophet's marriage to Umm Salamah. And in a short time, Khalid became a good Muslim.

And after the marriage to Umm Habibah, Abu Sufyaan, her father, no longer wanted to kill the Prophet (peace be upon him). Likewise marrying Juwairiyah and Safiyah made the two tribes stop all sorts of aggression against him and Islam. Moreover, Juwairiyah was one of the greatest sources of blessing to her own people. On the occasion of her marriage, the Prophet's Companions freed a hundred of her people.

The wives of the Prophet (peace be upon him), especially those who outlived him, played a very important role in conveying Prophetic traditions (Ahadith) to the people. Aishah, for example, related a large number of the Prophet's statements and deeds.

The treatment of the Prophet (peace be upon him) to his wives was of kindness always. Although the Prophet's life was hard, none of his wives complained. Anas said about the Prophet's life: "The Messenger of Allah (peace and blessings be upon him) has never had or tasted a flattened loaf in all his lifetime, nor has the Prophet ever seen roasted mutton."

Aishah said: "Over 2 months have elapsed, during which we have seen 3 crescent moons, but no fire has been kindled in the houses of the Messenger of Allah (peace and blessings be upon him) (they had no food to cook)." "What did you eat?" Urwah asked. Aishah said "Water and dates".

In spite of these difficulties, none of the Prophet's wives complained once.

The Prophet's family were so noble and kind that none of them desired 'the life of this world and the glitter' to the abode in the Hereafter.

Although the wives were many in number, no disputes occurred between them as it normally happen among co-wives. Some few cases could be the only exception, but they were fairly normal. Allah reproached the wives for that, and so they stopped doing such things.

These incidents are mentioned in At-Tahreem Chapter [66:1, 3]:

O Prophet! Why do you forbid that which Allah has allowed to you, seeking to please your wives?

وَٱللَّهُ غَفُورٌ رَحِيمٌ

And Allah is Oft-Forgiving, Most Merciful.

وَإِذْ أَسَرَّ ٱلنَّبِيُّ إِلَىٰ بَعْضِ أَزْوَاجِهِ حَدِيثًا فَلَمَّا نَبَّأَتْ بِهِ

And (remember) when the Prophet disclosed a matter in confidence to one of his wives, then she told it.

The Attributes and Manners of the Prophet

The Messenger of Allah (peace and blessings be upon him) combined both perfection of manners and perfection of creation. This impression on people can be understood by the bliss that filled their hearts and filled them with dignity. People's dignity and devotion of the Prophet (peace be upon him) were very unique and matchless. No other man in the history of humanity has been so loved.

Those who met him, loved him. People were ready to sacrifice their lives for the sake of saving even his nail from hurt. His Companions found that he was truthful and honest and so they loved him.

Below we list just a brief summary of his beauty and perfection. To try to list them all is truly beyond our capabilities.

Describing the Prophet (peace be upon him), who had passed by her tent, on his voyage of migration, Umm Mabad Al-Khuzaiyah said to her husband:

"The Prophet was bright and had broad expression. His manners were truly fine. Hi did not have a bulging belly nor had a head deprived of hair. His eyes were black and attractive and were finely arched by continuous eyebrows. His hair was black, a little curly, and he wore it long. His voice was beautiful and commanding. His head was large and well-formed and was set on a slender neck. His expression was sweet, thoughtful, and serene. Once you became intimate with him you felt attachment and respect. His speech was very well set and was free from wordiness, as if it were a rosary of beads. His stature was neither too small nor too high, just right. Every step he took, he was surrounded by his Companions. Whenever he said something, they listened with captivated attention, and if he issued a command, they competed with each other in carrying it out. His words were marked by sincerity and truth, free from all kinds of lies and falsehoods."

Ali ibn Abi Talib describing the Prophet (peace be upon him): "The Messenger of Allah (peace and blessings be upon him) was neither extremely short tall nor excessively tall. He was medium height among the people. His hair was both curly and wavy combined. It was in between, and it was not plain straight. His face was not fat, swollen, or meaty-compact. The face was fairly round. His teeth were white. The Prophet had black, large eyes, and with long haired eyelids. His limbs and shoulders were rather big. He had thick hands and thick fingers and toes. When walking, he lifted his foot off the ground as if walking in a muddy field. He is the Seal of Prophets, and the most generous and bravest. His speech was the most honest and reliable. The Prophet (peace be upon him) was the most attentive to people's trust, and was always careful to pay people's due in full. Seeing him unexpectedly you fear him and admire him. He who had acquaintance with him, loved him. I truly have never seen such a man neither before him, nor after him."

Abu At-Tufail said: "He was white and handsome. He was neither thin nor fat, and neither short nor tall."

Anas ibn Malik said: "He had unfolded hands and were pink-colored. He was neither brown nor white. He was in between. In both his beard and head there were about 20 grey hairs, and some grey hairs in his temples."

Jabir ibn Samurah reported that the Prophet (peace be upon him) had a broad face with wide eyes.

Al-Bara said: "He had the best character, and had the most handsome face. He had broad-shoulders. He was of medium height, and his hair went up to his earlobes. I once saw him dressed in a red garment and I have never seen someone more handsome. In the beginning he used to let his hair loose as the people of the Book, but later on, he used to part his hair. His face was moon-like.

Ar-Rabi bint Muawwidh said: "If you had seen him, you would feel the sun was shining."

Jabir ibn Samurah said, "I saw him one day at one full-moony night. I looked at him. He had on a red garment. I compared him with the moon and I found that he was better than the moon."

Abu Huraira said: "I have never seen someone nicer than the Messenger of Allah (peace and blessings be upon him). It seems as if the sunlight was moving within his face. I have never seen someone who was faster in pace than the Prophet (peace be upon him). It was as if the ground folded itself up to shorten the distance for him. We could not keep up the pace. We wore ourselves out while he was at full ease."

Ka'b ibn Malik said: "When he was pleased, his face shinned as the moon."

Whenever Abu Bakr saw him he would say: "He is the Messenger of Allah (peace be upon him). He is faithful and calls for forgiveness. He shines like the moon's light.

Jabir ibn Samurah said: "The Prophet's legs were gentle. He laughed quietly, which was no more than smiling. If you look at his eyes, you will say 'He is black-eyed though he is not.'"

Ibn Al-Abbas said: "The Prophet's two front teeth were divided a little so whenever he spoke, light went through them. His beard was thick. His forehead was broad. His eyebrows were as the metal piece attached to a lance. His nose had narrow nostrils. His chest was broad and flatted. He had long forearms. His shoes hardly touched the ground. When he walked away, he vanished quickly. Still he walked at ease (when he is not in a hurry). The Prophet (peace be upon him) walked leaning forward."

Anas said: "I have never touched silk softer than the palm of the Prophet's (peace be upon him). I have never I smelt a perfume or any scent nicer than his."

Abu Juhaifa said: "I took the Prophet's hand and I placed it on my head and I found that it was colder than ice and had a smell better than the musk perfume."

Jabir ibn Samurah, who was a little child, said: "When the Prophet (peace be upon him) wiped my cheek, I felt his hand. It was cold and scented as if his hand had been taken from a store of perfume."

Anas also said: "The Prophet's sweat was pearl-like."

Umm Sulaim said: "The Prophet's sweat smelt better than the nicest perfume."

Jabir said: "Whoever walks a path that has been trodden by the Messenger of Allah (peace and blessings be upon him), will certainly scent his smell and will know for sure that the Messenger of Allah (peace and blessings be upon him) walked that path."

The Seal of Prophethood that was similar in size to a bird's egg, was between the Prophet's shoulders on the left side having spots on it like moles.

The Perfection of Soul

The Messenger of Allah (peace and blessings be upon him) was known for superb eloquence and fluency in the Arabic language. He was a straightforward speaker. He was very familiar with the dialects and accents of every tribe. He was eloquent at both bedouin and town speech.

Even the best of men have their flaws, but the Messenger of Allah (peace and blessings be upon him), unlike all other men, the more he was hurt, the more gentle and patient he became. And the more insolence and disrespectful anybody exercised against the Prophet, the more enduring he became.

Aishah (RA) said: "The Messenger of Allah (peace and blessings be upon him), whenever he was given the choice between two affairs, he always selected the easiest and the most convenient. However, if the Prophet (peace be upon him) was certain that it is sinful, then he would walk away very far from it. He has never avenged himself. However, if the sanctity of Allah is violated he would. And that would always be for Allah's and never for himself. He was always the last one to get angry, and always the first one to be satisfied. His generosity and hospitality were matchless. He was a man that never feared poverty."

Ibn Abbas said: "The Messenger of Allah (peace and blessings be upon him) was the most generous. He was always the most generous in Ramadan, the times at which the angel Jibreel (Gabriel) (peace and blessings be upon him) came to see him. Jibreel (Gabriel) (peace and blessings be upon him) used to visit him each and every night of Ramadan to review the Quran with him. Verily the Messenger of Allah (peace and blessings be upon him) was more generous at giving charity than the blowing wind."

Jabir said: "The Messenger of Allah (peace and blessings be upon him) would never say no to anything that he was asked for."

The Prophet's courage, his succor (assistance and support in times of hardship and distress) and his might are distinguishable. The Prophet was the most courageous. The Messenger of Allah (peace and blessings be upon him) difficult times and stoodfast at them.

More than once, very brave men fled away leaving him alone, and yet the Prophet (peace be upon him) stood strong, and faced the enemy without turning his back.

Ali said: "Whenever the fight grew very fierce and the eyes of the fighters went red, we used to resort to the Messenger of Allah (peace and blessings be upon him) for succor (assistance and support in times of hardship and distress). He was always the closest to the enemy and not afraid of death."

Anas said: "One night the people of Madinah heard a loud sound. People ran towards the source of sound, but the Messenger of Allah (peace and blessings be upon him) had already gone ahead of them. He was riding the horse of Abu Talhah, which had no saddle. His sword was slung round his neck and back. The Prophet (peace be upon him) said to them: 'There is nothing to be afraid from.'"

The Messenger of Allah (peace and blessings be upon him) was the most modest, and always the first one to cast his eyes down.

Abu Said Al-Khudri said: "The Prophet (peace be upon him) was shier than a virgin in her bed. When the Prophet disliked something, we always could read it on his face. He never stared at anyone's face. He always lowered his eyes. He looked at the ground more than he looked sky-wards. He would never mention a person whom he had heard bad-news about, even if he disliked him. Instead the Prophet would say: 'Why do some people do such and such?'"

Those who have exchanged speech with the Prophet (peace be upon him), and even his own enemies, acknowledge his noble qualities. Even before he became the Messenger of Allah (peace and blessings be upon him), he was nicknamed Al-Ameen (the truthful and the trustworthy). Even during the Al-Jahiliyah (before Islam), people used to turn to him for consultation and judgment.

Ali said that Abu Jahl said to the Messenger of Allah (peace and blessings be upon him): "We never call you a liar. However, we do not have faith in what you have brought."

So in His Book, Allah said about them in Surah Al-An'am [6:33]:

قَدْ نَعْلَمُ إِنَّهُ لَيَحْزُنُكَ الَّذِي يَقُولُونَ فَإِنَّهُمْ لَا يُكَذِّبُونَكَ وَلَٰكِنَّ الظَّالِمِينَ بِآيَاتِ اللَّهِ يَجْحَدُونَ

6:33 We know indeed the grief which their words cause you; it is not you that they deny, but it is the verses of Allah that the wrongdoers deny.

وَلَقَدْ كُذِّبَتْ رُسُلٌ مِّن قَبْلِكَ فَصَبَرُوا عَلَىٰ مَا كُذِّبُوا وَأُوذُوا حَتَّىٰ أَتَاهُمْ نَصْرُنَا وَلَا مُبَدِّلَ لِكَلِمَاتِ اللَّهِ وَلَقَدْ جَاءَكَ مِن نَّبَإِ الْمُرْسَلِينَ

6:34 Verily, (many) Messengers were denied before you, but with patience they bore the denial, and they were hurt, till Our help reached them, and none can alter the Words of Allah. Surely, there has reached you the information about the Messengers (before you).

Even when Heraclius (He was the Emperor of the Byzantine Empire from 610 to 641) asked Abu Sufyaan: "Have you ever accused him of lying before he became the Messenger of Allah?" Abu Sufyaan said: "No."

The Prophet (peace be upon him) was most modest and far from being proud or arrogant. He forbade all people to stand up at his presence, as others do for their kings. Visiting the poor and helping them are some of the Prophet's habits. For example, if a slave invited him, he would always accept their invitation. The Prophet (peace be upon him) always sat among people as if he were like any ordinary person.

Aishah (RA) said that the Prophet (peace be upon him) used to repair his own shoes. He sewed, mended his own dress and cleaned the house. After all, the Prophet (peace be upon him) was a human being like all others. He often checked his dress (lest it has some insects on so not to harm them). He milked the she-sheep and cared for them. The Messenger of Allah (peace and blessings be upon him) was always the most truthful to his pledges, and he kept good and steady relationship with his relatives.

The Prophet (peace be upon him) was the most gentle, merciful, and amiable to everyone. His way of living was the simplest.

Bad manners and rudeness were two qualities completely alien to him. He never called anybody names. He never cursed nor ever made noise in the streets. He never exchanged offences with others.

The Prophet (peace be upon him) forgave people easily. Nobody was allowed to follow him like a bodyguard. He never showed that he was superior to others and not to men or women.

If someone served him something, he served them as well. Loving the needy and the poor and participating in their funerals were things the Messenger of Allah (peace and blessings be upon him) always observed. He never disgraced a poor person for their poverty.

Once the Prophet (peace be upon him) was travelling with his Companions and when they were hungry, someone brought a sheep. A man then said: I will slaughter it, another man said: I will skin it. A third man said: I will cook it. So the Prophet (peace be upon him) said: I will gather the wood for fire. They said: "No. We will collect it for you."

The Prophet replied: "I know that you can, but I do not want to be privileged. For Allah dislikes it very much to see a slave of his privileged to others." So the Prophet (peace be upon him) went and gathered fire-wood.

Hind ibn Abi Halah said: "The Prophet (peace be upon him) was continually sad and thinking perpetually. He never rested for a long time. And the Prophet (peace be upon him) only spoke when it was necessary. And whenever said something, he would end his talk with his jawbone but never out of the corners of his mouth snobbishly.

The Prophet's speech was always inclusive and decisive. It was never excessive nor short of meaning. He always glorified the bounty of Allah even if it was very little. If he did not like the food, he would neither criticize it nor praise it. He was always in control of his temper and would never get upset unless it was necessary.

When the Prophet (peace be upon him) pointed at anything, he would do so with his full hand-palm. If he was angry he would turn away both his face and body aside. When he was happy or pleased, he would lower his eyes down.

He stayed quiet unless something was said closely relevant to him. He established the brotherhood bond among his Companions, and so he made them close and he never implanted enmity among them.

Those who were honorable with their people, were honored and respected always by him. He visited friends and always asked if they needed anything. He stood by what was right, and he criticized the wrong, and he tried to undermine it. He was moderate in everything. Each situation or thing was dealt with in its proper due.

Righteousness was always his target, so the Prophet (peace be upon him) was never short of it, nor indifferent to it. Remembrance of Allah was a thing he always aimed at and was established whenever he sat down or stood up.

No certain position was ever assigned for him for sitting. He sat at the end of the group, seated next to the last person. And asked the people to do the same.

Anyone whoever interrupted him to asking for an advice would always be the first to start the conversation and the one to end it. The Messenger of Allah (peace and blessings be upon him) would listen to them patiently until they ended their speech. The Prophet (peace be upon him) never denied a request by anyone, if it was possible.

In justice, everyone were equal. No one was better than another except the person that loved and feared Allah the most. His assembly was always a meeting of clemency, patience, and honesty. Voices were never raised. They honored the old, and have mercy on the young. They assisted the needy and were kind to the guests.

The Prophet (peace be upon him) was always pleasant-tempered and lenient. He was never rude and was neither a reproacher nor a praiser. He overlooked what he did not like. He never reproached, disparaged nor did sought the shortages or defects of others.

He only spoke about things whose reward was Divinely desirable. When he spoke, the people would attentively listen lowering down their heads. The people only spoke when the Prophet was silent. They avoided disputes or arguments about who was to talk. He who talked would be listened to by everyone until he finished his talk.

The Prophet (peace be upon him) laughed at what the people laughed at and admired what the people used to admire. He would always showed patience with a stranger's loudness or harshness at talk.

The Prophet (peace be upon him) said: "When you see a person seeking an object sincerely, assist them. And never ask for a reward from them, except from the reward-Giver, Allah."

Kharijah ibn Zaid said: "The Messenger of Allah (peace be upon him) was the most honored among the people with whom he sat. The Prophet's limbs could hardly be seen. He was always silent and rarely said anything when speech was not a necessity. He turned away from speech that was impolite or rude."

On the whole the Messenger of Allah (peace and blessings be upon him) was ornamented with matchless attributes of perfection. He was even praised by Allah [68:4]:

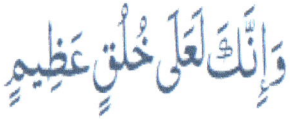

And verily, you are on an exalted character.

Those were the attributes and qualities of the Messenger of Allah (peace and blessing be upon him) which made the hearts of the people come close to him and love him.

Those traits made the Prophet (peace be upon him) very popular that the enmity and the restraint of his people grew less and they began to quickly embrace Islam in large crowds.

No one can ever claim to have full knowledge of all the beautiful attributes of the greatest man in history. No one can ever give this beautiful man his due description. He was an honest and sincere man that always sought Allah's light.

اللَّهُمَّ صَلِّ عَلَى مُحَمَّدٍ وَأَزْوَاجِهِ وَذُرِّيَّتِهِ،

O Allah! Send Your Mercy on Muhammad and on his wives and on his off spring,

كَمَا صَلَّيْتَ عَلَى آلِ إِبْرَاهِيمَ،

as You sent Your Mercy on Abraham's family

وَبَارِكْ عَلَى مُحَمَّدٍ وَأَزْوَاجِهِ وَذُرِّيَّتِهِ،

and send Your Blessings on Muhammad and on his offspring,

كَمَا بَارَكْتَ عَلَى آلِ إِبْرَاهِيمَ، إِنَّكَ حَمِيدٌ مَجِيدٌ

as You sent Your Blessings on Abraham's family,
for You are the Most Praiseworthy, the Most Glorious.

The Story of People of the Ditch The Boy and the King

Allah's Messenger (peace be upon him) said: "There lived a king before you and he had a (court) magician. As he (the magician) grew old, he said to the king: I have grown old, send some young boy to me so that I should teach him magic. He (the king) sent him a young boy so that he should train him (in magic). And on his way (to the magician) he (the young boy) found a monk sitting there. He listened to the monk's words and was impressed by them. It became his habit to pass by the monk and to spend the time with him listening to his teachings and then leave to the magician late. He (the magician) beat him because he was late. He made a complaint of that to the monk and he said to him: "When you feel afraid of the magician, say: Members of my family had detained me. And when you feel afraid of your family you should say: The magician had detained me." It so happened that there came a huge beast (of prey) and it blocked the way of the people, and he (the boy) said: "I will, come to know today whether the magician is superior or the monk is superior." He picked up a stone and said:

"O'Allah, if the affair of the monk is dearer to Thee than the affair of the magician, cause death to this animal so that the people should be able to move about freely." He threw that stone towards it and killed it and the people began to move about (on the path freely).

He (the young boy) then came to that monk and informed him, and the monk said: "Today you are superior to me. Your affair has come to a stage where I find that you would be soon put to a trial, and in case you are put to a trial do not give my clue."

The young boy began to treat the blind and those suffering from leprosy. He in fact began to cure people from (all kinds) of illnesses. When a companion of the king who had gone blind heard about him, he came to him with numerous gifts and said: "if you cure me, all these things collected together here would be yours."

He said: "I myself do not cure anyone. It is Allah Who cures and if you affirm faith in Allah, I shall also supplicate Allah to cure you."

He affirmed his faith in Allah and Allah cured him and he came to the king and sat by his side as he used to sit before. The king said to him: "Who restored your eyesight?" He said: "My Lord!" The king got astounded: "Should it mean that your Lord is another One besides me." He said: "My Lord and your Lord is Allah," so he (the king) took hold of him and tormented him until he gave a clue of that boy.

The young boy was thus summoned and the king said to him: "O'boy, it has been conveyed to me that you have become so much proficient in your magic that you cure the blind and those suffering from leprosy and you do such and such things." The boy said: "But I do not cure anyone; it is Allah Who cures."

The king took hold of him and began to torment him. Eventually the boy gave a clue of the monk. The monk was thus summoned and it was said to him: "You should turn back from your religion." He, however, refused to do so." He (ordered) for a saw to be brought (and when it was done) he (the king) placed it in the middle of his head and tore it into parts till a part fell down.

Then the courtier of the king was brought and it was said to him: "Turn back from your religion." And he refused to do so, and the saw was placed in the midst of his head and it was torn till a part fell down.

Then that young boy was brought and it was said to him: "Turn back from your religion." He refused to do so and he was handed over to a group of his courtiers.

The king ruled: "Take him to such and such mountain, and make him climb up that mountain and when you reach its top (ask him to renounce his faith) but if he refuses to do so, then throw him (down the mountain)." So they took him and made him climb up the mountain and he said: "O'Allah, save me from them (in any way)."

The mountain began to quake and they all fell down and he came walking to the king. The king said to him: "What has happened to your companions (the courtiers)? He said: "Allah has saved me from them."

He again handed him to some of his courtiers and said: "Take him and carry him in a small boat and when you reach the middle of the ocean (ask him to renounce) his religion, but if he does not renounce his religion throw him (into the water)." So they took him and the boy said: "O'Allah, save me from them and what they want to do." At that moment, the boat turned over and they were drowned and he came walking to the king, and the king said to him: "What has happened to your companions (the courtiers)? He said: "Allah has saved me from them, and he said to the king: "You cannot kill me until you do what I ask you to do."

And he said: What is that? He said: "You should gather people in a field and hang me by the trunk of a tree. Then take hold of an arrow from the quiver and say: 'In the name of Allah, the Lord of the worlds,' then shoot an arrow and if you do that then you would be able to kill me."

The king called the people in an open plain and tied the boy to the trunk of a tree, then he took hold of an arrow from his quiver and then placed the arrow in the bow and then said:

"In the Name of Allah, the Lord of the young boy." He then shot an arrow and it bit his temple. He (the boy) placed his hands upon the temple where the arrow had bit him and he died and the people said: "We affirm our faith in the Lord of this young boy, we affirm our faith in the Lord of this young man, and we affirm our faith in the Lord of this young boy."

The courtiers came to the king and it was said to him: "Do you see that Allah has actually done what you aimed at averting. They (the people) have affirmed their faith in the Lord." The king commanded ditches to be dug at certain points in the path. When these ditches were dug, and the fire was lit in them it was said (to the people): "He who would not turn back from his (the boy's) religion would be thrown in the fire or it would be said to them to jump in it." (The people courted death but did not renounce religion) until a woman came with her child and she felt hesitant in jumping into the fire and the child said to her: "O'mother, endure (this ordeal) for it is the Truth." (Transmitted by Imam Ahmed, Imam Muslim and An-Nasa'i from the Hadith of Hammad Ibn Salamah).

Some scholars claimed that the incident of the ditch was repeated many times in the past more than once. Ibn Abu Hatim said: "I was told by my father after Abul Yaman after Safwan Ibn Abdur Rahman Ibn Jubair as saying: The incident of the ditch took place in the Yemen during the lifetime of Tubba. And, it took place in Constantinople during the lifetime of Constantine who set the fires in which he threw the Christians who were sticking to their religion (Islamic Monotheism).

It also took place in Iraq, in the land of Babylon during the lifetime of Bikhtin-assar who erected an idol and ordered that all people must prostrate themselves before it. Daniel, Izrya and Mashayl refused and thereupon, he set a great fire and threw them into it. However, Allah Almighty saved them from the fire and caused the 9 men who transgressed over them to fall into the fire that they made.

Concerning Allah's Statement that reads: "Cursed were the people of the Ditch," As-Sadiy said: "There were three ditches: one in Sham (Syria), another in Iraq, and the third in the Yemen." (Narrated by Ibn Abu Hatim)

Good Books to Read

Stories of the Prophets
   ISBN 9781643543109

Stories of the Koran
   ISBN 9781095900796

Great Women in Islam
   ISBN 9781505398304

The Path to Guidance
   ISBN 9781643540818

The Battles of the Prophet
   ISBN 9781092642507

Purification of the Soul (part 1)
   ISBN 9781643541389

Tafseer Ibn Kathir
   ISBN 9781512266573

Kalid Ibn Al-Walid
   ISBN 9781508435204

The Ideal Muslim Woman
   9781643543192

Al-Fawaid: Wise Sayings
ISBN 9781727812718

The Book of Hajj
ISBN 9781072243335

40 Hadith Qudsi
ISBN 9781070655949

40 Hadith Nawawi
ISBN 9781070547428

The Legacy of the Prophet
ISBN 9781080249343

Heaven's Door
(Purification Part 2)
ISBN 9781643541396

Soul's Journey after Death
ISBN 9781643541365

Koran: English – Easy to Read
ISBN 9781643540924

www.ingramcontent.com/pod-product-compliance
Lightning Source LLC
Chambersburg PA
CBHW071213080526
44587CB00013BA/1361